**books**online

Read SAP PRESS online also

With booksonline we offer you online access to leading SAP experts' knowledge. Whether you use it as a beneficial supplement or as an alternative to the printed book – with booksonline you can:

- Access any book at any time
- Quickly look up and find what you need
- Compile your own SAP library

Your advantage as the reader of this book

Register your book on our website and obtain an exclusive and free test access to its online version. You're convinced you like the online book? Then you can purchase it at a preferential price!

And here's how to make use of your advantage

1. Visit www.sap-press.com
2. Click on the link for SAP PRESS booksonline
3. Enter your free trial license key
4. Test-drive your online book with full access for a limited time!

Your personal **license key** for your test access including the preferential offer

qygp-knx5-e8uc-msf4

Welcome to the Galileo Press *Discover SAP* series. This series was developed as part of our official SAP PRESS imprint to help you discover what SAP is all about and how you can use the wide array of applications and tools to make your organization much more efficient and cost effective.

Each book in the series is written in a friendly, easy-to-follow style that guides you through the intricacies of the software and its core components. Beginning with this book, "Discover SAP," you'll find a detailed overview of the core components of SAP, what they are, how they can benefit your company, and the technology requirements and costs of implementation. Once you have a foundational knowledge of SAP, you can explore the other books in the series covering CRM, Financials, HCM, BusinessObjects, and more. In these books you'll delve into the fundamental business concepts and principles behind the tool, discover why it's important for your business, and evaluate the technology and implementation costs for each.

Whether you are a decision maker who needs to determine if SAP is the right enterprise solution for your company, you are just starting to work in a firm that uses SAP, or you're already familiar with SAP but need to learn about a specific component, you are sure to find what you need in the *Discover SAP* series. Then when you're ready to implement SAP, you'll find what you need in the SAP PRESS series at *www.sap-press.com*.

Thank you for your interest in the series. We look forward to hearing how the series helps you get started with SAP.

Jenifer Niles
Vice President
Galileo Press America

SAP PRESS

SAP PRESS is a joint initiative of SAP and Galileo Press. The know-how offered by SAP specialists combined with the expertise of the Galileo Press publishing house offers the reader expert books in the field. SAP PRESS features first-hand information and expert advice, and provides useful skills for professional decision-making.

SAP PRESS offers a variety of books on technical and business related topics for the SAP user. For further information, please visit our website: *www.sap-press.com.*

Ingo Hilgefort
Reporting and Analytics with SAP BusinessObjects
2010, app. 500 pp.
978-1-59299-310-0

Naeem Arif, Sheikh Tauseef
SAP ERP Financials: Configuration and Design
2008, 467 pp.
978-1-59299-136-6

Marc O. Schäfer, Matthias Melich
SAP Solution Manager, Enterprise Edition
2009, 555 pp.
978-1-59299-271-4

Martin Murray
SAP MM – Functionality and Technical Configuration
2007, 588 pp.
978-1-59299-134-2

Nancy Muir and Ian Kimbell

Discover SAP®

Second Edition

Galileo Press

Bonn • Boston

Galileo Press is named after the Italian physicist, mathematician and philosopher Galileo Galilei (1564–1642). He is known as one of the founders of modern science and an advocate of our contemporary, heliocentric worldview. His words *Eppur se muove* (And yet it moves) have become legendary. The Galileo Press logo depicts Jupiter orbited by the four Galilean moons, which were discovered by Galileo in 1610.

Editor Jenifer Niles
Developmental Editor Kelly Grace Harris
Copyeditor Julie McNamee
Cover Design Jill Winitzer
Photo Credit Getty Images/Creativ Studio Heinemann
Layout Design Vera Brauner
Production Editor Kelly O'Callaghan
Assistant Production Editor Graham Geary
Typesetting Publishers' Design and Production Services, Inc.
Printed and bound in Canada

ISBN 978-1-59229-320-9

© 2010 by Galileo Press Inc., Boston (MA)
2nd Edition

Library of Congress Cataloging-in-Publication Data
Muir, Nancy, 1954–
    Discover SAP / Nancy Muir, Ian Kimbell. — 1st ed.
        p. cm.
    Includes bibliographical references and index.
    ISBN-13: 978-1-59229-320-9 (alk. paper)
    ISBN-10: 1-59229-320-4 (alk. paper)
    1. Management information systems—Computer programs. 2. Business—Data processing—Computer programs.
3. SAP ERP. 4. Integrated software. I. Kimbell, Ian. II. Title.
    HD30.213.M84 2010
    650.0285'53—dc22

                                                                    2009042513

Contents at a Glance

Contents

PART II SAP Products

PART III   Essential SAP Tools

13   Understanding SAP Composite Applications 255

14   User-Friendly SAP — Duet™, Alloy™, and Adobe® Interactive Forms 265

15   Sustainability 283

Preface

In writing this book originally, and in this second, updated edition, we tried to address what we felt was a gap in the available information about SAP by providing an easy to understand overview of SAP, its products, and its approach to enterprise computing.

Our objective was to provide a simple and straightforward look at SAP and its products. We made every effort to explain SAP product features, not in technical jargon or by using marketing brochure product features, but by simply describing all of the benefits and by being specific about what these products can *do* for your business.

Since the first edition of this book was published, SAP has been busy updating the product suite and purchasing new solutions to enhance and expand the complete offerings. The most notable of these acquisitions was the purchase of BusinessObjects, a market-leading business intelligence solution offering the capability to unlock information, enable insight, manage performance, and govern compliance, regardless of the underlying business applications and data stores. SAP had successful business intelligence tools, but with the integration of BusinessObjects, it now offers the industry leading solution. This acquisition has involved the merging and purging of tools, but the current

SAP BusinessObjects portfolio offers best-of-breed tools, which are covered in Chapter 12, SAP BusinessObjects Solutions.

The following sections outline who can benefit from this book, how we structured the book, and what topics are covered.

Who Will Benefit from This Book?

If you're a business decision maker considering implementing SAP products in your business, this book will help you become familiar with the terminology, concepts, products, and technology you will be encountering.

If you're a manager who is dealing with new SAP products in your group, and you want to help your people succeed and become more productive, this book gives you the information you need to appreciate how all of the various features and tools in SAP products might make your people more efficient.

If you're an IT person who has never worked with SAP technologies and products, you'll get a quick, solid grounding in both and be able to make the connection between how those technologies and products solve business problems.

If you're a consultant considering entering the world of supporting SAP products, this book can serve as a kind of tutorial to help you better understand the SAP universe, including SAP's extended partner community and how it works to support customers.

What You'll Discover

Our goal in writing this book was to introduce and explain in simple language, enterprise computing concepts and terms; SAP as a company and how it approaches solving real-world business problems; the technology behind SAP products; and what you can expect during an SAP implementation.

We also provide an overview of each of SAP's major products with actual case studies so you can see how each product works in a real business.

We were careful to define the most current business and enterprise computing terms throughout the book so anyone from an IT specialist unfamiliar with business terms to a business person unfamiliar with technology terms can understand the information we provide. We also made every attempt to give you examples and case studies to make SAP and its products relevant to you, your business, and your industry.

Navigational Tools for This Book

Throughout the book, you will find several elements that will help you access useful information. We have used the following icons to help you navigate:

> **Tip**: When you see this icon you know that you'll find useful information as well as special tips and tricks that can make your work easier.

> **Note**: Notes call out information about related ideas, other resources to explore, or things you should keep in mind.

> **Technical Information**: This icon highlights technical details and issues related to SAP products that will help you in making decisions.

> **Flash**: When you see this icon, you know you will be given some news, latest developments, or important information about SAP.

> **Example**: Here you'll encounter real-life scenarios and exercises.

Additionally, marginal text provides a useful way to scan the book to locate topics of interest for you. Each appears to the side of a paragraph or section with related information.

This is a marginal note

What's in This Book?

This book is organized into five parts. We move from basic information about SAP and its approach to enterprise computing products and services, to more specific chapters on SAP products themselves. We then explore some of the tools you find in all SAP products that provide features such as self-service and risk management. Finally, we look at the technology behind those products and advise you about what to expect if you implement SAP solutions in your organization. Here's an overview of what the book covers.

Part I SAP and Enterprise Computing — The Basics

Read the book in sequence or go to specific chapters or sections as needed

Chapter 1

SAP: The Company is where we look at the history of SAP, that is, how it has grown and developed products to address various business processes over the years. We provide an overview of SAP today, including its different enterprise computing solutions.

Chapter 2

The SAP Approach to Enterprise Software is where we define enterprise computing and explain how SAP approaches finding and providing solutions to enterprises of all sizes and types.

Chapter 3

Business Suite 7 Overview explains how the modular approach to enhancing technical functionality, can help companies reduce the costs and time associated with software implementations.

Part II SAP Products

Each of the chapters in this part covers one or more SAP software products, explaining what the product is, how it fits in an enterprise setting, and specific product features and tools, as well as offering a case study with a real-world example of the product in place. Here are the products covered in these chapters:

Chapter 4

SAP ERP Financials addresses all of the financial functions of a business, which most readers will find very valuable. SAP ERP Financials is one of the most often implemented applications of SAP.

Chapter 5

SAP ERP Human Capital Management covers solutions related to human resource, again a very important part of the SAP landscape.

Chapter 6

SAP ERP Operations deals with Product Development and Manufacturing, Procurement and Logistics, and Sales and Service products.

Chapter 7

SAP Customer Relationship Management helps you obtain, service, and retain your customers.

Chapter 8

SAP Supplier Relationship Management deals with the sourcing, procurement, and supplier enablement features.

Chapter 9

SAP Product Lifecycle Management covers the pieces of a product's life, from inception, to development, and through to obsolescence.

Chapter 10

SAP Supply Chain Management introduces features for keeping inventory moving in and out of your company in a way that can have a big impact on your bottom line.

Chapter 11

SAP's Strategy for Small to Midsize Enterprises deals with SAP's complete portfolio of solutions, including SAP Business One, SAP Business All-in-One, SAP Business ByDesign, and BusinessObjects Edge.

Chapter 12

The *SAP BusinessObjects Portfolio* gives you a detailed look at the new BusinessObjects portfolio, including Enterprise Performance Management, Business Intelligence, Governance, Risk, and Compliance, and Information Management.

Part III Essential SAP Tools

This part covers important tools that you might encounter in an SAP implementation. Let's get a quick recap of these chapters now:

Chapter 13

Understanding SAP Composite Applications looks at composite applications, applications built using pieces of SAP software. These composite applications are small prepackaged business processes that you can use to customize your own solutions.

Read all of the chapter descriptions to get an idea of what's included in each

Chapter 14

User-Friendly SAP — Duet, Alloy, and *Adobe Interactive Forms* highlights three tools intended for users of SAP software. Duet is a joint project between SAP and Microsoft, which provides the functionality of SAP through the Microsoft Office interface so familiar to knowledge workers. Alloy allows employees to continue using Lotus Notes while providing access to data within the SAP Business Suite. And SAP Interactive Forms is software by Adobe that uses Adobe Acrobat technology to make easy-to-use interactive forms, which SAP embeds within business processes.

Chapter 15

Sustainability is the focus of cross-functional organization within SAP. In this chapter you will discover what support they provide to customers establishing their own sustainability initiatives.

Chapter 16

User Productivity Tools for Information Workers is where you learn about role-based portals, which are work areas customized to each worker in your company to make them more productive. In addition, we explain how employee self-service (ESS) and manager self-service (MSS) functions allow your people to initiate many processes themselves, thereby saving them time and you money.

Part IV Technology Overview

Chapter 17

Service-Oriented Architecture is the chapter where we go into more depth about the way that SAP builds and customizes enterprise solutions with collections of services.

Chapter 18

SAP NetWeaver as a Technology introduces you to SAP NetWeaver, the technology platform on which all other SAP products rest.

Part V The Solution in Place

Chapter 19

Preparing for an SAP Implementation provides advice about how to prepare for putting SAP in place, from your assessment of your own company and its needs, to the programs, people, and services that can help you be successful.

Chapter 20

SAP Solution Manager is a useful tool built into SAP NetWeaver that guides you through every step of your SAP implementation and even provides useful documentation about the specific solution you implement.

Chapter 21
Conclusion sums up what was covered in the whole book and gives you some direction for the future.

Appendix

We provide four useful appendices for your reference:

> **Appendix A**
A glossary of SAP and enterprise computing terminology.

> **Appendix B**
Provides information about various resources for help and information related to SAP and its products.

> **Appendix C**
Gives you a useful collection of SAP solution maps that you can use as a quick reference for looking up the product and features you need.

> **Appendix D**
A bibliography that includes the source material we used in putting this book together.

In addition, the book includes an index that you can use to go directly to certain points of interest.

Use the index as a navigational tool

We hope that this straightforward overview of SAP and its technologies and products will give you the information you need to assess your own business needs, determine which SAP products and services to explore further with an SAP account representative, and help you take advantage of the many benefits that SAP has to offer for solving enterprise challenges.

Acknowledgments

Writing this comprehensive book and updating it in this second edition required the knowledge and input of many people, who we would like to acknowledge here. First, we wish to thank SAP, whose solutions and products have helped to transform thousands of companies and organizations to become "best-run," and will continue to do so as SAP focuses on helping its customers integrate and optimize their operations, while being flexible enough to respond to just about any challenge.

We would especially like to thank the following people, who acted, sometimes unknowingly, as a sounding board for this book:

> Jeff Anders
> Byron Banks
> Amy Funderburk
> Rajeev Goel
> Marie Goodell
> Fergus Griffin
> Matthias Haendly
> Patricia Harris

> Tesha Harvey
> Richard Howells
> Nir Kol
> Paige Leidig
> David Ludlow
> Matthias Melich
> Wolfgang Oelschlaeger
> Thomas Ohnemus
> Emily Rakowski
> Katharina Reichert
> Judith Ross
> Philip Say
> Marc Oliver Schaefer
> Ulrich Scholl
> Sabine Vogler
> Bernd Welz
> Sheila Zelinger
> Michaela Zwinakis

Last but most certainly not least, we wish to thank our editor for this second edition, Jenifer Niles, for trusting us with this project and shepherding it through every step of the way. Thanks also to our developmental editor, Kelly Grace Harris, and our copy editor, Julie McNamee, who made sure that all our i's were dotted and our t's were crossed.

Nancy Muir
Ian Kimbell

PART I
SAP and Enterprise Computing – The Basics

SAP: The Company

With this book, you will get a solid foundation in SAP products and services. And although subsequent chapters deal with the nuts and bolts of SAP applications, underlying technology, and support, and how they may be useful in your enterprise, no product exists independently of its creator. This holds true especially for SAP, whose origins, growth, and philosophy have had an impact on what it creates and how its customers benefit from its products.

So let's start with an overview of SAP, the company, and its history to help you understand how to successfully interact with SAP today.

The Beginnings of SAP

SAP was founded in 1972 by five IBM colleagues who struck out on their own. Dietmar Hopp, Hans-Werner Hector, Hasso Plattner, Klaus Tschira, and Claus Wellenreuther founded SAP in Mannheim, Germany, where it began as a small regional company.

In the earliest days, the founders couldn't afford to buy computers because they were so expensive. Instead, they arranged with another company, ICI, in neighboring Oestringen, to use their computers at night. You should note that this was long before the personal com-

Overview and history

puter came on the scene. In those days, all of their work was produced on punch cards.

> ### ⊕ Tip
>
> You can impress people with your SAP knowledge if you know that the company name SAP is the acronym for *Systems Applications and Products* in data processing. And remember, never pronounce SAP to rhyme with *rap*; instead, simply pronounce each of the three letters, S.A.P.

In an era of development of simple business tools such as calculating software, which evolved into spreadsheet programs, and relatively simple word processors, these five men recognized the need for more sophisticated applications that could support the way businesses function.

R/1 System
They spent the next year developing applications that would support real-time processing of business tasks. Their first product was a financial accounting software package. This software was at the core of what would later become known as the *R/1 system*. The *R* in this case stands for real-time data processing.

But R/1 was just the beginning; the next few decades were to bring about tremendous growth for SAP and the world of enterprise computing.

Examining the Growth of SAP

R/2 system, enterprise
During the 1970s, the term *enterprise* was just coming into general use, and today almost any business can be considered an enterprise, if it has a focus on an ability to respond to changes in the market and innovate. SAP developed what it referred to as its *database and dialog control system*, which eventually became known as *R/2*. The system was essentially a business application software suite run on a mainframe computer. R/2 was the cornerstone of enterprise resource planning (ERP) applications used by major companies throughout the coming decades.

SAP in the 1980s

In the 1980s, SAP grew quickly and moved into its first building in Walldorf, Germany, near Heidelberg. Early in the decade, SAP counted half of the top 100 German industrial firms among its customers, such as ICI, BASF, and John Deere. But growth beyond Germany's borders was imminent.

Development of R/2 systems during the 1980s took into account the potential of the multinational customer base, and SAP paid a lot of attention to enabling its products to handle a variety of languages and currencies, thus reflecting the plethora of country-specific legal requirements. This multinational approach to software development continues today.

During this period, SAP technology also focused on making applications adaptable by programmers to fit into individual enterprises. For example, SAP development maintained a flexible approach, allowing the software to run on many different databases and platforms (operating systems) seamlessly.

Flexible approach to development

In the mid- to late 1980s, SAP launched its first sales group outside of Germany (in Austria), passed the $52 million revenue mark, and began to make its presence known at major computer shows. In 1988, SAP GmbH became SAP AG, and later that year began trading on the Frankfurt and Stuttgart stock exchanges.

The decade ended with SAP subsidiaries located in Denmark, Sweden, Italy, and the United States, thereby firmly establishing SAP's foothold in the international technology marketplace.

SAP's Unique Approach

One of the things that set SAP apart as it grew over the years was the way it married technology with the requirements of running a business. An SAP programmer would sit down with a salesperson to explain the software. The salesperson would then go to the customer and demonstrate the functionality. The feedback that companies provided was then shared with the programmers to help them build applications that were closely aligned with real workplace functionality. In this way, business process knowledge was coded into SAP's systems. Other companies took a different path, stringing together functionality in a way that didn't always reflect their customers' business processes.

Much later, SAP developed tools called *SAP Best Practices* that make the technical implementation of best practices in a workplace setting much

SAP Best Practices

easier. These Best Practices are documented prototypes on which you can base an enterprise solution, similar to the way an expense report template in a spreadsheet program provides you with the structure of a standard business form to save you time.

SAP built a successful business foundation during the 1980s, and in the 1990s developed a truly international business approach and presence.

SAP in the 1990s

SAP grew internationally in the 1990s, with business outside of Germany exceeding 50% of its total income. Customers such as Shell Oil, Kodak, and Procter & Gamble joined SAP's European clients, and, in 1998, the company was listed on the New York Stock Exchange.

SAP R/3 SAP R/3, introduced in the 1990s, was a giant leap in computing for business enterprises. It moved enterprise computing from the mainframe and the world of programmers writing code to the world of databases, applications, and interfaces that made SAP's offerings more accessible to end users.

Client/server architecture SAP R/3 was based on something called *three-tier client/server architecture*. This is basically an approach to computer networking that divides the computer requesting data from the computer that stores the data and the end-user interface.

In this setting, a client computer (e.g., a computer where a user sits working on a report) requests something from an application (this might be on a network or web server) that works with a database (the third layer, as shown in Figure 1.1). This division allows for a great deal of flexibility as each layer is scalable in itself; if more database capacity is needed, it can be added easily in the server layer, while the client layer is focused on other jobs, such as showing more sophisticated graphical reports.

Client/server architecture became integral to creating web-based applications, for example, where services can be made available from the application layer.

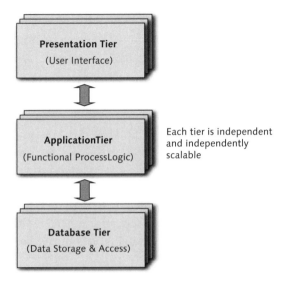

Each tier is independent and independently scalable

Figure 1.1 Three-Tier Client/Server Architecture

Another important focus for SAP was the concept of *abstraction*. Abstraction is a method of hiding technical complexity behind the scenes so users, and even the programmer customizing an application, don't have to tinker with the underlying technology. Think of abstraction this way: When you turn on a radio, you don't need to see or understand how radio waves function to appreciate the music you hear. In the same way, abstraction in SAP R/3 helped to make access to data easier and seamless for end users.

Abstraction

The approaching new millennium brought both challenges and tremendous opportunity as SAP continued to explore new models of technology and business productivity.

Entering the New Millennium

Toward the end of the century, SAP announced plans to integrate its products with e-commerce and web technologies. Using the Internet model, SAP placed the end user at the center of enterprise computing. The growth of e-business had shifted the thinking of businesses toward establishing a more collaborative environment for users.

By 2004, SAP AG had revenues of €7.5 billion and was working with partners in 25 industries to develop its next generation of enterprise solutions. SAP became the third-largest independent software vendor in the world, after Microsoft and IBM.

Though it's useful to understand where SAP came from, to truly understand how it could work with your business, you need to get a feel for what SAP is doing today.

SAP Today

Today SAP produces business solutions for a wide variety of industries in every major market in the world. SAP's approach to developing software is collaborative, in that it works with business partners to develop product features to reflect real-world computing needs. The company, which is still based in Walldorf, Germany, has more than 48,500 employees in more than 50 countries.

> **☼ Did You Know?**
>
> Are you concerned about how your existing computing systems will interact with SAP systems? Because SAP embraces many open standards and is actively involved in the establishment of worldwide technology standards, it is striving to ensure that enterprise-wide solutions, which often involve a combination of applications and technologies, are more efficient and seamless to implement.

Service-oriented architecture (SOA) The development of a blueprint for enterprise computing called *Service-Oriented Architecture* (SOA) outlined in more detail in Chapters 2, The SAP Approach to Enterprise Software, and Chapter 3, Business Suite 7 Overview), and a technology platform called *SAP NetWeaver* constitute the latest SAP model.

SAP's customers now number more than 89,000. This customer base translates into well over 91,500 installations in 120 countries (systems installed in companies), with more than 12 million users (those using the system at varying levels). See Figure 1.2.

Service-Oriented Architecture is a very important concept for SAP's products, but equally important is the way SAP interacts with customers and partners to grow its business in innovative ways.

Figure 1.2 Some of SAP's Customers

> **Note**
>
> At one point, SAP called its approach to service-oriented architecture ESA, or Enterprise Services Architecture. In 2006, that changed to enterprise service-oriented architecture, or enterprise SOA, and is currently called service-oriented architecture.

SAP's Approach to Growing Its Business

Today SAP is the number one business in enterprise computing and is still the third-largest software company in the world.

One key to SAP's success has been the way it has collaborated with businesses and consultants to integrate best business practices into its software applications. Through these partnerships, SAP has been able to build an industry focus that allows its products to be used in a variety of industry settings, such as manufacturing, pharmaceuticals, and healthcare. SAP has also developed a huge support network of consultants, who are educated by SAP in how to work with their solutions through annual conferences, certification programs, and consultant education programs, such as SAP Academy.

 Tip

> For a detailed list of support programs and information resources for SAP, see Appendix B.

Three communities that SAP supports are vital to these partnerships:

> **SAP Business Community**
> This is a forum for the exchange of ideas and solutions with member experts and business leaders.

> **SAP Developer Network (SDN)**
> This network includes developers, consultants, and business analysts focused on sharing technical knowledge.

> **User Groups**
> These user groups are independent, non-profit groups made up of SAP customers and partners who share knowledge and experiences through conferences and online interaction.

⚙ **Customer Competence Centers (CCC)**

> In 1994, SAP created the CCC program to assist customers in setting up and optimizing their own support operations. The program focuses on sharing best practices, providing operational tools, and creating operations standards across all organizations involved with SAP IT service and application management.

BusinessObjects and enhancement packages

SAP continues to grow its business with new acquisitions such as the purchase of BusinessObjects, an industry leader in business intelligence. While SAP applications house the data and processes that make your organization operate smoothly, BusinessObjects brings to the table the tools to provide in-depth analysis of that data and display the results in the form of reports, dashboards, or scorecards (which can be displayed on your office computer or mobile device). This enables you to have all of the information you need, at the time you need it, to make the best decisions possible. See Chapters 11, SAP's Strategy for Small to Midsize Enterprises, and Chapter 12, the SAP BusinessObjects Portfolio, for more details about BusinessObjects.

SAP is also strengthening support for mid-market users of enterprise computing. This mid-market consists of companies with as few as a hundred to a few thousand employees, with more out-of-the-box products that require less customization to get going. SAP continues to work toward hiding underlying technical complexity to make the end-user experience a comfortable and productive one.

See Chapters 20 and 21 for more about how SAP supports its products

Lastly, today's economy requires companies to monitor and justify their IT expenditures. So SAP's enhancement packages were developed to let you select only those features and processes that you want to upgrade at the time you want to upgrade them. No longer will you have to perform a costly full-system upgrade with extensive coding, downtime, and training just to improve one aspect of your business. Enhancement packages increase your flexibility to implement those features you need to remain competitive but at a time when your budget can afford to do so.

So exactly what products does SAP bring to the table? In the next section, we provide an overview of SAP software and technologies.

SAP Products: An Overview

SAP continues to focus on software applications and technologies that support enterprises with a variety of individual applications that handle processes, such as SAP Supply Chain Management (SAP SCM) and SAP Customer Relationship Management (SAP CRM). In addition, SAP NetWeaver provides the ideal technology platform on which those applications can run.

The SAP NetWeaver platform helps to integrate all of the other applications SAP provides, as well as applications from other enterprise computing companies that your enterprise may have in place. SAP NetWeaver provides tools that are useful across all parts of an enterprise, such as Business Warehouse (SAP NetWeaver BW), which helps you centrally store and organize information, and tools to help you modify or create new business processes.

Tip

SAP has made an effort to support open systems, which means that its products can be run with a mix of products from other vendors, if that is the most efficient and cost-effective route for a customer to take.

Business Suite 7 SAP's main offering is the *SAP Business Suite*. The launch of SAP's new Business Suite 7 emphasizes the modular nature of its applications, which allows you to lower your total cost of ownership by purchasing just the modules you need initially and then adding others as appropriate.

Business Suite 7 incorporates best practices from 25 industries while still allowing you the flexibility to customize and integrate your own company-specific processes. All applications within Business Suite 7 use the "switch framework." This means that when you purchase one of the applications, such as SAP CRM, the features and functions are all turned off so that you can activate, or switch on, only those features that are most beneficial to your company.

The SAP Business Suite includes the following applications:

It's E.R.P, not erp
> **SAP ERP**
> Named for the enterprise resource planning tools and features it includes, is for dealing with key business functions such as financials and human capital management. (Also, be sure to spell out E. R. P., rather than pronouncing "erp" to rhyme with "burp.")

> **SAP Customer Relationship Management (SAP CRM)**
> Is intended for managing customer-related processes such as customer support.

> **SAP Product Lifecycle Management (SAP PLM)**
> Is for handling the creation and implementation of new products.

> **SAP Supply Chain Management (SAP SCM)**
> Helps you deal with procurement, inventory, and other supply chain processes.

> **SAP Supplier Relationship Management (SAP SRM)**
> Helps you when you're working with various suppliers.

> **SAP Composite Applications**
These applications work across the various areas and processes of a business, including analytic blueprints from SAP (formerly called SAP xApp Analytics) for generating useful reports and SAP composite applications for Mobile Business to help your employees who work outside the office with their mobile computing needs.

See Chapter 13 for more about composite applications

In addition to SAP Business Suite, new offerings for small to midsize companies include

> **SAP Business One**
This application provides one system for the management of sales, finances, purchasing, inventory, and manufacturing operations.

> **SAP Business All-in-One**
These packages offer preconfigured solutions based on SAP Business Suite.

> **SAP Business ByDesign**
This too is an *on-demand* solution fully managed by SAP, so no upgrades or large IT infrastructure is required.

> **Industry-specific applications**
For all of the SAP applications, there are specialized products that support individual industry needs, as well as regulation compliance and risk management.

Lastly, SAP has a Business User Group that specifically looks at the needs of the information worker. This group is working on end-user integration with products such as Duet and Microsoft Office (shown in Figure 1.3) and Adobe forms technology. This makes it simpler for people using technology to make it work for them in their day-to-day jobs.

See Chapter 2 for individual SAP solutions

In addition, the Business User Group is looking at ways of bringing key performance metrics to the desk of every professional with analytics, and ways of taking care of compliance with SAP BusinessObjects Governance, Risk, and Compliance.

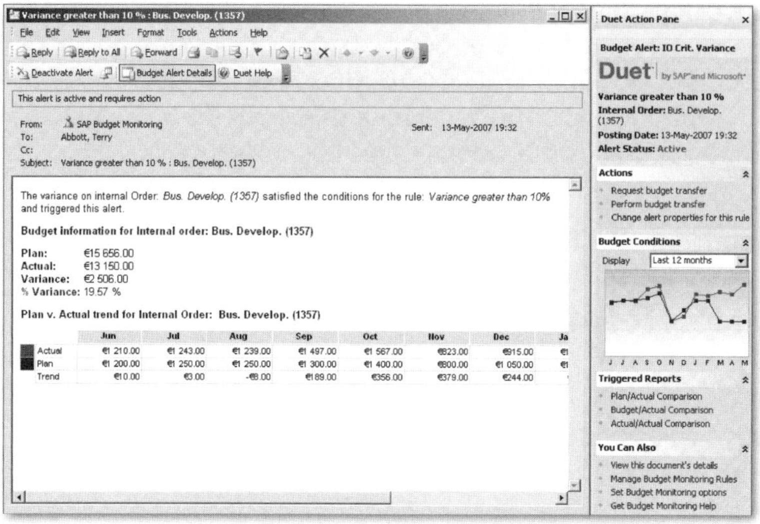

Figure 1.3 Integration with Microsoft Office Through Duet

See Part II for more about SAP products

In Part II of this book, Essential SAP Tools, we provide you with more detailed explanations of each of SAP's products.

Conclusion

In this chapter, we provided you with some context for understanding SAP as a company by sharing the following:

> A discussion of the history of SAP as a company

> An overview of SAP today

> An introduction of SOA as a fundamental approach to enterprise computing

> Information about SAP's approach to growing its business in collaboration with SAP communities and customers

> A quick look at SAP's major product offerings

In Chapter 2, The SAP Approach to Enterprise Software, we'll introduce some basic concepts and terms from the world of enterprise computing, discuss how SAP fits into that world with tools for integration and tools to support business processes, and look at where SAP is headed in the next several years.

The SAP Approach to Enterprise Software

IT systems serve the purpose of helping enterprises implement their business strategies more effectively and optimize the coordination of their operational processes. The fundamental aim of enterprise software is to "pour" business processes into software, that is, to link technology with operational workflows within an enterprise.

This chapter provides an overview of the key concepts relating to enterprise software. It introduces the central ideas and lays down the essential technical foundations. These include the SAP approach to service-oriented architecture, the SAP NetWeaver technology platform (on which all SAP applications can run), and technologies that help end users access SAP systems as part of their daily work. SAP's approach to the development of enterprise software is also presented.

Enterprise Resource Planning (ERP)

An *enterprise* is a unit or organization that operates as a commercial entity. Enterprises may range from charitable organizations with just two employees to large global corporations. Most enterprises use one or more software solutions. The scale of the requirements that must be fulfilled by these software solutions depends on the size of the enterprise and on the complexity and diversity of its business activities.

An IT system that supports business processes is referred to as an *ERP system*. ERP stands for *enterprise resource planning*. An ERP system comprises a range of software applications designed to support business processes, such as submitting a sales order or material procurement for production. SAP software, with SAP ERP at its core, is one of the ERP systems most widely used by enterprises.

➕ Tip

Explanations of the various terms and acronyms used in enterprise resource planning are provided in the glossary at the back of this book, as well as on the inside front cover at the start of the book.

SAP software integrates functions and information in an enterprise. *SAP Business Suite*, as discussed in Chapter 1, is a package of software applications designed to support the most prevalent workflows in enterprises. The SAP ERP portion of the Business Suite focuses on financials, human resources, operations, and corporate services. Other portions of the Business Suite handle customer resource management, purchasing, and other areas of enterprise functionality.

⚙ How Large Does an Enterprise Have to Be to Use ERP?

The first implementations of ERP systems took place in large corporations with tens or hundreds of thousands of employees in dozens or even hundreds of locations. Enterprises of this size require software solutions capable of mapping diverse information and processes on a large scale. However, many midsize enterprises also use SAP. In addition, SAP applications have been developed for small enterprises in recent years. For more information, refer to Chapter 11, SAP's Strategy for Small and Midsize Enterprises.

Information Makes the World Go Round

In this much-lauded information age, data relating to consumer goods has become an important economic tool. Incorrect or incomplete information — about internal processes or about events outside enterprises — may result in financial losses in the millions. It is therefore considered essential to ensure that information is as accurate and accessible as possible. The concept behind enterprise software is to make information available as quickly as possible and in real time to support business processes.

Economic conditions as well as changing consumer and user expectations are placing tremendous pressure on companies to make critical decisions in a shorter amount of time. Companies used to have the luxury of gathering and compiling data from multiple sources, analyzing the data, and then reaching a conclusion. Now, to stay competitive, access to all data must be instantaneous and delivered via all means of communication, such as smart phones. To achieve this, SAP's current marketing push is that an organization needs something called clarity.

Clarity and sustainability

Clarity, according to SAP, means that all information is available to everyone who needs it at the time they need it; as a result, your business is leaner and more flexible. With clarity, your organization reacts more quickly to changing economic conditions and consumer wishes because it has the best information to make strategic decisions. Even if you're in an airport waiting for a flight, a clear organization makes it possible for you to view your business network's data from afar, drill down into that data, and view analytics in real time.

In addition to being a clear organization, companies in today's world need to be sustainable. *Sustainability* means employing green practices within your organization, that is, employing practices that are economically and environmentally consuming and replenishing the earth's resources (see Chapter 15, Sustainability, for more details).

 Example

A computer manufacturer decides to switch to purchasing competitively priced components and assembling computers from them, instead of building computers from standard components, which also have to be stored. Because the enterprise can access pricing information in real time, the manufacturer is always able to purchase the most cost-effective components and increase the enterprise's profit margin.

The following sections describe the evolution of standard business software. Key terms and concepts are discussed in several places, which will give you a deeper insight into the world of the enterprise in terms of IT requirements.

The Origins of Standard Business Software

Business applications

Applications were developed by SAP and other software providers to help enterprises more effectively manage and use information and business processes; for example, information about customers, products, or finances. These applications were called *business applications*. The foundations for their development were laid in the 1970s, and these applications served, above all, to support data processing in financial accounting and human resources.

Centralized data storage and ease of access to information also enabled the creation of reports on this data. Thanks to the availability of very powerful processors, these reports can now be used to run analyses that provide a basis for strategic and operational decision making. Instead of merely generating a list of all customers, it is now possible, for example, to show which customer generated the greatest profit. Or, users responsible for customer accounts can access precise data that may reveal conflicting information about sales orders.

Figure 2.1 shows evaluations of sales in the various branches of a car dealership group, broken down by region and model.

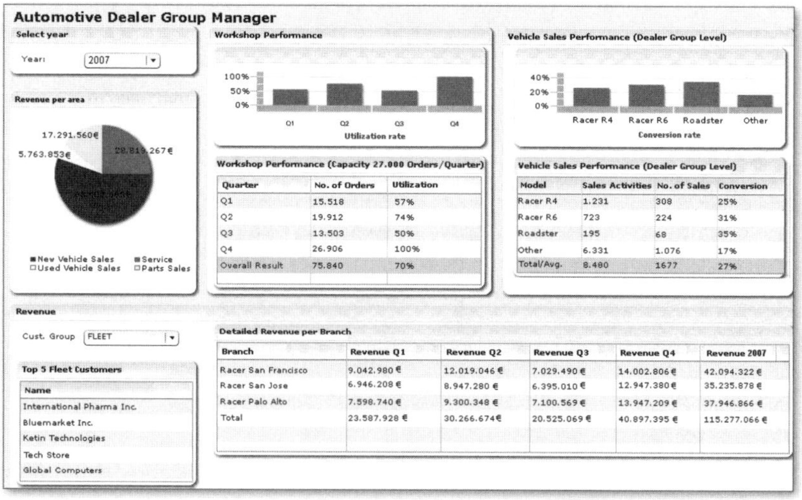

Figure 2.1 Generating Reports from Centrally Stored Data in SAP ERP

In the early years, SAP limited its software applications to accounting and HR. A little later, however, functions were extended to cover other areas within an enterprise. Today, ERP software can be used to help an enterprise manage finance, HR, logistics, sales and distribution, production, purchasing, and services. An ERP system is now capable of handling a wide range of processes, including anything from the planning of a business trip to the tracking of a sales order.

Which areas are covered by ERP?

However, the need to cover various business areas was not the only challenge for ERP systems. It was also necessary to enable collaboration across departments, countries, or enterprises using the same data.

The Challenge of Integration

In the earliest years of enterprise software, huge data stores were created for each large department in an enterprise, so, for example, the finance department may have had a different set of customer data than the sales department. As a result, a sales employee was unable to access the accounting database to view billing data or the shipping department database to check whether an order had already been processed. Practically, though, all of the various people or departments involved in a business process in an enterprise need to be able to access the same data. For example, the purchasing, marketing, and accounting departments all need to be able to check the status of an order to print a catalog. It is not a particularly efficient way to run an enterprise if the purchasing department manages the order data and the marketing department has to ask the purchasing department to access this information on their behalf.

It was therefore essential to find a way to avoid this inefficient division of information. The answer was *integration*, and SAP was to play a pioneering role in this development. SAP and other providers of ERP software searched for a solution to link the "data silos" that contained information and functions from different areas and to enable access to these across the entire enterprise.

Avoiding data silos

In an integrated enterprise environment, a sales order is available to the sales department, finance, customer service, and shipping department to enable seamless processing and order fulfillment. As a result, the sales department can provide the customer with precise information about the order status and improve customer satisfaction. Centralized and fast updating of data means that the enterprise can be flexible in its response to change.

SAP NetWeaver   The level of integration was consistently improved in each new product generation, from SAP R/1, R/2, and R/3 right through to SAP ERP. SAP NetWeaver (see Chapter 18, SAP NetWeaver as a Technology Platform) is the latest technology for data integration from SAP. All SAP products are based on this platform.

Overview of SAP NetWeaver

SAP NetWeaver is the technology platform on which the SAP Business Suite runs. A key capability of SAP NetWeaver consists of the integration options that allow various programs and applications in the IT systems to communicate with one another. This means that you can access data from various sources without having to open and close other software applications or log on to systems and log off again. It is also possible to run business applications across various departments and to run these faster, more efficiently, and more seamlessly than before.

SAP NetWeaver essentially supports integration at the following four levels:

> **Integration of people**
  User productivity is mentioned many times in this book. Users need to be able to use the system without difficulty. It is therefore essential to provide them with an accessible user interface. A single user interface can be used for both SAP and non-SAP applications so that users can access all of the data they require.

> **Integration of information**
  All necessary information must be quickly and easily accessed within the enterprise and must be of a high quality. SAP NetWeaver Business Intelligence meets this information requirement.

> **Integration of processes**
  Today, it is almost impossible to imagine that all business processes were once covered by a single software solution. Efficient processes

need to be universally defined across various systems or even across enterprises.

> **Integration of applications**
Direct communication between various applications is ensured, and the popular programming language Java is supported in addition to ABAP, SAP's own programming language.

SAP NetWeaver contains several components that are used by all SAP applications:

> SAP NetWeaver Process Integration

> SAP NetWeaver Portal

> SAP NetWeaver Application Server

> SAP NetWeaver Business Warehouse

> SAP NetWeaver Mobile

> SAP Auto-ID Infrastructure

> *http://www12.sap.com/usa/platform/netweaver/dataunification.epx*

> *http://www.sap.com/platform/netweaver/components/IDM/index.epx*

Learn more about these components in Part IV, Technology Overview, of this book

SAP NetWeaver also has a repository of services, which you can use to modify your business applications. The Services Repository can be compared to a collection of text modules, which can be used again and again each time you want to write a new letter.

The SAP NetWeaver integrated technology platform is used to run all SAP applications and to exchange information with other applications. SAP NetWeaver supports the integration of business applications and data, and it offers tools for creating new applications (Figure 2.2). In other words, it represents a development environment for SAP applications.

SAP NetWeaver as a development environment

SAP NetWeaver technology can be used to implement a service-oriented architecture. The range of services provided in SAP NetWeaver and the applications for using these services are intended to support individual business processes (such as the creation of a sales order) and analytical applications (such as the creation of reports based on underlying data).

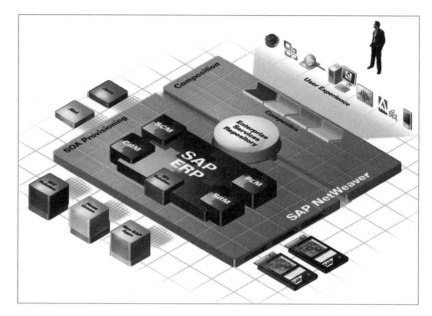

Figure 2.2 The SAP NetWeaver Platform for SAP Applications

Moreover, SAP NetWeaver is a means of building a bridge between IT and business departments.

Uniting IT and Business Requirements

SAP NetWeaver acts as an interface between IT practices and business processes. A business process could be, for example, the creation of sales orders by a sales employee, and an example of an IT practice is the joining together of several applications originating in different systems with a single user interface. A key task for an IT department is to make it easier for users to use the system in order to work more efficiently.

User Productivity
Enablement

The IT practice implemented in SAP NetWeaver is known as *User Productivity Enablement*. Increased user productivity is enabled, for example, by the SAP NetWeaver Portal, which makes it easier for end users to access the SAP system thanks to various personalization options. This IT practice may include a range of specific options that can be implemented in SAP NetWeaver to support business processes. As a result, the customers and employees of an enterprise can optimize their access to the data they need.

Ex Example

> You can create a website with SAP NetWeaver Portal, and you connect it to an order entry system, and then your customers can use it to place orders. You can also use SAP NetWeaver for mobile devices (e.g., smartphones), which sales employees use to enter orders while working outside of the office.

IT employees no longer need to program new solutions. Instead, they can build them from business process components, which means that employees from the IT department and other departments can finally speak the same language.

At this point you should consider your own IT landscape and ask yourself if it could be integrated into an SAP environment. This integration is facilitated by the open application environment of SAP NetWeaver.

Open Application Environment

You can use SAP NetWeaver's open application environment together with a range of applications and technologies from various sources. This means that you can continue to use the technology that is already in place alongside SAP NetWeaver, and save you the cost of purchasing a brand new system.

The concept of *open standards* was explained in Chapter 1, SAP: The Company

For example, if your environment includes systems from Oracle and SAP, SAP NetWeaver provides all functions required to allow these systems to communicate and exchange data. In addition to integration options, SAP NetWeaver also provides tools you can use to create and modify your own businesses' applications, which are then known as composite applications.

Third-party systems

Using Composite Applications

Applications that consist of various modules (known as *services*, which are explained in the next section) are referred to as *composite applications*. These applications are used to implement business processes. They allow you to re-use components from existing business applications to create new applications. A combination of functions from various applications then executes a business process (e.g., sales order entry).

In the past, changes like this required a complete re-programming of the ERP system. Composite applications allow you to implement these changes more easily in your enterprise.

SAP NetWeaver
Composition
Environment

The *Composition Environment* (CE) is based on SAP NetWeaver and provides a development environment in which you can create business applications from services. Chapter 13, Understanding SAP Composite Applications, presents the SAP NetWeaver CE in more detail and includes a range of examples of composite applications. Composite applications are used in various business areas and processes, for example, *analytic blueprints from SAP* (formerly called *SAP xApp Analytics*) for creating analyses, or *SAP xApps for Mobile Business* for mobile sales force employees who use mobile applications.

The next section provides a brief insight into the basic concept behind service-oriented architecture.

Service-Oriented Architectures

Web services

A service-oriented architecture (SOA) is a system architecture that encapsulates individual services or "software modules," so to speak, for business processes in such a way that they can be flexibly combined and re-used. The business processes that these services map can, in turn, be combined to map more complex business processes. This makes software development easier and more cost-effective. The individual services are often made available via the Internet as *web services*. As a result, the complexity of the individual applications is not visible to the user. SOA builds on the use of web services as modules to create software that enables the integration of various applications and the shared use of functions and information.

What Is a Service?

Reusability

A *service* is a module of program code that serves a specific business function. It is usually linked with other services and functions and therefore represents part of a business processes. A simple example of a service is one that calculates the amount of value-added tax to be added to a sales order. After a service has been created, it can be re-used in a range of processes.

Web services can similarly be kept in reserve and re-used as required, just as you can take clothes of a certain style and color from your wardrobe but leave other items in place before hanging up new ones. An SOA approach to enterprise computing therefore offers greater flexibility, while also saving time and money. For this reason, SOA is now a key component of the SAP strategy.

The SAP Approach to Enterprise Services

SOA is a generic approach to the design of IT practices, and web services are not only used in an SAP context. However, SAP provides special functions for modeling business processes, which are tailored to the requirements of enterprises and the use of SAP software.

A service can be used to generate a purchase order, for example. For this purpose, you do not need to program an extensive application. Instead, you can simply use a web service, which you can modify to suit the existing business processes in your SAP system and also re-use in various other business processes from other business areas. The services provided by SAP are referred to as *enterprise services*. Enterprise services comprise a range of functions that are required to process a specific task.

Enterprise services

> ▶ **Note: Name Changes**
>
> The SAP approach to SOA was initially called *Enterprise Services Architecture* (ESA). In 2006, this term was replaced by enterprise SOA. Today, we refer to SAP's approach as just SOA — service-oriented architectures.

SAP goes one step further and uses services to create entire *scenarios*. A scenario comprises several services that are used to execute a complete business process, such as purchase to pay. As you can see in Figure 2.3, purchase to pay begins with coverage analysis, which includes the creation of a request for quotation. The process continues with steps including generating a purchase order, receiving goods, and generating payment. This process involves various departments, including purchasing, warehouse management, accounts payable (invoice verification), and controlling. The individual steps in the process (❶ to ❼) can be brought together in a single scenario, which is more easily processed or even outsourced to a service provider.

Scenarios

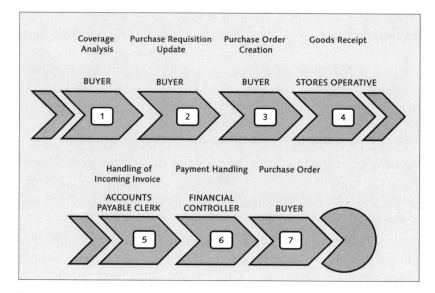

Figure 2.3 Business Process Based on Services

SAP has already created a range of scenarios based on services, and more will follow. Chapter 17, Service-Oriented Architecture, explains how you can develop and test your own processes based on services.

SAP Support for Business Processes

The unique feature of SAP's approach is the fact that it unites technology and business processes. This section provides more details of how this works in practice. By collaborating with a network of strategic partners, SAP became familiar with business processes used in many different industries, gained insight into the individual processes and best practices, and received feedback on its products from these partners.

The solutions developed by SAP are based on these best practices, which serve, so to speak, as the enterprises' individual recipes for success. However, the software still had to be modified to meet the requirements of each customer. To fulfill this requirement, SAP developed applications that could be tailored to meet the specific needs of individual customers, while at the same time offering a framework for the needs specific to individual industries.

🛟 Tip: Best Practices

Best practices comprise expert knowledge from various industries or relating to specific processes in an enterprise. SAP makes these best practices available in the form of technical and business-related documentation and pre-configured content in SAP systems. These can be regarded as "turnkey" resources that facilitate and accelerate the implementation process.

In the past, enterprises that had implemented an SAP system often required the assistance of external consultants to adapt the SAP ERP system to their specific requirements. It could take years for the implementation process to be completed. In previous years, SAP optimized this process by integrating modification options and best practices into components or services that could be easily adapted.

To provide enterprise solutions, providers such as SAP first had to understand business processes and then learn how to implement these in a marketable software product; in other words, they had to develop software applications that could be sold as a package based on business principles. Over the years, SAP developed many business applications to automate various business processes (the various stages of development were described in Chapter 1, SAP: The Company). These products are now part of the SAP Business Suite.

Table 2.1 lists the most important SAP applications, their acronyms, and how they are typically used (note that the first six categories are part of SAP ERP). You will find more information about the component of the SAP Business Suite in Part II of this book, Essential SAP Tools.

Various SAP applications

Category	Typical Areas of Use
Financials	Financial accounting/controlling, financial supply chain management, enterprise planning, preparation of financial statements, corporate governance
Human Capital Management (HCM)	Personnel administration, recruitment, workforce deployment

Table 2.1 SAP Applications

Category	Typical Areas of Use
Procurement and Logistics Execution	Logistics, warehouse management, purchasing, purchase order processing
Product Development and Manufacturing	Production planning, manufacturing, product development, document management
Sales and Service	Order processing, customer service, services
Corporate Services	Real estate management, plant maintenance, travel management, quality management, occupational health and safety, environmental protection
Product Lifecycle Management (PLM)	Management of a product's lifecycle
Customer Relationship Management (CRM)	Customer acquisition, customer retention, front office
Supplier Relationship Management (SRM)	Automation of procurement processes, vendor evaluation and negotiations, collaboration with vendors

Table 2.1 SAP Applications (Cont.)

In the past, many SAP products required extensive modifications to make them match the individual requirements of an enterprise — a process known as *Customizing*. Today, many ERP solutions are delivered as "out-of-the-box" solutions, which can be used in the organization with little or no modification. However, the fact that SAP products come with pre-configured content makes them no less flexible and adaptable.

▶ **Note**

In Customizing, you adapt a standard software application to the specific requirements and organizational structures of your enterprise. Many SAP applications are only ready for use after you have made the necessary changes. Customizing settings are made when an SAP system is implemented or enhanced, as well as during release changes or upgrade projects.

They also come with *integrated* best practices that exist for the most frequently used business processes. This means that an application such as SAP CRM (see Figure 2.4) can be used with only very slight changes in customer service or in sales order processing.

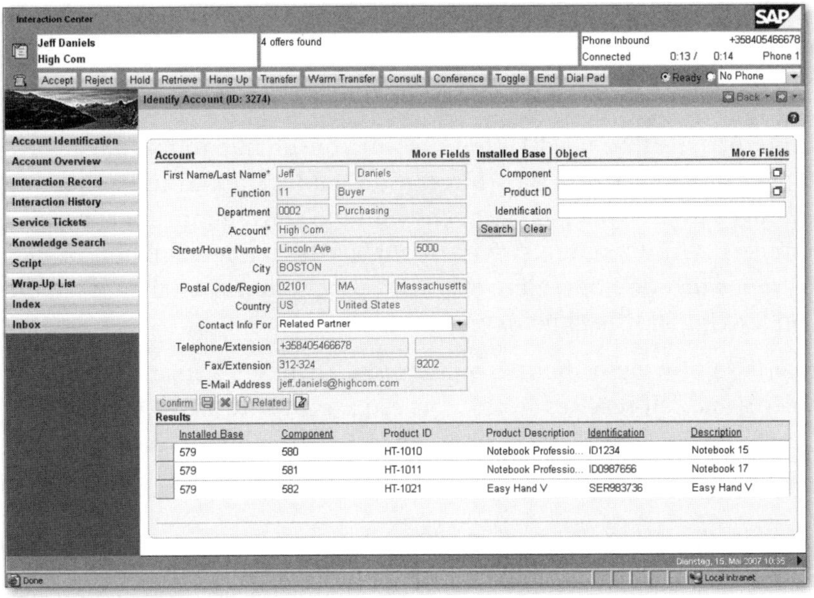

Figure 2.4 SAP CRM Tools for Maintaining Customer Relationships

SAP Business One, *SAP Business All-in-One*, and *Business by Design* include solutions designed especially for small and midsize enterprises. For more information, refer to Chapter 11, SAP's Strategy for Small to Midsize Enterprises.

Solutions for SMEs

Because SAP is itself an enterprise that is growing and learning all the time, new products and technologies will continue to evolve in the future. For this reason, we turn to the matter of SAP's focus at the present time and for the coming years.

Where Is SAP Headed?

SAP's focus remains firmly fixed on providing enterprises with technologies, software, and services to help them respond more flexibly to change, reduce operating costs, and enhance their internal processes to collaborate more efficiently with customers, vendors, and partners. One of SAP's key objectives is therefore to allow enterprises to acquire and analyze reliable data. Thanks to enhanced user interfaces and easy access options, SAP also makes it easier for end users to do their work in the SAP system. SAP realizes these goals in various ways. So let's look into the issues currently in SAP's focus.

An Invisible Enabling Technology

Enterprises often need large teams of consultants to customize SAP applications, perform data integration, and train end users. Making changes to the system is frequently a time-consuming and expensive process. SAP therefore strives to enable the implementation of ERP systems that do not require extensive programming or changes to the underlying Basis technology.

User interfaces

SAP also provides various *user interfaces*. Thanks to personalized work-places and self-services areas, users can execute processes without having to request information from other departments. These tools facilitate access to the SAP system, regardless of the size of the enterprise.

User-Friendly Access for End Users

Users in the enterprise have various options for accessing enterprise software. The integration of Microsoft Office and the use of Adobe form technology are two examples of new developments to facilitate system access. These topics are discussed in detail in Chapter 14, User-Friendly SAP — Duet™, Alloy™, and Adobe® Interactive Forms, but here's a brief overview.

Duet and Microsoft

The *Duet* (see Figure 2.5) product was jointly developed by SAP and Microsoft. It allows employees to use popular Office applications such as Microsoft Excel, Word, or Outlook in the ERP environment. Duet allows you to access enterprise data and tools to help with decision making (e.g., reports and analyses) and to use these in conjunction with Office applications.

Adobe forms

SAP Interactive Forms by Adobe provides functions for easy and efficient creation and completion of forms. These forms can be integrated into business processes, efficiently filled out, and sent to the right people.

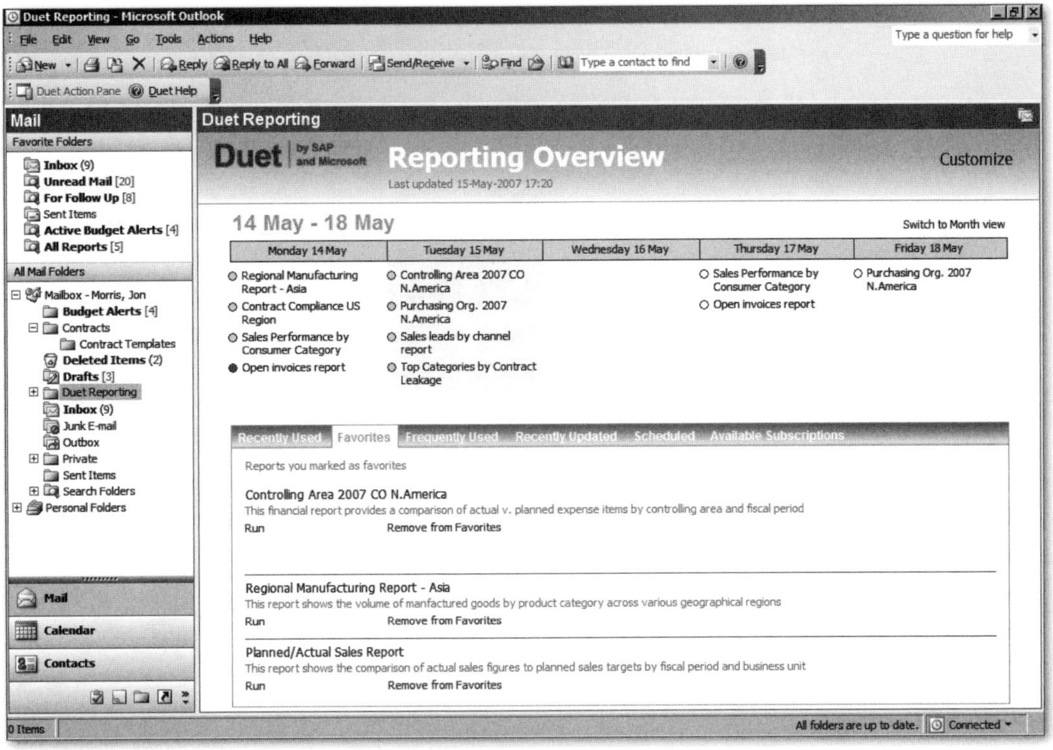

Figure 2.5 Using the Familiar MS Outlook Interface with Duet

Another form of user access is portals, so we look at these next and then move on to roles and access authorizations for specific portal content, and finally to self-service functions.

The Portal as an Interface with Users

The underlying architecture or technology of the SAP system is invisible to end users. All they see is the data they need to do their work.

In many SAP applications, the *SAP NetWeaver Portal* user interface is used to display this data. This interface, which allows users to access functions, information, and services, is similar to the web interfaces with which you are familiar from using the Internet.

For example, the portals that SAP refers to as *workplaces* provide employees with the specific data and functions they need for day-to-

Portals, roles, workplaces

day work. *Work triggers* allow data to be assigned to users via these portals based on their roles in the enterprise.

You can manage your calendar, contacts, email, and so on in the portal. You can also add the information and analyses you need for your daily work. Figure 2.6 shows a typical portal area.

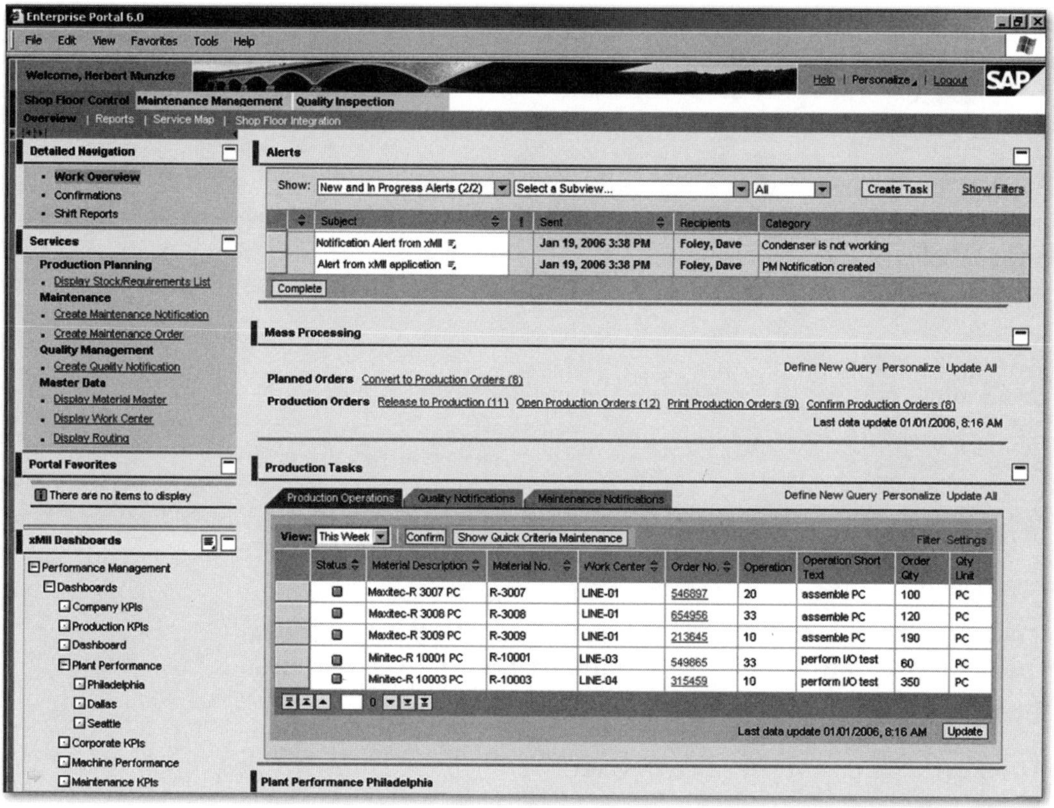

Figure 2.6 Typical Portal with Various Data and Alerts

It's important to note that the use of portals depends on the employees' role-based access.

The Role Concept

The concept of *roles* is a key aspect of portals. Each employee in an enterprise is assigned at least one role, and specific information and functions are required to fulfill the tasks associated with each role.

Example

> Everyone in an enterprise is an employee of that enterprise, and as such requires access to information from the HR department, such as details about training courses and leave requests. An employee may also be part of the management team, and, in this case, requires data about the tasks and productivity of the employees in his department. A manager may simultaneously be an engineer and require information about technological developments or new equipment. These three titles — employee, manager, and engineer — are examples of different roles.

An enterprise can assign specific roles to an employee. Based on these roles, the employee can access the required functions and data in the SAP system. Data and notifications (alerts) can also be sent to the employee automatically via his workplace.

Various authorizations are defined in the SAP system for each role. This allows employees to access the data and processes they need, while at the same time preventing them from displaying or changing data for which they do not have authorization.

Authorization concept

Roles are also of central importance to the employee self-service function, so let's look at the use of self-services next.

Self-Services for Increased Efficiency

SAP NetWeaver and the applications in the SAP Business Suite provide enterprises with self-service areas. *Self-service* means that employees and managers can complete certain tasks without any help from other employees — just like in a self-service store. Self-services are comparable with Internet services, which allow you to make purchases, find information, and communicate with other users without having to go to your local store, library, or post office.

Self-service

These self-service functions are provided by the SAP NetWeaver Portal, which allows users to access content via a browser interface. Tools are provided to guide users step-by-step through the process. These tools, referred to as *guided procedures*, will be familiar to you from using the Internet to make reservations (e.g., to reserve plane tickets).

Guided procedures

Example

> If employees want to check their remaining vacation for a year, they usually have to request this information from the HR department and wait for an answer. With self-services, employees can check their remaining vacation in the system themselves and also request vacation time without having to contact the HR department. This procedure reduces the workload of HR staff, who can then devote more time to other tasks.

Various examples of self-services are shown in Figure 2.7.

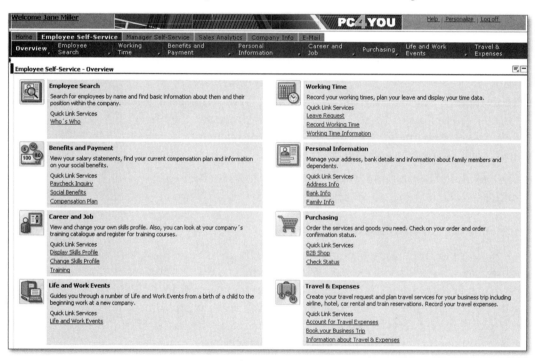

Figure 2.7 Integration of Self-Services in a Workplace

ESS and MSS

SAP offers self-services for both employees (Employee Self-Services) and managers (Manager Self-Services) in an enterprise.

Employee Self-Services (ESS) currently includes the following functions:

> Time management
> Time recording corrections

> Travel management
> Life and work event management
> Management of benefits
> Purchasing

Manager Self-Services (MSS) includes:

> Budgeting
> Personnel planning
> Performance management
> Purchase requisitions
> Equipment management

More information about self-services is provided in Chapter 16, User Productivity Tools for Information Workers.

Another focal point for SAP, which was also mentioned earlier, is the enhancement of its product portfolio for small and midsize enterprises.

Enhancing Functionality for Small and Midsize Enterprises

All over the world, many large corporations use an enterprise software solution, and in many cases, it is SAP. SAP will continue to offer software, support, and new technologies to these enterprises in the future. In addition, SAP is currently focusing on customer-specific solutions that can be quickly implemented in small and midsize enterprises. In the future, SAP will develop increasing numbers of complete software packages and add-ons for frequently used business products to help increase the productivity of users. The guided procedures used in self-service scenarios will reduce the time needed to train new employees in these new products.

Benefits Offered by SAP

The purpose of enterprise software is to help enterprises meet their strategic objectives. Therefore, the way SAP ERP and other applications can enhance business processes is the primary concern, not the technology used. If you are considering implementing an ERP system, your focus will be on the capabilities of the software, which must fulfill your specific requirements.

Therefore, the following concepts are all important when considering the use of enterprise software:

> **Return on investment (ROI)**
> The ratio of profit made on an investment in a software solution relative to the amount of capital invested.

> **Total cost of ownership (TCO)**
> The total costs involved in operating the software, which should be kept to a minimum.

> **Compliance**
> Adherence to various legal or internal regulations.

> **Outsourcing**
> The option of subcontracting parts of the business process to external providers.

A key argument in favor of implementing an integrated enterprise software solution is the possibility of automating processes, a step that reduces costs while increasing efficiency. Thanks to centralized data storage, you can also run reports and analyses to help you make the right decisions for your business. For many enterprises, meeting customer requirements as quickly as possible is absolutely essential to remaining competitive in the face of market changes. In other words, the time it takes to position a product in the market after it has been developed (*time to market*) must be minimized to give the enterprise a competitive edge.

To sum up, the following core capabilities are essential to the success of an enterprise:

> **Differentiation**
> The ability of an enterprise to set itself apart from its competitors.

> **Productivity**
> The ability to work efficiently and cost-effectively.

> **Flexibility**
> The ability to react quickly to change.

These are all concepts that you will encounter again and again when using an SAP system or reading SAP publications.

Conclusion

This chapter introduced you to several fundamental concepts and terms relating to the SAP environment, including the following:

> Definitions of the terms "enterprise," "enterprise software," and "ERP"

> The history of the development of enterprise software and current concepts relating to ERP

> The meaning of data integration

> SAP's focus on business processes

SAP has developed an ERP system that offers a flexible approach to the use of services and is based on an open technology platform that facilitates the integration of users, data, and processes. To help you understand the technological basis of SAP applications, in this chapter we discussed the following topics:

> SAP's approach to service-oriented architecture

> The role of SAP NetWeaver as a platform for SAP applications

> Open architectures, composite applications, and the ways in which these simplify processes

> Tools such as portals and self-services, which help employees work more efficiently

Now that you're familiar with the basic concepts and technologies in SAP, let's move onto Chapter 3, Business Suite 7 Overview, which provides more information about SAP's applications that support common business functions.

Business Suite 7 Overview

Technology and its link to the global economy shows us just how quickly consumers' want and need change, and how that rapid change can have an impact on your company's ability to meet these needs in a timely fashion. To stay competitive, enter a new market niche, or maintain your current market share, you must be able to drive and direct how quickly your company adapts to new changes or meets current customer demands.

Keeping IT applications and business processes up-to-date and tuned to quickly respond to these needs is a challenge facing many organizations. Large enterprises today have to undergo three major phases before they are up and running with the latest and greatest software applications. First, there is the technical upgrade to ensure your hardware can handle the new applications. Next, many new software packages make you look at your current business processes and tweak them, add new processes, or retire old ones.

Meeting your customers' needs during changing market conditions

Lastly, you add the new software to get the desired new changes in functionality and then spend time training your employees on how to use the new package. What does this mean to you? Extensive time and money will be spent on what turns out to be a full-fledged upgrade, which also includes a lot of features and functions that have nothing to do with the enhancements you wanted to make. When IT budgets are already under scrutiny, and you are doing more with less, this becomes a tough business case to make. To help you reduce your total cost of ownership (TCO) and provide your organization with the ability to implement only those functions you need at the time you need them, SAP has developed the Business Suite 7 package.

SAP's new Business Suite 7 helps lead the trend away from costly and time-consuming upgrades. Released in 2009, Business Suite 7 helps larger enterprises adapt a modular approach to enhancing their technical functionality, while also reducing the costs and time associated with software implementations.

Business Suite 7 is an integrated suite of products consisting of SAP ERP, SAP Customer Relationship Management (SAP CRM), SAP Supplier Relationship Management (SAP SRM), SAP Product Lifecycle Management (SAP PLM), and SAP Supply Chain Management (SAP SCM). This integrated lifecycle set of applications provides you with built-in business expertise, as well as tools and best practices that reduce efforts directed toward testing and customization. This allows you to more quickly deploy new innovations and products, which improves your response to changing market conditions and allows you to better meet your customers' needs. We'll take a look at each of these applications next.

Modular upgrade approach

Overview of Business Suite Solutions

As we've mentioned, one of the biggest draws to using the Business Suite 7 solutions is their ability to be implemented in modular fashion. This allows you to focus on the critical areas of your business while keeping IT costs in line. So let's look at SAP ERP, the core product in the Business Suite package.

SAP ERP

The SAP ERP application lets you hone your company's financial, human capital, operations, and corporate services practices to ensure they are aligned with the overall corporate strategy.

> **SAP ERP Financials**
> Includes tools for core accounting and reporting capabilities, financial links to supply chain processes, functions to keep you in com-

pliance with government and global financial regulations, and help to monitor your incoming and outgoing cash flow while minimizing financial risks to your organization.

> **SAP ERP Human Capital Management**
> Empowers your employees to manage their personal information, such as marriage, birth of a child, and benefits coverage, as well as work events such as time recording and signing up for training (Figure 3.1). Likewise, supervisors participate in the employee development and compensation processes, and collaborate with other departments during the development of a corporate budget.

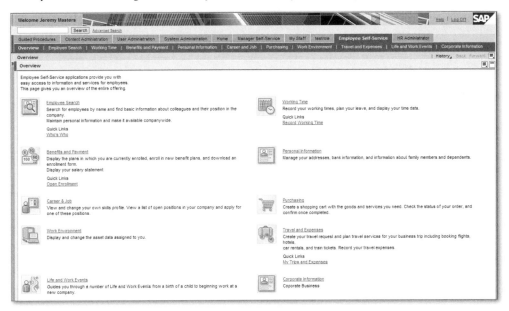

Figure 3.1 Employee Self-Service Portal for Benefits Management

> **SAP ERP Operations**
> Tools that help you manage and streamline the day-to-day activities within your organization. With SAP ERP Operations features, you can automate processes to reduce costs and waste, manage your production cycle, and provide self-service opportunities for your customers.

> **SAP ERP Corporate Services**
> Functions in the SAP ERP Corporate Services segment manage external activities associated with real estate, corporate travel, corpo-

rate assets, and environmental health and safety issues. If you have an international organization, the Global Trade Services portion of SAP ERP Corporate Services keeps you in compliance with trade, tariff, and documentation requirements.

The SAP ERP tools keep your organization running smoothly for your employees and management staff.

SAP Customer Relationship Management

SAP CRM

The SAP Customer Relationship Management (SAP CRM) tools focus on one of your most important assets, your customers. To stay competitive, you need to find a way to maintain your current clientele and attract new customers by differentiating yourself from others in your industry. See how SAP's CRM tools can help you achieve your long-term goals in this area.

Marketing, sales, service, and e-commerce

> **Marketing**
> Features in the marketing area help you with brand and loyalty management, market segmentation, managing your market campaigns, and finding new ways to reach out to customers through e-marketing campaigns.

> **Sales**
> These tools promote collaboration between your marketing and sales forces so that customer needs are met. Functions in the sales portion of SAP CRM help you determine what sales areas are profitable, and how to deliver the most positive customer experience to build brand loyalty and return sales.

> **Service**
> With service tools, you take a proactive stance to servicing your customers by providing your staff with all of the information they need to know at just the right time. Other features allow you to manage your service agreements and contracts, and set up alerts to notify the customers when their contracts are about to expire. Inventory management tools allow you to keep track of the parts and materials on hand, which enables you to quickly address customer issues as soon as they arise. SAP CRM service tools also let you establish secure web portals to provide an additional means of interaction between you and your customers.

> **Contact Center**
> Customers like to feel they have received personalized service from you. With the Contact Center tools, you can deliver your sales, marketing, and service message to your customers over a variety of channels to meet their individual needs.

> **E-Commerce**
> Take advantage of today's Internet technology to reach your customers with SAP CRM's e-commerce features (see Figure 3.2). These tools provide a means for you to analyze trends resulting from your e-commerce business, as well as a way for your customers to order your products and report service issues online.

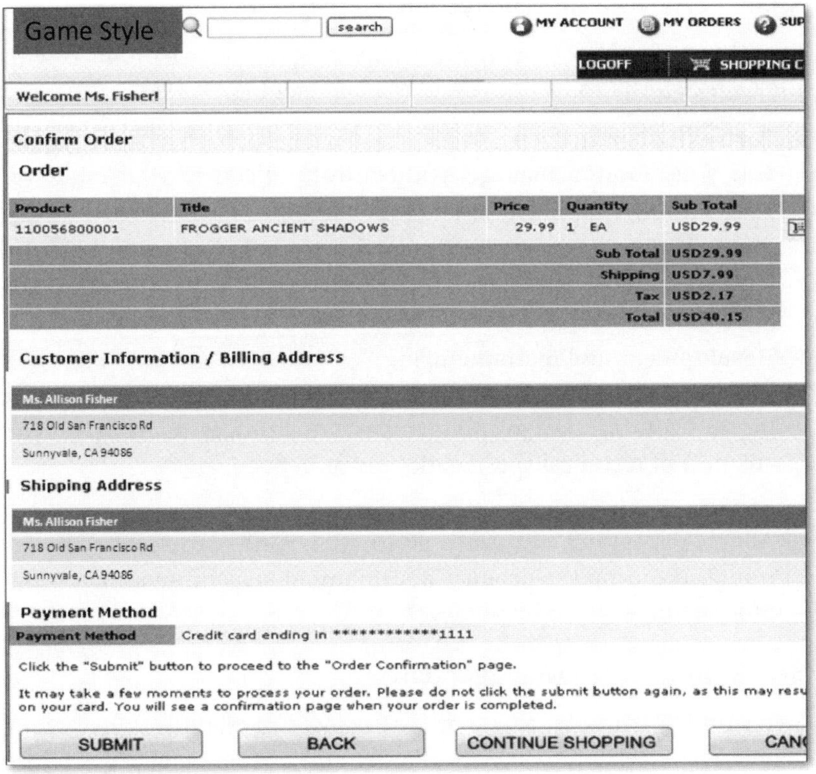

Figure 3.2 Ordering Your Products Online

SAP CRM products help bring your business to the forefront for your customers and let your business prosper even during tough economic times.

SAP Supplier Relationship Management

Having streamlined your daily operations and developed prosperous customer relationships, SAP Supplier Relationship Management (SAP SRM) helps you focus your efforts on your relationship with your suppliers and vendors. Here, you examine your procurement process to maximize efficiency from the initial contract bidding through the receipt of final payment. To help your staff have materials and supplies on hand when they need them, other features in SAP SRM help you evaluate your suppliers' performance and provide a portal for collaboration between your purchasing group and your vendors.

1.1.4 SAP Product Lifecycle Management

Stay ahead of your competition by delivering innovative products with the help of SAP Product Lifecycle Management (SAP PLM).

> **Portfolio planning**
> Lets you monitor, manage, and control projects in your organization from inception through implementation. These tools also help you rank and prioritize your projects through collaboration efforts between various department members to ensure your projects align with strategic corporate initiatives.

> **Development and manufacturing**
> Allows you to accelerate the development of new products by helping you with the design and manufacturing processes, as well as the creation of technical specification documents.

> **Service**
> Allows the service, warranty, and maintenance processes to be introduced during the product development stage, providing a view of the complete product lifecycle.

SAP Supply Chain Management

SAP Supply Chain Management (SAP SCM) has features to help your supply chain respond faster to market and economic changes while keeping the focus on the customer.

> **Planning**
> Lets you optimize planning activities involving safety stock, the supply network, supply distribution, and supply chain design.

> **Execution**
  Monitors costs and efficiencies in your supply chain during order fulfillment, procurement, transportation, and warehousing.

> **Collaboration**
  Connects you with suppliers, customers, and manufacturers so that information can be shared, and your supply chain can function without disruption.

We've given you a brief overview of each of the Business Suite 7 components and their features; now we'll show you how they benefit your business.

Business Suite 7 Benefits

SAP Business Suite 7 covers all aspects of your business and brings you tools to help you reduce costs, be more efficient, and bring new innovations to fruition faster. SAP also worked with its customers and partners to develop value scenarios, which are industry-specific processes that take you end-to-end to achieve desired outcomes. For example, if you are in the retail industry, customers' buying habits can determine how your business operates. With the "inspired shopping experience" value scenario, retail management learns how their business must change or adapt to maintain customer and brand loyalty (see Figure 3.3).

Industry-specific value scenarios

Overarching Goals			
Operational Excellence	Integrated Sourcing and Procurement	Efficient Manufacturing Operations	Delivering Efficient After Sales Service
Responsive Supply Networks	Collaborative Demand and Supply Planning	Manufacturing Network Planning and Execution	Logistics and Fulfillment Management
Product and Service Leadership	Integrated Product Development	Continuous Product and Service Innovation / Embedded Product Compliance	Product Delivered as a Service
High Performing Assets	Asset Visibility and Performance	Optimized Asset Operations and Maintenance	Asset Safety and Compliance
Superior Customer Value	Optimizing Sales and Marketing Investments	Differentiation through Service Excellence (Discrete) / Accelerating Lead-to-Cash	Differentiation through Service Excellence (Final Services)

Figure 3.3 Value Scenarios Transcend Corporate Boundaries

Business Suite includes SAP's BusinessObjects analytics

Business Suite 7 has incorporated the analytics features from its BusinessObjects portfolio (see Chapter 11, SAP's Strategy for Small to Midsize Enterprises) to provide you with better insight into how well your organization is performing and meeting its strategic goals. The ability to monitor all aspects of your business provides you with the information and flexibility you need to make decisions or alter your strategy to meet your business objectives.

Ability to get information from all sources

The modules of the Business Suite 7 package are built with SOA architecture (see Chapter 17, Service-Oriented Architecture) and SAP NetWeaver technology (see Chapter 18, SAP NetWeaver as a Technology Platform). What this means is that the suite integrates with existing SAP applications as well as your non-SAP applications. You can access data from all sources to help you in decision making, strategy execution, and product development.

Harmonized user interface

In addition to helping you reduce costs and streamline processes through value scenarios, you can also reduce the need for extra training each time you add on another Business Suite application. All Business Suite applications are designed with the same user interface, which means they all have the same look and feel. Your employees will spend more time using the applications than trying to understand how they operate.

Reduce deployment time with enhancement packages

Perhaps one of the biggest benefits of SAP's Business Suite 7 is that it is less expensive to deploy. Your company purchases only the application for the area it wants to improve, instead of purchasing an entire software application package. Your deployment is then a matter of switching on only those features within the module that contain the enhancements or functionality you need. When the enhancements are turned on, they are immediately incorporated into your current business processes. Enhancement packages then provide the opportunity for you to add additional industry-specific features to your system on an as-needed basis. Again, by turning on only the features you want, your company avoids the time and expense associated with a major system upgrade.

Synchronized release schedule for all Business Suite modules

Regardless of which Business Suite 7 applications you have purchased, SAP has synchronized the release of its upgrades for all applications. For example, if you purchased the SAP SCM application, and then two years later purchased the SAP CRM application, when the next software release comes out from SAP, you can upgrade your two modules simultaneously. This ensures your software always has the most current features and functionality, and that only one upgrade is necessary for all parts of the Business Suite.

Being able to add software in an on-demand fashion helps your business react more quickly to market changes, pushes new products through the pipeline faster, and keeps your business prosperous even during rough economic periods. In the next chapters, we'll examine the individual applications in more detail.

Conclusion

SAP Business Suite 7 applications connect all facets of your operation and provide you with greater insight and access to the information you need to analyze your business, make better informed decisions, and strategically position yourself for growth. With the ability to upgrade via enhancement packs and the inclusion of more than 24 industry-specific best practices, you'll be able to reduce your TCO and more quickly realize the benefits to your company, and at the same time reduce inefficiencies and streamline your processes.

In the next chapter, we'll begin our review of the SAP products, beginning with SAP ERP Financials.

PART II
SAP Products

4

SAP ERP Financials

SAP's first product offering back in the 1980s was the Financials package for enterprises. Because financial activity is vital to the life of any company in any industry, this was a logical starting point. Today SAP ERP Financials is more robust than ever, with tools that allow companies to not only automate routine financial activities such as managing their general ledger but also to improve their ability to budget and forecast using analytics, smooth their cash flow to make themselves more profitable, and stay on track with local and global financial compliance requirements.

In this chapter, we look at the role of SAP ERP Financials in an enterprise and the specific features that SAP's financial software provides. We conclude the chapter with two case studies that show you how SAP ERP Financials provides benefits in real-world settings.

How SAP ERP Financials Fits in an Enterprise

For most business people, it's not hard to imagine the benefits of efficient, accurate accounting software tools. However, the scope of what SAP ERP Financials can do for an organization goes far beyond keeping numbers accurate. In this section, we look at the ways in which SAP ERP Financials helps you handle your cash flow better, deliver

Specific SAP
Financials features

reports and data that help you make key decisions, and support alignment with financial requirements to keep your company in compliance (Figure 4.1).

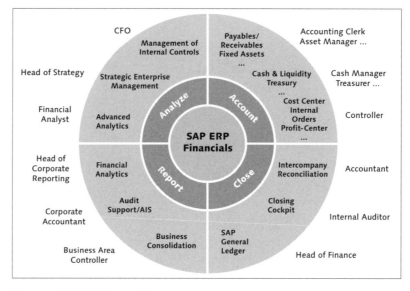

Figure 4.1 SAP ERP Financials

Optimized Cash Flow

Cash is the lifeblood of any organization, and keeping it flowing in a timely way is vital to your profitability and sometimes even to your survival. The ability to manage the cash in your enterprise is part of the SAP ERP Financials package.

Cash flow cycle; financial supply chain

SAP ERP Financials includes tools you can use to manage the financial supply chain and cash flow cycle from end to end. By automating several procedures, you can reduce the time it takes to collect cash from your sales, which can make a big difference to your bottom line. SAP ERP Financials consists of the following:

> **Financial Supply Chain Management**
> Provides tools to access online invoices and payments, analyze customers' credit worthiness, facilitate online billing disputes, and prioritize payment collection to reduce the number of overdue accounts.

> **SAP BusinessObjects Planning and Consolidation**
> These functions help consolidate your individual department plans

and budgets into one corporate plan while providing what-if scenarios to help you test your budget assumptions. At the same time, you have a well-documented audit trail to provide the compliance and reporting you need internally and externally.

Four key financial areas that SAP ERP Financials supports (see Appendix C for SAP ERP Financials Solution Map details) are the following:

> **Financial Supply Chain Management**
> This area enables you to handle electronic invoicing, payments, and dispute and collections management.

> **Treasury**
> Provides tools for risk management, cash and liquidity management, and bank communication management.

> **Financial Accounting**
> This area has features such as consolidations, general-ledger management, and accounts receivable and payable.

> **Management Accounting**
> This area enables you to handle activities such as profit center accounting, project accounting, and revenue and cost planning.

Of course, all of these management tools are very useful, but when it comes down to it, the key to keeping your cash flow moving along in a productive way is having the information you need to make good decisions. That's where SAP ERP Financials' strong analytic tools come in.

Better Business Insight

Today more than ever, in addition to cash, information drives your business. With easy and instant access to financial data, employees can be more productive in their work. They have the correct information they need to complete transactions, report on their activity, serve customers, and plan future activities based on solid forecasts.

In describing SAP ERP Financials, SAP states that "SAP ERP provides a complete analytical framework to consolidate and dissect business information generated in your industry solutions or your core enterprise processes." This simply means that you can access business data in real time, use that data to make better business decisions, and produce impressive reports and analyses from that data (see Figure 4.2). This is possible because of the data integration capabilities of SAP

SAP ERP Financials rests on SAP NetWeaver

NetWeaver, the platform that SAP ERP Financials rests on, and the analytical tools built into SAP ERP Financials.

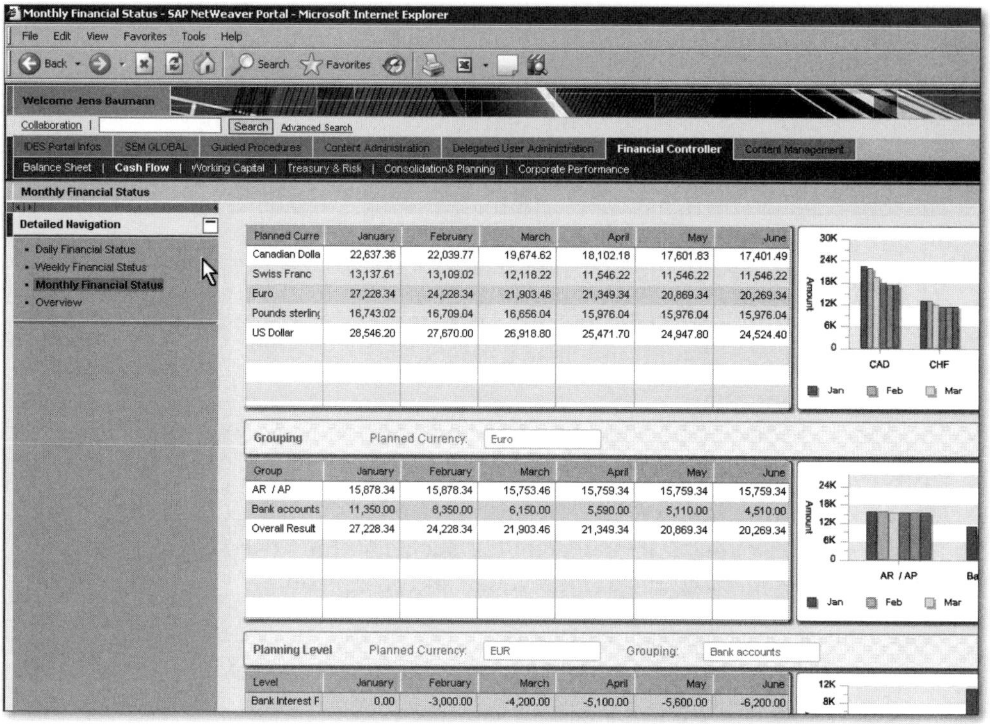

Figure 4.2 Analytical Tools Provide a Wealth of Information

Portals, work centers

SAP ERP Financials allows all of the various sets of data and financial activities in your business to be integrated, so that your employees can use *key performance indicators* (KPIs) in the context of their everyday work. By using the portal technology supported by SAP NetWeaver, individual workers can have reports and analytics pushed into their desktop work centers (i.e., their centralized online data, schedule, and tools page). Based on employee roles in the company, financial data that matches each person's needs can appear in work centers without anyone having to ask for it.

➕ Tip

Because the design of SAP ERP Financials is intuitive, most employees have a fast learning curve and can get to work with minimal training.

SAP ERP Financials and Analytics

So, what can you actually do with SAP ERP Financials and its analytic capabilities? You can get all kinds of reports, forecasts, and analyses that help you decide how and when to spend your money and make changes in your operations.

SAP BusinessObjects BPC and SAP NetWeaver BW

Through the use of SAP BusinessObjects Planning and Consolidation (BPC), and SAP NetWeaver Business Warehouse (SAP NetWeaver BW), which you'll learn more about in Chapters 12 and 18, SAP ERP Financials allows you to perform the following analytical activities:

> Generate consolidated financial and statutory reports.

> Plan, budget, and forecast.

> Run cause and effect analyses.

> Analyze profitability by criteria such as unit, profit center, or geographical location.

> Calculate and manage risk.

> Analyze product and service costing.

> Review payment behavior.

> Calculate overhead costs.

In other words, if you have good information, you can use it in a variety of ways to help you manage your business. SAP ERP Financials not only provides the information, it also provides the tools you need to calculate, analyze, and display financial information to others.

The final piece of the SAP ERP Financials functionality is the ability to help you stay in compliance with a world of financial requirements in today's global economy.

Calculate, analyze, and display financial information

Improved Compliance

When you consider the financial scandals that have rocked the business world in recent years, the need to comply with regulations regarding your company's financials is pressing. If you're in senior management, you're well aware that corporate executives can be held personally responsible for not meeting current accounting standards.

Although the need for accountability is strong, compliance isn't always easy. Different regulations exist when you're doing business in differ-

Sarbanes-Oxley Act

ent countries or industries. The Sarbanes-Oxley Act (SOX) that is in effect in the United States, for example, does not provide a set of business practices so much as a direction about what business records to store and for what period of time. It also includes regulations for the storage of electronic records, which has an impact on your IT department. If a transaction involves other countries, you must ensure that you are complying with all regulations for record retention.

GAAP, IFRS, Basel II
One of the functions of SAP ERP Financials is to help you comply with regulations that demand quality financial reporting and strong internal controls, such as the SOX, US Generally Accepted Accounting Principles (GAAP), International Financial Reporting Standards (IFRS), and Basel II.

> ### New GAAP and IFRS Regulations
>
> Beginning in 2012, US companies will be required to do dual-reporting in both GAAP and IFRS. Beginning in 2015, US companies will be required to report only in IFRS.

SAP ERP Financials, in conjunction with SAP BusinessObjects, provides several tools to stay in compliance, as shown in Figure 4.3. In addition, as you can see in Figure 4.4, you get tools for managing access control, global trade, environment, and process control, in addition to risk management features.

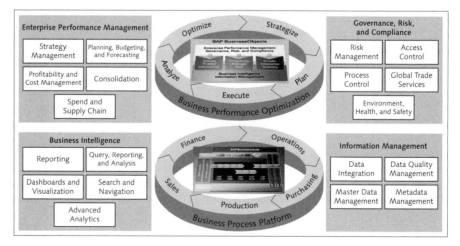

Figure 4.3 SAP ERP Financials Combines with SAP BusinessObjects

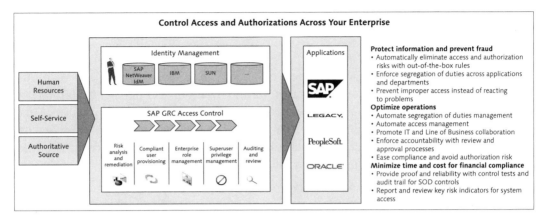

Figure 4.4 Built-in Access Controls Help Keep Your Financials in Compliance

With SAP ERP Financials and SAP BusinessObjects, you get tools to support the following compliance-related activities:

SAP BusinessObjects is covered in detail in Chapter 12

> Audit information systems

> Management of internal controls

> Whistleblower complaints

> Transparency to comply with financial regulations

Now that you have an overview of how SAP ERP Financials addresses cash flow, analytics, and compliance issues, let's look at the specific features in SAP ERP Financials that help you to achieve these benefits.

A Closer Look at SAP ERP Financials

Because you now have an idea of how SAP ERP Financials fits into a business, it's time to explore the specific functions and components included in SAP ERP Financials and see how they work in a real-world business setting.

Key Features and Functions

SAP ERP Financials provides a framework to help you manage the financial side of your business. But you may be wondering what exactly these features allow you to do. Here are some of the features and functions in SAP ERP Financials and how they support business activities:

> **Biller Direct**
> Give your customers online access to their monthly and yearly invoices, account status, bill itemization, and payment information. Customers can then save or print this information in a format that is useful to them. This data is also readily available to other departments within your company, such as call center agents, who may need it to resolve customer inquiries.

> **Cash and Liquidity Management**
> Manage and streamline your accounts receivable process so that your cash is available when you need it. Cash Liquidity Management also enables you to pinpoint where and how your cash is being spent so that you improve your cash forecasting. Lastly, tools are provided to support electronic bank interfaces that help you reduce manual reconciliations and establish in-house banking to give you more control over your cash.

> **Fast Close Cockpit**
> Efficiently generate reliable and consistent financial closing information from all sources, while providing one central point of data control and monitoring. Accurate financial reports are then available for regulatory and reporting purposes. The Fast Close Cockpit automates many tasks associated with the closing process, and reduces the reliance on manual processes and spreadsheets.

Meet financial reporting needs

> **Financial and Management Reporting**
> Use this set of standard analyses that meet the reporting needs of a wide variety of roles in your organization, such as senior executives, line-of-business managers, and sales assistants. The usefulness of these reports isn't limited to internal people; reports can be designed to meet the needs of shareholders, banks, and other financial institutions.

> **Planning, Budgeting, and Forecasting**
> These tools handle anything from traditional budgeting to rolling forecasts. You can use Financials tools for collaborative planning, such as cost center planning. The analytical planning workbench allows you to model planning scenarios, with preconfigured planning applications that support your operational planning.

> **Strategy Management and Scorecards**
> Link and align operational and strategic plans and develop key performance indicators (KPIs) that support a number of popular *scorecard* methodologies. Scorecards are a type of financial report that typically color code and set up data so that it's easy to analyze. Supported scorecard methodologies include balanced scorecard, economic value added, and activity-based costing methods.

Scorecards

> **Cost and Profitability Management**
> Assign overhead costs, manage the costs of producing products and services, and analyze the profitability of various products and services.

> **Working Capital and Cash Flow Management**
> Manage your capital with functions that support your processes and improve your liabilities and receivables management. You can manage cash flow, including cash flow calculations and middle- and long-term planning.

 **Tip**

You can also manage receivables by analyzing payment histories and determining the Days Sales Outstanding (DSO), which allows you to optimize payment schedules.

To get an idea of the breadth of features that you get with SAP ERP Financials, Table 4.1 shows the various categories of functions that are included with the applications they contain.

Category	Application
Financial Supply Chain Management	Credit Management
	Electronic Bill Presentment and Payment
	Dispute Management
	Collections Management
Treasury	Treasury and Risk Management
	Cash and Liquidity Management
	In-House Cash
	Bank Communication Management

Table 4.1 SAP ERP Financials Solution Map

Category	Application
Financial Accounting	General Ledger
	Financial Statements
	Accounts Receivable
	Accounts Payable
	Contract Accounting
	Fixed Assets Accounting
	Bank Accounting
	Cash Journal Accounting
	Inventory Accounting
	Tax Accounting
	Accrual Accounting
	Local Close
	Travel Management
Management Accounting	Cost Center and Internal Order Accounting
	Profit Center Accounting
	Project Accounting
	Investment Management
	Product Cost Accounting
	Profitability Accounting
	Transfer Pricing
Corporate Governance	Audit Information System
	Management of Internal Controls
	Risk Management
	Whistleblower Complaints
	Segregation of Duties

Table 4.1 SAP ERP Financials Solution Map (Cont.)

Industry-Specific Financial Management

Functionality for
more than 25
industries

In addition to all of the standard financial functions, SAP ERP Financials can also provide industry-specific financial management functions. In more than 25 industries, including automotive and pharmaceuticals, SAP has developed sets of best practices that help implement processes that match your business's core accounting and reporting requirements. For example, if you work in the automotive industry sector, dealer management features and service parts management are best practices tools that help you manage tasks specific to your industry.

There are also cross-industry best practices available for functions such as customer resource management and human capital management.

Best practices

 Example

> Consider funds management in the public sector area. The traditional organization and processes of government agencies are under scrutiny today because of shrinking funds and more involved and savvy citizens. SAP ERP Financials can help a government entity plan and control the flow of revenues and expenditures with a modern, double-entry bookkeeping method that increases cost transparency. The public sector solution also offers active availability controls to monitor financial appropriations (such as funds appropriated for specific initiatives). Special planning techniques uniquely useful in funds management make it possible to differentiate provisional budget plans, which may have to undergo a lengthy approval or vote process.

Keep in mind that SAP ERP Financials is an open solution that can dovetail with other complementary analytical solutions from SAP or third parties.

So what does SAP ERP Financials look like in a specific company setting? We provide two case studies that demonstrate how the product works in two different industry settings.

SAP ERP Financials Case Study 1

Review Table 4.2, which gives you a snapshot of a case study, and then read the rest of this section to see SAP ERP Financials in action.

SAP ERP Financials in a real-world setting can help solve a variety of problems based on careful analysis of an individual business's needs and processes. In this case study, an international company, which places strong emphasis on building brand identity, was looking for a way to enhance its capital management processes. The company had implemented some core components of SAP ERP, so it found that the SAP Treasury and Risk Management application in SAP ERP Financials provided a fit.

Company	International liquor distributor
Existing Solutions	Core components of SAP ERP
Challenge	To enhance its capital management processes internationally
SAP Solutions	SAP ERP Financials SAP Treasury and Risk Management application
Benefits	More consistent data for bank reconciliations, direct connection with bank payment systems to avoid lost data, automating of collection processes, linking of daily cash investments to daily cash positions, and more

Table 4.2 SAP ERP Financials Case Study 1

SAP Treasury and Risk Management

The company went with SAP because it found strategic value in the integration of cash management, automated bank statements, accounts receivable, and accounts payable features. The company proceeded to implement pieces of the cash management solution in four phases, which we describe next.

Phase 1: Cash, Debt, and Investment Management

In this first phase, the company focused on managing working capital. It set goals of reconciling bank accounts on a daily basis: concentrating cash, calculating an amount of cash to borrow or invest each day, improving control and accuracy, and reducing its workforce.

SAP ERP Financials vendor payments

During this phase, every cash entry was set up to go through a single system. That system created automatic journal entries for the general ledger; this helped employees avoid repeated rekeying, which can introduce errors. Bank reconciliations became easier because the general ledger and bank were always aligned.

In addition, by using SAP ERP Financials, authorized individuals could view the same current bank statement information so no one had to route the information internally. Phase 1, the longest of the four phases, also implemented the following capabilities:

> **Vendor Payments**
> These payments were set up to upload directly into bank payment systems, which helped to avoid lost data. Payment files are now

saved in SAP data interchange file format (DIF) and can be sent using an electronic data interchange (EDI) translator so that they can be read by banking systems, which can then release payments.

> **Customer Receipts**
  These receipts allow customer payments to be directly uploaded into SAP applications from bank systems. Customer receipts are automatically posted into customer records in the Accounts Receivable module and the General Ledger.

> **Global Bank Account Information Management**
  This now automates the collection and processing of global bank account information (refer to Figure 4.3 for an example) and reconciles accounts for the United States and most international accounts on a daily basis. Domestic cash balances are centralized into one account, which means that the company receives a higher overnight rate of interest. Reports about current and previous-day balances help management make decisions about how to fund disbursement accounts.

> **Reduction in Number of Bank Accounts**
  This reduction was due to a function that allows for the postprocessing of bank statements to remove discrepancies. Without these discrepancies, it's easier to manage multiple complex types of transactions from a single account rather than maintaining separate accounts by transaction type.

> **Treasury Management for Debt and Investments**
  This feature supports the linking of investment contracts to daily cash positions, along with performance reporting and investment-tracking capabilities. The system automatically calculates debt and investment interest or fees. Settlements are prepared for the treasury department's banking and financial institution business partners based on established settlement instructions. At the end of each month, the system automatically calculates and posts accruals and foreign currency revaluations for investments, as well as debt.

SAP ERP Treasury Management

Phase 2: Global Cash Visibility

In the second phase of implementing SAP ERP Financials, the company focused on expanding the benefits of SAP ERP Financials by bringing six foreign subsidiaries into the reconciliation system. This centralization of account reconciliation helped make all financial information more visible to the company's accounting group. It involved uploading bank information for the subsidiaries to SAP ERP Financials to help the treasury department have access to worldwide cash positions. By centralizing this international banking activity, the company was able to close several more bank accounts. In addition, more and more payments were handled electronically, eliminating the need to maintain lockboxes.

Phase 3: Straight-Through Processing

Now it was time to tackle the *straight-through processing (STP)* payment process. Using this process, rather than uploading payments through banking software, payments are sent directly to the bank from SAP ERP Financials Accounts Payable payment data. This process works regardless of what form the payment might take, such as a foreign exchange draft or wire.

The resulting system is akin to an in-house bank that instructs an external bank to pay on their behalf. Because this cuts out some steps and automates journal entries, it keeps cash in-house longer, lowering costs. STP also allows for better internal controls because vendors' own banking information in the SAP ERP Financials Accounts Payable vendor master file is used to make payments.

Automated Clearing House (ACH)

The company also implemented an STP process for receivables. Because about 80% of domestic collections use Automated Clearing House (ACH) as its network for processing debits to customer accounts, the company can now send a payment file directly to the bank. This cuts out one internal processing step to save time.

In addition, during phase 3, the company improved vendor file accuracy using SAP ERP workflow to manage vendor master files, which eliminated duplicate activity and ensured better control of vendor file information.

Phase 4: Hedging of Foreign Exchange

Foreign exchange rate fluctuations

To help deal with fluctuations in foreign exchange rates, all foreign exchange contracts are now recorded in SAP ERP Financials. Each exchange trade creates a trade ticket, which in turn causes a confirmation of trade to be returned to the system. During this phase, the company integrates its commodities by hedging contracts into their accounting system using SAP ERP Financials. This removes the need to use a third-party foreign exchange management system.

SAP ERP Financials also enabled the company to use intercompany contracts, which allowed them to handle foreign subsidiaries that have to record foreign exchange hedge contracts locally. Those local contracts are now integrated with the company's core SAP data and with subsidiaries that report at the parent-company level.

Lastly, the company was required to perform auditing reviews to comply with the Sarbanes-Oxley Act. Through careful implementation of SAP software, auditing tasks were simplified, and controls were established to ensure compliance. Controls were therefore put in place at the front of workflow processes so the company didn't need controls at the backend.

Compliance controls

The company implemented segregation of duties for payment processes required by SOX. One example of this was the way that the company controlled wire transfers to set up STP so that changed vendor information couldn't be accessed inappropriately.

SAP ERP Financials Case Study 2

Let's look at another case study regarding SAP ERP Financials. First, review Table 4.3, and then read the remainder of the section.

Company	Large European hospital
Existing Solutions	Some SAP and some non-SAP software
Challenge	To improve their ability to manage patient treatments, reduce administrative workload, and reduce costs
SAP Solutions	SAP ERP Financials with SAP Patient Management application
Benefits	Improved ability to organize care system, reduced treatment time and lower costs, negotiation with insurers, and enhanced view of all activities and services delivered

Table 4.3 SAP ERP Financials Case Study 2

This technologically advanced hospital was looking for ways to meet the growing needs of patients by modifying its care process. This is a large regional hospital with a staff of more than 3,000 and more than 1,000 hospital beds. They implemented SAP ERP, including the Financials features, to help keep rising healthcare costs under control.

The Challenge

Rising healthcare costs and an aging population are putting all medical organizations under pressure. Any new system had to support business and administrative processes, as well as patient care processes.

Additional challenges involved dealing with a merger, changes from government to private funding, inflation, and the conversion to the Euro form of currency.

The Solution

At the time, only one vendor offered a solution for the healthcare sector. The hospital implemented SAP Patient Management, an application from an SAP partner, and SAP ERP Financials to help them control their cash management, sales and distribution, and materials management. These solutions provided tools for electronic patient management (EPR) as well as the ability to reduce administrative workload and save costs.

SAP Patient Management

SAP Patient Management also helped the hospital make connections between treatments and costs, enabling the hospital to negotiate rates with insurance companies and reduce patient waiting lists. SAP Workflow capabilities helped the hospital work with patient records as a clinical pathway to enable the best treatment decisions.

The improvements are being shared with other hospitals to help them also find a way to improved treatment and cost controls.

Conclusion

In this chapter, you learned about the following features of SAP ERP Financials that help to drive your enterprise:

> Financial and management accounting (including basic accounting processes)

> Corporate governance to keep your company in compliance with global regulations and requirements
> Financial supply chain management to ensure that you keep your cash flow as healthy as possible

In Chapter 5, SAP ERP Human Capital Management, we will explore another integral part of SAP ERP, which deals with the people in your company from a human resource perspective.

5

SAP ERP Human Capital Management

Every company in the world, whether small or large, involves people. In fact, *human capital,* as they are called, can be a company's greatest asset. People have the personal skills and experience that make your systems work. They bring vital social skills to your sales, customer, and vendor relationships. And they come up with new product ideas and enhancements for your company that enable you to make innovative leaps and stay competitive.

In recent years, great strides have been made to develop processes that help a company recruit, retain, and support talented people, as well as measure a workforce's productivity. Those who work in the human resources area at a company will find useful tools in SAP ERP Human Capital Management (SAP ERP HCM) for recruiting and retaining talent, running training programs, and administering compensation programs. In addition, managers can use these tools for recording employee performance, attendance data, and more. Employees can use self-service tools for tasks such as checking available leave, educating themselves on benefits, and reporting their time worked on projects. This self-service aspect of SAP ERP HCM frees up human resource professionals to focus on other, more innovative tasks.

SAP ERP HCM
in action

In this chapter, we explore the value of efficient HCM systems to your organization, examine the specific features in SAP ERP HCM, and look at some case studies of SAP ERP HCM in action.

How SAP ERP HCM Fits in an Enterprise

SAP ERP HCM provides tools for human resource professionals and others in an enterprise that supports them in four areas: Workforce Process Management, Talent Management, Workforce Deployment, and End User Service Delivery (Figure 5.1). We will explore each of these important areas in the following sections.

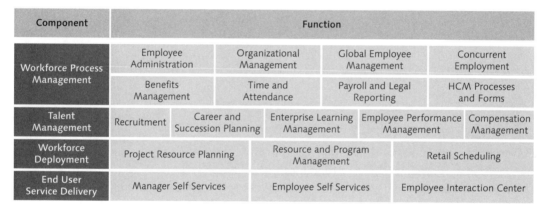

Component	Function			
Workforce Process Management	Employee Administration	Organizational Management	Global Employee Management	Concurrent Employment
	Benefits Management	Time and Attendance	Payroll and Legal Reporting	HCM Processes and Forms
Talent Management	Recruitment	Career and Succession Planning	Enterprise Learning Management	Employee Performance Management	Compensation Management
Workforce Deployment	Project Resource Planning	Resource and Program Management		Retail Scheduling
End User Service Delivery	Manager Self Services	Employee Self Services		Employee Interaction Center

Figure 5.1 The SAP ERP HCM Solution and Its Components and Functions

Workforce Process Automation to Improve Efficiency

Workforce Process Management addresses several vital HR functions for any enterprise, including benefits management, time and attendance, and payroll.

Automate basic
processes

Workforce Process Management is also the area of SAP ERP HCM that allows you to automate basic processes for managing employee information such as vacation time availability or job training; managing your organizational structure and policies, including employee handbooks; and tasks such as coordinating employee relocation activities (i.e., the transition of employee records).

⚙ Keeping Time Under Control

An important feature of the Workforce Process Management element of SAP ERP HCM is time management. You can coordinate activities such as the calculation of wages or employee time accounts, in which employee vacation, sick time, and other time off are accrued. SAP ERP HCM also offers a special working environment for time administrators where, from a single screen, they can record bonuses, change working times, approve overtime, view time account balances, and so on. Calendar views provide information about employee availability in a snapshot. In addition, by using web-based SAP Employee Self-Service (ESS), you can move time-management processes online so that employees can record their own time, request time off, and access their own data, even while out of the office.

Improving Talent Management

Hiring the right people, growing their skills, and recognizing their usefulness to an enterprise is one of the most important jobs that human resource professionals do. The Talent Management processes included in SAP ERP HCM help you with everything from recruiting and getting new employees onboard to managing their training and helping them improve their job skills. This is all done while ensuring that they get appropriate performance and compensation reviews, so you can develop the leaders you need to take charge of your enterprise in the future.

Talent management

➕ Tip

You can also use SAP ERP HCM to link performance reviews and assessment ratings directly to compensation programs to help managers make more accurate decisions on pay changes.

More Efficient Workforce Deployment Management

Workforce Deployment Management involves managing the human resources in your enterprise so that their workflow and assignments are handled efficiently. It also involves enabling employees to track their own activities, which can save project managers from having to rekey employee-reported hours and help prevent potential rekeying errors.

End User Service Delivery

The very nature of HR leads to high volumes of transactions and numerous HR, employee, and manager interactions. The End User Service Delivery component is designed to ensure that your company can deliver its HR services to its customers in an efficient, standardized, and cost-effective manner. It can do this by providing employees and managers with their own web-delivered self-service tools to manage their own data and the tasks related with managing their team, with little or no input from the HR team. Interactions between employees, managers, and the HR department that cannot be handled automatically by the self-service applications are handled by the Employee Interaction Center, a powerful relationship management tool that enables companies to deliver consistent, standardized, and cost-effective employee and manager services from anywhere in the world.

Gaining Insights Through SAP ERP HCM Analytics

Though workforce analytics is no longer a separate part of SAP ERP HCM, it's important to note that throughout SAP ERP HCM, you can use SAP analytic tools to improve reporting, analyze centralized data, and measure activities. Once you have access to vital HR data in useful forms, you can make better decisions about your HR initiatives.

Workforce analytics in SAP ERP HCM include the following:

Make vital HR decisions

> Workforce planning to monitor workforce trends and demographics
> Workforce cost planning and simulation
> Workforce benchmarking to measure workforce processes against external benchmarks
> Workforce process analytics and measurement for processes, including payroll, time management, and benefits
> Strategic alignment of business activities and overall business goals using a balanced scorecard framework
> Workforce analysis with reporting and analysis tools to monitor success factors and key performance indicators (KPIs)
> Talent management analytics and measurement to get a handle on your pool of talent, recruiting processes, learning, succession programs, and more

Now that we've provided you with a look at the types of activities SAP ERP HCM can help you deal with, let's examine the specific tools you use to control these activities.

A Closer Look at SAP ERP HCM

As you've seen so far in this chapter, SAP ERP HCM offers capabilities to manage talent, including recruiting and learning how to use add-on packages.

SAP ERP HCM also provides improved workforce analytics and performance management tools. All of these features of SAP ERP HCM can be combined with self-service capabilities (see Figure 5.2) that enable real-time access by managers and employees throughout an organization, giving them instant access to information and processes, freeing up HR staff time, and providing more direct access to work processes for users. In this section, we outline the specific pieces of SAP ERP HCM that help you achieve these results.

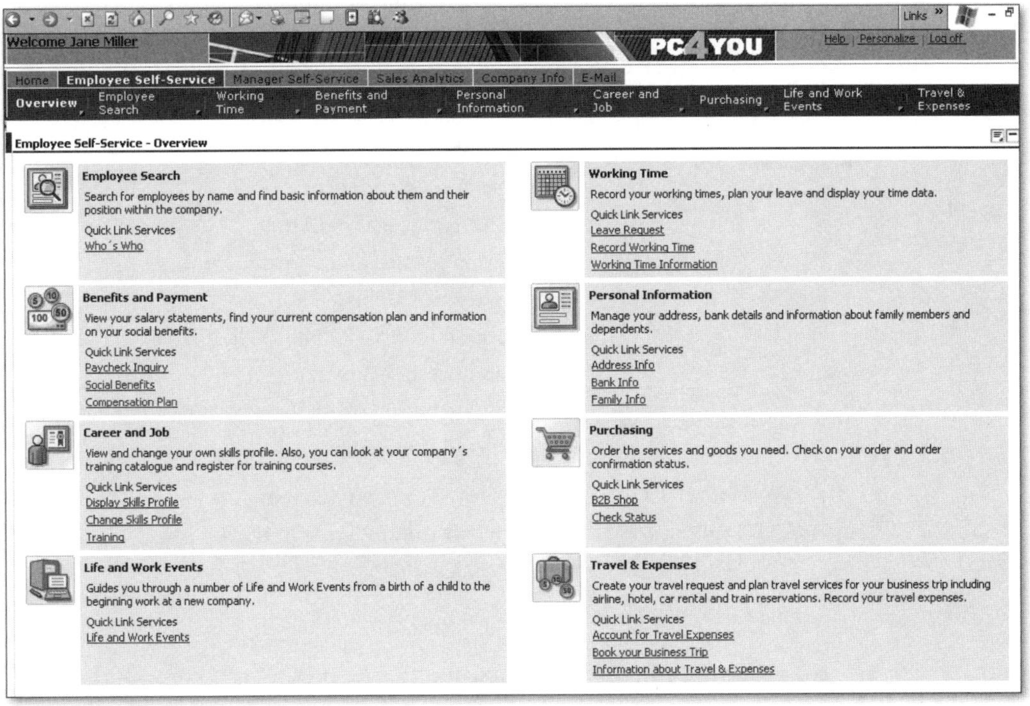

Real-time access by managers and employees

Figure 5.2 Typical Employee Self-Service Page

Key Features and Functions

SAP ERP HCM provides capabilities and benefits in four key areas of your business. Table 5.1 outlines these areas based on SAP's solution map. The sections that follow explore these categories in more detail.

SAP ERP HCM
solution map

Category	Application
Talent Management	Competency Management
	Recruiting
	Employee Performance Management
	Talent Review & Calibration
	Employee Development
	Enterprise Learning
	Succession Management
	Compensation Management
	Talent Management Analytics
Workforce Process Management	Employee Administration
	Organizational Management
	Global Employee Management
	Benefits Management
	Healthcare Cost Management
	Time and Attendance
	Payroll and Legal Reporting
	HCM Processes and Forms
	Workforce Planning
	Workforce Cost Planning & Simulation
	Workforce Benchmarking
	Workforce Process Analytics & Measurement
	Strategic Alignment
Workforce Deployment Management	Project Resource Planning
	Resource and Program Management
	Retail Scheduling

Table 5.1 SAP ERP HCM Solution Map

Category	Application
End User Service Delivery	Manager Self Services
	Employee Self Services
	Employee Interaction Center

Table 5.1 SAP ERP HCM Solution Map (Cont.)

Talent Management

The Talent Management processes in SAP ERP HCM include the following capabilities:

> Recruitment enabled by SAP E-Recruiting

> Career management to help managers review employee profiles and help employees manage their own career paths through self-service features

> Succession management to ensure that the right people are identified and actively developed, so that new leadership is always prepared to step in

> Enterprise learning management enabled by SAP Learning Solution

> Employee performance management to handle tasks such as objective setting and employee reviews

> Compensation management to help you establish performance and competency-based pay and long-term incentive programs

In the past, processes such as recruitment and training might have happened independently, with data stored in different systems. SAP ERP HCM makes it possible to have an integrated talent management system through a centralized data warehouse for every employee. With this integrated data system, all employee data is available to managers and HR professionals, ensuring a seamless system for hiring, training, and promoting people.

Enable integrated talent management

Let's say you have a job opening in your department. Using SAP ERP HCM, you can search across a talent warehouse of potential candidates, and, after deciding on a candidate, you can easily transfer that person's data into your employee records upon hiring. After an employee is on board, you can offer predefined or personalized learning programs, using the data a manager has entered about the employee to pinpoint areas of weakness. You can also match the employee with the right training opportunity (see Figure 5.3). HR can also use SAP ERP HCM tools to measure learning program effectiveness. Using self-service, your new employee can help to plan his own career and update skills data in his personnel records.

SAP Learning Solution

SAP Learning Solution can be used with SAP ERP HCM to integrate back-office ERP functionality with a learning management system (LMS) and a learning content management system (LCMS). SAP Learning Solution supports e-learning with synchronous and asynchronous interactions and in-person training. Using SAP Learning Solution, you can author content and manage that content with a learning portal.

Analytical features allow you to build in assessments of learning so you can improve the quality of education that you deliver to your employees. You can also add a training simulation tool called *SAP Tutor* to the learning solution. SAP Tutor helps you create, edit, and deliver interactive electronic training. Because your employees can access this self-learning training, it frees up training or HR staff for other tasks.

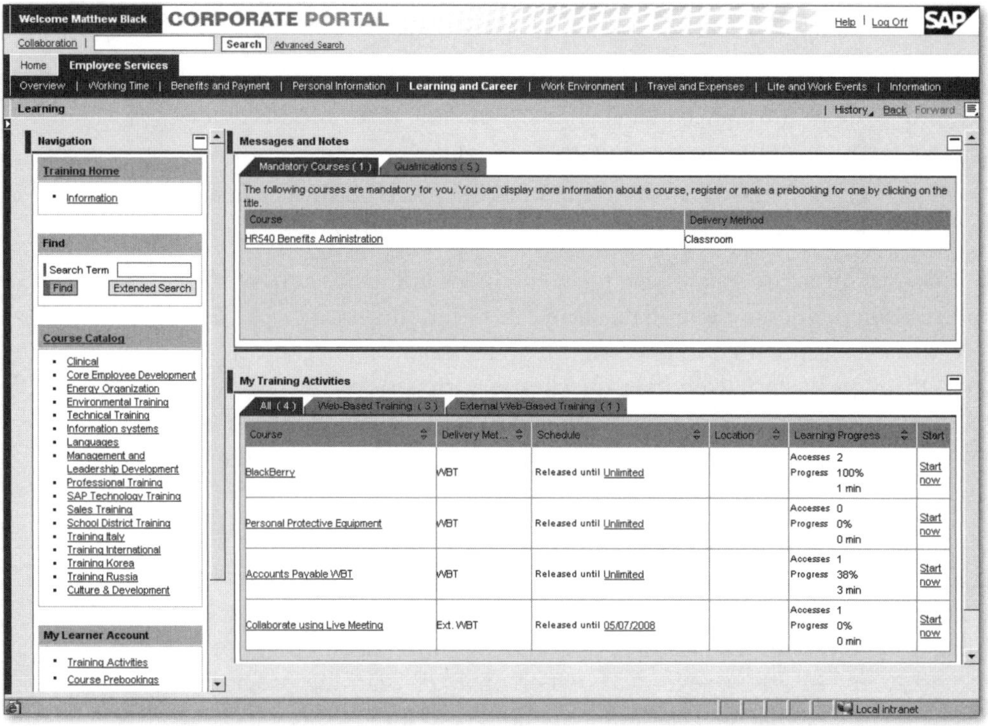

Figure 5.3 Manage Learning with a Convenient Self-Service Interface

Workforce Process Management

There are three categories of features in Workforce Process Management:

> The benefits management feature allows an organization to customize benefits offered to new employees and to define benefits plans on a broader level.

> Time and attendance features provide tracking, monitoring, record-keeping, and evaluation of employee time data that you can tie into various projects.

> The payroll capabilities in Workforce Process Management support legal regulations in 47 countries to help ensure compliance and can easily handle issues of different currencies, languages, and collective agreements.

In addition, by taking advantage of the SAP Interactive Forms software by Adobe, processes such as hiring, termination, reassignment, and taking a personal leave of absence can now be handled without leaving a lengthy paper trail. Electronic forms can be transmitted instantly and are easier to track, complete, and modify. The forms-handling capabilities of SAP ERP HCM can be based on workflow templates that are included with the software. By using the concept of defined user roles, you can give the employees access to the forms they need.

Using electronic forms

Workforce Deployment Management

Workforce Deployment Management involves the vital area of resource management. Resource planning for projects and teams is accomplished with a workforce scheduling application (see Figure 5.4).

In addition, you can align project tracking with employee time tracking and financial data. It also includes the capability to schedule retail staff. If you take into account customer traffic, shifts, and employee skills, you can allocate people in a way that matches your specific retail operation.

Workforce scheduling application

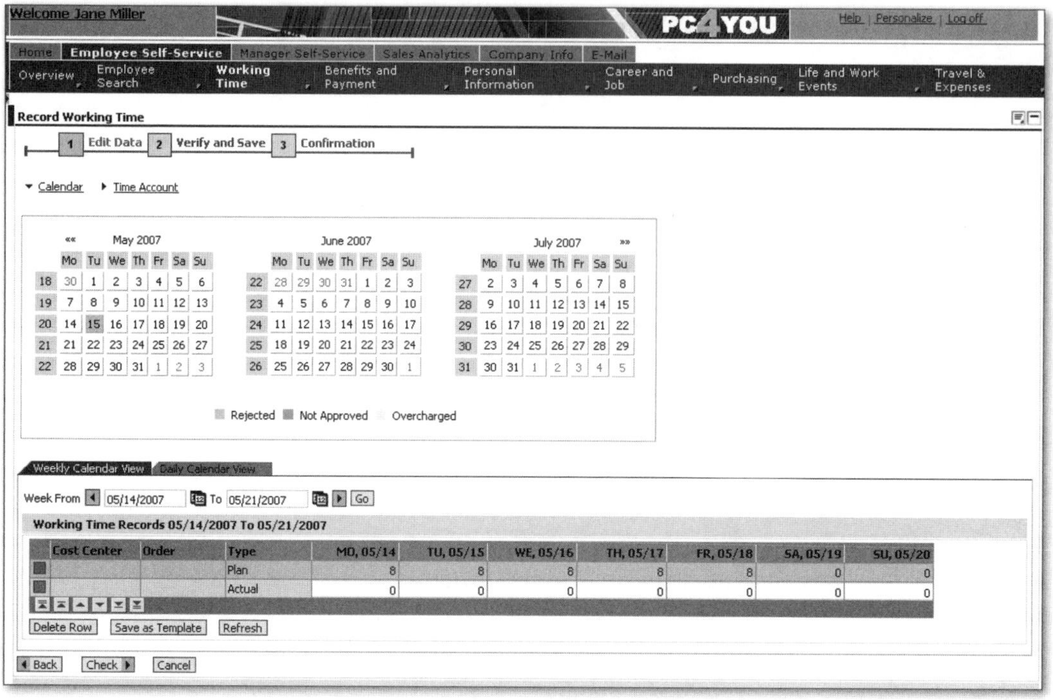

Figure 5.4 Manage Resources from a Central Location

Ex Example

A chain of grocery stores that are open 24 hours a day with three shifts of workers will have different scheduling needs than a chain of walk-in clinics open from 9:00 a.m. to 4:00 p.m., four days a week.

End User Service Delivery

End User Service Delivery empowers both employees and managers to take responsibility for their own HR-related tasks via self-service applications and provides a powerful tool for enabling excellent customer service to employees through an employee interaction center (EIC).

> *Employee Self-Services* gives employees quick access to their own data using a simple-to-learn employee-specific portal. Employees can maintain their own data, check their payslips online, process leave requests, complete forms and checklists, and check their ben-

efits entitlements. Changes to employee data completed via Employee Self-Service can be instantly reflected in the core HR system or sent for approval from either the HR team or the employee's manager.

> *Manager Self-Services* uses the benefits of the SAP Enterprise Portal to empower managers to take control of their own teams, giving them the ability to manage employee-related transactions such as recruitment requests, team budgets, and project management tasks and produce their own reports.

ESS and MSS

> *Employee Interaction Center* offers companies a centralized employee customer service program, that provides an integrated tool enabling administrators to manage employee requests via phone, email, chat, or fax. It uses a sophisticated call tracking and monitoring tool to ensure that employees get excellent, correct, and consistent service no matter from where in the world the service is provided.

To see how SAP ERP HCM functions in the workplace, read through the following case studies.

SAP ERP HCM Case Study 1

Table 5.2 gives you a quick overview of the first case study regarding SAP ERP HCM. Go through it before you read the rest of this section.

Company	British university
Existing Solutions	Older COBOL-based system
Challenge	To improve and lower the cost of payroll, to improve access to HR data, and to reduce errors in data entry
SAP Solution	SAP ERP HCM, SAP Employee Self-Service (ESS)
Benefits	Lower costs of payroll processing, freeing up HR staff, improved reporting and access to data, reduced errors

Table 5.2 SAP ERP HCM Case Study 1

A large British university located in London had a collection of legacy systems in place for HR and payroll procedures. They used a labor-intensive COBOL-based system that had been around for many years;

so many years, in fact, that they were having trouble finding IT people who were trained to work with the system. The system left staff performing many calculations manually, and the awkwardness of the older system was costing the university time and money.

Moving from legacy HR and payroll procedures

SAP ERP HCM, with a SAP for Higher Education & Research industry solution portfolio, allowed the university to streamline its systems and automate its processes. The university also took advantage of the SAP Employee Self-Service (ESS) application. In this case study, we look at the challenges faced by the university, the SAP solution, and the benefits that resulted.

The Challenges

The university faced several challenges at the outset. First, it needed to improve its HR and payroll operations and reduce the cost of its payroll systems. In addition, the university sought to improve the way management controlled and reported employee activities. The existing systems allowed for duplicate data entry, which resulted in data errors that can occur when keying data. Lastly, the university needed a way to improve access to important HR data to help management make good business decisions.

At the time the university was reviewing its existing system, there was also an increased need to improve reporting to meet government requirements. New funding regulations demanded more data and reports than the current systems could generate.

The SAP Solution

The university chose an SAP solution in part because of the company's track record working with universities, which have different needs from private-sector companies. Moreover, SAP's offerings could run on the existing Microsoft SQL Server database and could handle the UK's public-sector specific payroll requirements.

Automate HR

The first goal was to automate manual HR and payroll activities. Then, the university needed to set up ESS capabilities. Finally, the university needed to implement a solution that consolidated data entry and improved reporting capabilities.

To achieve these improvements, the university implemented SAP ERP HCM software, including payroll, recruitment, and training and events features. University employees worked with a consulting partner with experience in higher education, who trained the university's own team in how to work with this software.

The solution automated payroll calculations, which reduced the time it took to prepare payroll and also improved accuracy. In addition, the implementation consolidated several applications so that data would only be entered once. Data cross-checking and audit reports now help with correcting any errors that exist with the data.

Free up HR staff

The SAP ESS application the university put in place allows employees to update a great deal of their own personnel information, freeing up HR staff for more important activities such as recruitment and maintaining employee relations.

Reporting features improved both the quality and accuracy of reports. The easy-to-use, uniform interface the university adopted makes the system simple for people to use. Interfaces that were built between the SAP software and a number of non-SAP applications allowed university employees to leverage the features of both. For example, the university's online recruitment website interacts with the HCM software, enabling users to export information onto the website and import it back into the SAP system.

Looking Toward the Future

The university hopes to build on its SAP solution by adding more ESS initiatives supported by the portal component of SAP NetWeaver. This would allow people to view payslips, update personal data, schedule training, and submit information, such as timesheets, sick days, and expenses online. The university also plans to add the SAP Manager Self-Service (MSS) application to enable managers to automate approvals and reporting.

SAP ERP HCM Case Study 2

To help you understand how SAP ERP HCM works in real life, we've included a second case study. Table 5.3 gives you a quick snapshot of this study.

Company	German automobile manufacturer
Existing Solutions	Legacy systems
Challenge	To improve HR processes to better support flexible scheduling and sophisticated leave management
SAP Solution	SAP ERP HCM
Benefits	Improved system operation with a single interface and optimized personnel administration

Table 5.3 SAP ERP HCM Case Study 2

The Challenge

This German automaker has a reputation for innovative, flexible resource scheduling, including a very sophisticated leave management operation. The company needed an HR system that could support optimized processing of all employee data, from new hires to payroll for its 120,000 employees. The company also needed to manage pension programs for 75,000 retired employees.

The automaker decided to restructure its entire personnel management, time management, and payroll processes to achieve the speed, accuracy, and flexibility required.

The SAP Solution

The company assigned a group of 50 people to work with SAP Consulting to implement SAP ERP HCM. Using SAP's ASAP methodology, the group performed an analysis of existing processes and established a blueprint for meeting HR requirements using SAP's solution.

ASAP methodology

The in-house team created a quality management system to check, recheck, and document test cases. They established 850 new work agreements and resource regulations to work with SAP ERP HCM. A production environment was created with hardware partner HP.

SAP solutions included organizational and time management functions, tools for managing the company pension plan, and a web-based manager workplace.

The Benefits

Today, SAP ERP is used to process 750,000 transactions every day and can even handle peak operations of 1 million transactions. All HR-related legal requirements and work schedules are stored in a single system. Automatic workflows have improved work scheduling and helped employees complete tasks faster.

Approximately 8,000 HR users can access payroll and time management records easily. Because of built-in standard features in SAP ERP HCM, it's easy to modify processes as needs change, but such change requires little custom programming.

Conclusion

In this chapter, we looked at the Human Capital Management portion of SAP ERP, which helps your HR professionals manage your staffing and ongoing employee needs. This solution supports enterprises in the following areas:

> Talent management with features such as recruiting and career planning
> Workforce deployment for planning and managing resource activity
> Workforce process management for dealing with issues such as benefits and time and attendance
> End User Service Delivery to bring Self Service capabilities to employees and managers

In Chapter 6, SAP ERP Operations, we'll explore the features of SAP ERP Operations, including the areas of product development and manufacturing, procurement and logistics, and sales and service.

6   SAP ERP Operations

Businesses today are focusing more and more on delivering products and services quickly and efficiently. SAP ERP Operations offers a way to make the entire operational product chain more efficient by providing tools in six areas that help you control your operations for the following:

> Product Development and Collaboration
> Procurement
> Operations: Sales and Customer Service
> Operations: Manufacturing
> Enterprise Asset Management
> Operations: Cross Functions

In this chapter, you'll discover how you can use SAP ERP Operations to automate your business processes, ranging from requisitioning and receiving materials to order entry, production planning, and shop floor management.

As with all of SAP ERP, you'll also have access to SAP ERP Analytics and data management functions, which will allow you to stay on top of your operations and quickly modify them if necessary. In addition, you'll find out how role-based self-service functions allow your employees to access the features of the system easily.

SAP ERP Operations Overview

SAP ERP Operations helps you streamline and automate operations-related processes such as procurement and manufacturing, which goes a long way toward creating customer satisfaction and cost savings. Take a look at the three main areas of SAP ERP Operations and how they can work to benefit your business.

Product Development and Collaboration

Product Development and Collaboration covers the entire lifecycle of your products from conception and requirements-gathering to retirement of the product. Having information about your products — such as specification documents, formula recipes, materials management, or compliance documents — readily available helps you quickly adapt to changing market conditions and improve your strategic planning.

Product Development and Collaboration

Suppose the requirements for the new machine you are developing require gold-plated fittings. You realize that the current price of gold now makes these fittings cost prohibitive. With SAP ERP Product Development and Collaboration, you can gather all documents related to this project and work with internal and external sources to find an alternative solution that meets your needs and maintains the quality of your product. Because of document management tools, all documents can be updated to the latest version and routed to the appropriate people for review and approval.

Procurement

End-to-end procurement processes

Purchasing has become a highly complex area, in which having the necessary solid data can help you manage procurement in a way that can save you a significant amount of time and money. With complete support for procurement, you can manage end-to-end procurement processes, from self-service requisitioning to optimized flow of materials, and a flexible invoicing and payment system.

You can also manage all of your critical documents, including bills of material, routing data, computer-aided design models, recipes, project plans, and parts information.

Procurement in SAP ERP Operations helps your company efficiently manage the ordering, receiving, and financial settlement areas of purchasing, and helps you ensure compliance with regulations and collaboration with suppliers. For example, if your company manufactures MP3 players, Procurement features of SAP ERP Operations allow you to find the right supplier for those little plastic headphones that you package with your product, set up systems to receive and warehouse the headphones, pay your supplier, and control their distribution to your various manufacturing plants.

Handling these procurement and logistics tasks helps you improve your customer service because your products get out faster, and information about orders is consistent and accurate.

Operations: Sales and Customer Service

Sales and Customer Service is where you put the focus on your customer orders. You can automate the sales ordering process, including providing customers with quotes and generating orders and contracts. You can use the most profitable sales and interaction channels, reduce your administrative costs by automating sales order management, and increase customer satisfaction by having access to on-time information about their orders.

Automate sales ordering processes

This portion of SAP ERP Operations not only helps with products but also supports services with service-order processing and service delivery. The ability to track sales and service activity for billing or cost analyses helps you oversee your company's profitability. You can also manage aftermarket processing of warranty claims, service orders, and returns, as well as the calculation of incentives and commissions.

Imagine a retail appliance chain that has to keep track of after-sale issues, such as warranty expirations, service calls, and product returns. With SAP ERP Operations Sales and Service features, these tasks are all centralized and connected, leading to much greater efficiency in serving customers.

SAP ERP Operations Sales and Service

Operations: Manufacturing

Manufacturing

Manufacturing is the area in which you can improve and automate your production planning and automate your manufacturing process. All of the documents and specifications for your products can be managed using these tools, and they can be connected with your shop-floor systems to ensure that you maintain quality standards.

If your company is in the business of delivering high-end espresso machines to consumers, for example, you might use Manufacturing tools to plan, schedule, and sequence your production line to produce the highest quality machines on a faster schedule. You can also gather production information right from your shop floor to help you see how many espresso units are being produced each day, and, therefore, keep a tighter control on the dispatching of parts such as filter baskets and steam valves throughout your manufacturing cycle.

In addition, consistent quality enhances customer satisfaction, while automating production processes can lower operating costs.

Enterprise Asset Management

Asset management

Keeping your company running smoothly not only entails making sure you have the materials on hand to make your products and that your product line is churning smoothly but also that things like your building and fleet vehicles can handle your operation. Enterprise Asset Management lets you manage the life span of physical assets from purchase through their retirement, sale, or disposal.

Operations: Cross Functions

Standardized processes

The tools within Cross Functions let you establish standards that can be used across all operational aspects of your business, such as quality, safety, receipt and shipment of goods and materials, and project management.

Collaborating with Value Chain Partners

Supplier order collaboration

One of the key features of SAP ERP Operations is how it enables you to collaborate with various entities and people in managing your operations. For example, scenarios will be developed for SAP ERP Operations that help you manage temporary staffing needs when you gear up your production line for high activity. You can also manage supplier order collaboration, which allows suppliers to use self-service features to negotiate and process purchase orders, and verify payment status.

You can even work more easily with people or partners in the field through the use of mobile data collection technologies such as RFID (Radio Frequency Identification). Figure 6.1 shows a solution map for such technologies. To see RFID in action, simply walk through your local grocery store and watch employees scan inventory into a handheld device.

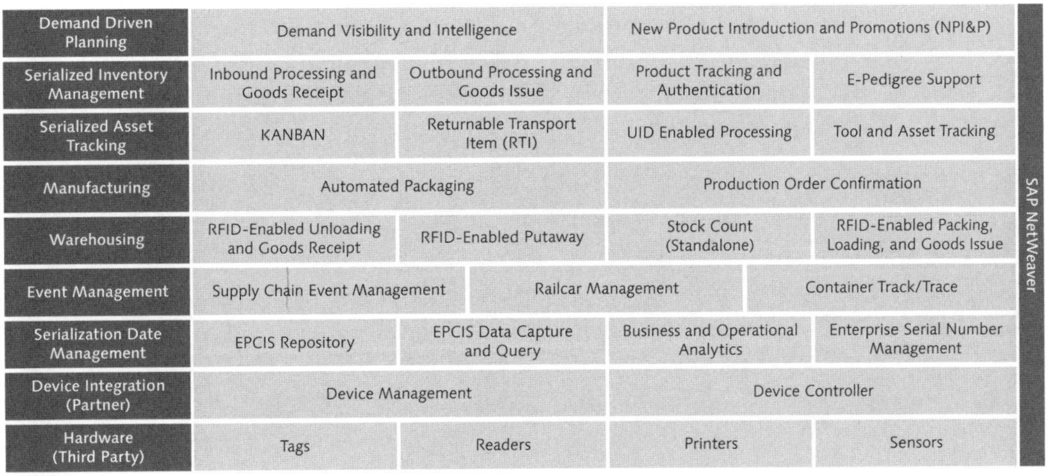

Demand Driven Planning	Demand Visibility and Intelligence		New Product Introduction and Promotions (NPI&P)	
Serialized Inventory Management	Inbound Processing and Goods Receipt	Outbound Processing and Goods Issue	Product Tracking and Authentication	E-Pedigree Support
Serialized Asset Tracking	KANBAN	Returnable Transport Item (RTI)	UID Enabled Processing	Tool and Asset Tracking
Manufacturing	Automated Packaging		Production Order Confirmation	
Warehousing	RFID-Enabled Unloading and Goods Receipt	RFID-Enabled Putaway	Stock Count (Standalone)	RFID-Enabled Packing, Loading, and Goods Issue
Event Management	Supply Chain Event Management	Railcar Management		Container Track/Trace
Serialization Date Management	EPCIS Repository	EPCIS Data Capture and Query	Business and Operational Analytics	Enterprise Serial Number Management
Device Integration (Partner)	Device Management		Device Controller	
Hardware (Third Party)	Tags	Readers	Printers	Sensors

SAP NetWeaver

Figure 6.1 Tracking Inventory and Sales Data with RFID and Other Technologies

➕ **Tip**

SAP ERP Operations can work with SAP Manufacturing and SAP Product Lifecycle Management (SAP PLM).

In the following section, we'll take a closer look at the features of SAP ERP Operations to give you a better idea of the specific tools you can use to achieve all of the benefits of SAP ERP Operations discussed so far.

A Closer Look at SAP ERP Operations

Exactly what tools and features provide the benefits we've covered in the previous sections? Let's start by reviewing the solution map for SAP ERP Operations, shown in Figure 6.2, to see what SAP ERP Operations consists of.

SAP ERP Operations Solution Map

Efficient
management
of processes

As seen in Figure 6.2, SAP ERP Operations consists of eight line items from the larger SAP ERP solution map: Human Capital Management, Financials, Product Development and Collaboration, Procurement, Operations: Sales and Customer Service, Operations: Manufacturing, Enterprise Asset Management, and Operations: Cross Functions. Together, these areas help you manage your operations more efficiently.

Human Capital Management	Talent Management		Workforce Process Management		Workforce Deployment		End-User Service Delivery	
Financials	Financial Supply Chain Management		Treasury		Financial Accounting	Management Accounting		Corporate Governance
Product Development and Collaboration	Product Development	Product Data Management	Product Intelligence		Product Compliance	Document Management		Tool and Workgroup Integration
Procurement	Purchase Requisition Management		Operational Sourcing		Purchase Order Management	Contract Management		Invoice Management
Operations: Sales and Customer Service	Sales Order Management				Aftermarket Sales and Services			
Operations: Manufacturing	Production Planning			Manufacturing Execution		Manufacturing Collaboration		
Enterprise Asset Management	Investment Planning and Design	Procurement and Construction	Maintenance and Operations	Decommission and Disposal	Asset Analytics and Performance Optimization	Real Estate Management		Fleet Management
Operations: Cross Functions	Quality Management	Environment, Health, and Safety Compliance Management	Inbound and Outbound Logistics	Inventory and Warehouse Management		Global Trade Services		Project and Portfolio Management

Shared Service Delivery — SAP NetWeaver

Figure 6.2 SAP ERP Operations Solution Map

Overview of SAP ERP Operations

Product Development and Collaboration, Procurement, Operations: Sales and Customer Service, Operations: Manufacturing, Enterprise Asset Management, and Operations: Cross Functions are the core functions you use to control the manufacturing and service of products in your organization. The benefits of each of these areas were already discussed, but an overview of the features of each is provided in the remainder of this section.

Table 6.1 outlines the key areas of SAP ERP Operations, based on SAP's solution map, excluding SAP ERP Financials and Human Capital Management, which we covered in earlier chapters.

Category	Application
Product Development & Collaboration	› Product Development › Product Data Management › Product Intelligence › Product Compliance › Document Management › Tool and Workgroup Integration
Procurement	› Purchase Requisition Management › Operational Sourcing › Purchase Order Management › Contract Management › Invoice Management
Operations: Sales and Customer Service	› Sales Order Management › Aftermarket Sales and Service
Operations: Manufacturing	› Production Planning › Manufacturing Execution › Manufacturing Collaboration
Enterprise Asset Management	› Investment Planning & Design › Procurement & Construction › Maintenance & Operations › Decommission & Disposal › Asset Analytics & Performance Optimization › Real Estate Management › Fleet Management
Operations: Cross Functions	› Quality Management › Environmental, Health, and Safety Compliance Management › Inbound and Outbound Logistics › Inventory and Warehouse Management › Global Trade Services › Project and Portfolio Management

Table 6.1 SAP ERP Operations

> ## ➕ Tip
>
> If you need additional features for dealing with suppliers, consider SAP Supplier Relationship Management (SAP SRM), covered in Chapter 8. Also, the SAP Customer Relationship Management (SAP CRM) application (see Chapter 7) provides its own sales, marketing, and service feature set.

Product Development and Collaboration

The first area of SAP ERP Operations involves all aspects of product development and innovation within your organization.

Product Development

Product Development is the application that allows you to manage the new product development and introduction (NPDI) process. You can define what your product will be, set requirements, and locate supplier resources. Tools help you collaborate in the design and development processes, including tracking information that moves between various internal departments and external partners.

Product Data Management

With Product Data Management tools, you manage the master data for all materials used in the production of your goods. For example, if there is an engineering change to a product, you will see all materials impacted by this change so you can react accordingly if material orders need to be adjusted.

Product Intelligence

Product Intelligence lets you retrieve all product data from internal sources, such as Finance and Supply Chain, to your external sources, such as your supplier or distributor.

Product Compliance

Product Compliance features keep your products in compliance with global regulations throughout the world.

Document Management

With Document Management, you have a central repository for all documents related to your products, such as schematics, requirements, change notices, material orders, and parts lists. If a change is required, all documents can be easily retrieved and reviewed to help with the decision process.

Tool and Workgroup Integration

The Tool and Workgroup Integration segment allows integration of most major CAD/CAM tools with SAP ERP Operations.

Procurement

Procurement is all about ordering the materials or products you need to run your business. You can provide Employee Self-Service (ESS) through the catalog features, and you can connect product designers, suppliers, manufacturers, and customers to automate your procurement activities. The Procurement application shown in Figure 6.3 helps you manage the entire procure-to-pay process and includes the following:

> Manage the procure-to-pay process

> Requisitioning

> Purchase request processing

> Trading contracts

> Purchase order processing

> Invoice processing

> Delivery schedule management

> Sourcing

In Figure 6.4, you can see how tools for finding and viewing information on a variety of procurement-related items are combined in one employee's role-based work center. This person can check information about purchase requisitions, purchase orders, and vendors, and inspect items by delivery date, vendor, material code, and more.

> Employee role-based work center

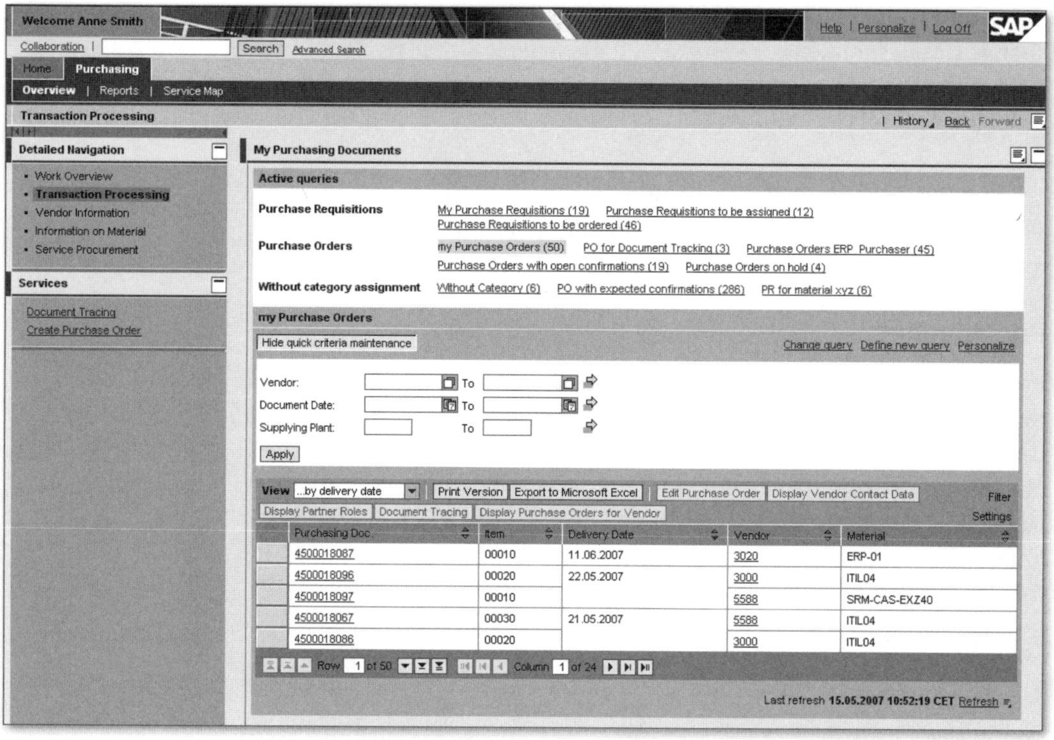

Figure 6.3 Tracking Various Stages of Procurement Through Useful Dashboards

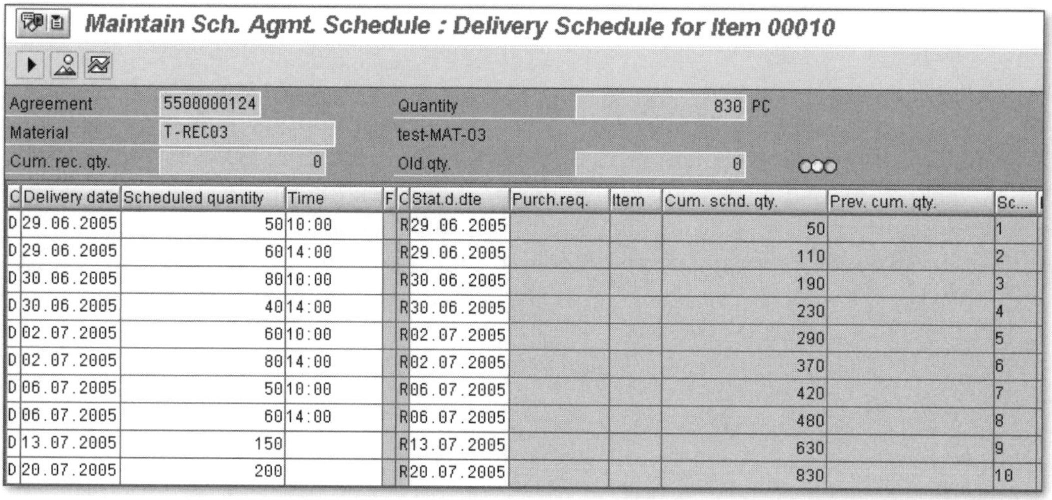

Figure 6.4 Delivery Schedule Management with Sophisticated Tools

Purchase Requisition Management

Purchase Requisition Management contains the tools for creating a purchase requisition for products or services required by your company. Purchase requisitions can be created directly in the Purchase Requisition area, where the requisitions information is manually entered, or the requisition can come in as a result of being triggered by another SAP component such as Plant Maintenance.

Operational Sourcing

Operational Sourcing looks at the requisition and then determines the best source from which to obtain the products or services requested. There may be enough inventory on hand to cover the request, or an outside source can be automatically checked to determine if it has the desired quantity of product in stock.

Purchase Order Management

Purchase Order Management lets you follow and monitor the purchase order as it is created and then sent to the supplier. Delivery schedules can then be created and tracked along with ticklers to remind you to follow-up with the supplier if necessary.

Contract Management

Contract Management involves establishing contracts with your suppliers to set quotas on the amount of product they are to supply you with over a specific period of time. By doing this, you ensure that you do not run out of products at a critical time and that you have a backup supply ready should you need it. It also allows you to set up all of your vendor information in a central location.

Invoice Management

When goods are received from your suppliers, you can use the Invoice Management tools to receive, verify, and process the invoices. The invoice is compared to the goods received for quantity and price, and then, if correct, can be used for payment processing. All data is then stored and updated in Materials Management and Financial Accounting.

Operations: Sales and Customer Service

Each of the areas of Sales and Service in SAP ERP Operations provides a rich set of tools, which we've included here.

Sales Order Management

E-commerce platform

Sales Order Management helps you handle everything from customer inquiries to quotations and placing orders. The e-commerce platform in SAP ERP Operations enables you to manage online orders. There are even tools to help you control sales incentives and commissions. Specifically, Sales Order Management includes the following:

> Account Processing
> Internet Sales
> Managing Auctions
> Inquiry Processing
> Quotation Processing
> Trading Contract Management
> Sales Order Processing
> Mobile Sales
> Inbound Telesales
> Contract Processing
> Billing
> Incentive and Commission Management
> Returnable Packaging Management
> Consignment

If you take sales orders, and most companies do, you'll find these tools invaluable.

Aftermarket Sales and Service

Support your customers

Aftermarket Sales and Service deals with all of the details that come up after you've made the sale; this is the time when your customers are concerned with getting the product installed or arranging for ongoing service support. These tools help you support customers with planning issues, including production installation, service contracts, and warranties.

Operations: Manufacturing

This area of SAP ERP Operations includes Production Planning, Manufacturing Execution, and Manufacturing Collaboration. If you manufacture products, you can use this part of SAP ERP Operations to figure out your production processes, capture real-time production data, and work with other companies or vendors to complete the production process. The following features help you to automate your entire manufacturing operation:

> **Production Planning**
> Helps you create strategies for your production sequence and schedules. With these tools, you can set up your factory floor optimally so you can deliver customer orders as promised.

Production Planning

> **Manufacturing Execution**
> Provides a tool for gathering actual production data, managing production processes, and allocating resources to get work done. You can keep track of inventory during the manufacturing process and dispatch inventory as needed.

Manufacturing Execution

> **Manufacturing Collaboration**
> Provides a means for integrating product data from outside sources into SAP.

Enterprise Asset Management

To manufacture goods or provide a service, you need physical assets such as land, an office or plant, machinery, computers, and perhaps a fleet of trucks to deliver your products or cars for your sales force. With the features of Enterprise Asset Management, you can plan for the purchase of these items, their maintenance and optimal performance, as well as manage their depreciation, disposal, sale, and replacement when necessary. Enterprise Asset Management consists of the following applications:

Asset procurement, performance and disposal

> Investment Planning and Design
> Procurement and Construction
> Maintenance and Operations
> Decommission and Disposal
> Asset Analytics and Performance Optimization

> Real Estate Management

> Fleet Management

Operations: Cross Functions

The Cross Functions tools allow you to establish standards for your products and company that can be applied across the board. This area includes the following:

> **Quality Management**
Lets you set standard quality practices throughout your organization that also help you focus on prevention and process improvement.

> **Environment, Health, and Safety Compliance Management**
Practices for environmental, health, safety, regulatory compliance, and corporate responsibility.

> **Inbound and Outbound Logistics**
Allows you to control the movement of products and materials into and out of your operation. You can manage your warehouse's in-yard activities and monitor the posting and distribution of outbound goods, including the calculation of duties and customs requirements.

> **Inventory and Warehouse Management**
Includes features to handle *cross docking* (a logistics procedure that avoids inventorying stock by breaking down received shipments on the dock and immediately shipping them out again), warehousing and storage, and physical inventory. You can keep close track of the value of inventory, and control goods receipts, storage, picking and packing, and stock transfers.

> **Global Trade Services**
Contains tools to help you stay in compliance with foreign regulations, import and export tariffs, customs regulations, licenses, permits, and trade agreements such as NAFTA.

> **Project and Portfolio Management**
Houses the functions for project selection, prioritization, resource allocation, budgeting, metrics, scheduling, and risk management. Because most organizations usually have multiple projects running at the same time, program managers can easily determine the status and progress of each project in their portfolio using the features in the Project and Portfolio Management area.

The following case study shows you how an agricultural firm discovered that the savings in time and money they could gain with SAP ERP Operations were substantial.

SAP ERP Operations Case Study 1

Table 6.2 is a snapshot of the first case study related to SAP ERP Operations. You should review it before moving on to the rest of this section.

Company	Leading European agricultural firm
Existing Solutions	SAP R/3
Challenge	To unify business processes and extend them to international divisions
SAP Solutions	SAP ERP Operations, SAP NetWeaver
Benefits	Ability to track materials flow, use of analytics for strategic planning, reduction of manual input

Table 6.2 SAP ERP Operations Case Study 1

A leading European agricultural firm with almost 50 companies under its umbrella specializes in producing animal feed and feeding systems. The company is also involved in the industrial electronics industry.

The Challenges

With so many companies forming a single entity, it was important to find a way to unify the business processes across the entire enterprise. At the same time, the company was looking toward international growth and finding ways to deal with a changing market.

Unifying business processes

The company's international growth meant it had to have standards in place for processes that could be extended to international divisions and offices.

The SAP Solution

The company implemented SAP R/3 in 2000, which went a long way toward standardizing processes. By upgrading to SAP ERP Operations, the company could take advantage of the new system's ability to support an entire business process throughout an organization.

SAP NetWeaver
Application Server

SAP ERP Operations was put in place with about 80 users but provided a connection for approximately 350 remote users by using the SAP NetWeaver Application Server (SAP NetWeaver AS). SAP ERP Operations was useful in several areas. First, the company built new production plants to extend its sales abroad and used the features of SAP ERP Operations to streamline its production line. In addition, features of SAP ERP Operations helped the company deal with a variety of distribution methods in different countries. The company was able to flexibly adapt its systems to support these differences, including distributing from central warehouses, or enabling salespeople to pick up and deliver products to customers.

A single common IT system supports processes such as production and materials management for the whole international enterprise. Support for additional languages helped the company adjust to a more global business, and transparency of operations to satisfy international regulations further helped to support international expansion.

The Benefits

The company is using analytics in SAP ERP Operations to help find a strategic future for the company. The ability to manage the overall flow of materials using SAP ERP Operations has helped the company get a handle on internal transactions between divisions. And because this planning of the flow of materials is automated, manual input and administration of the system is much easier and less labor-intensive.

SAP ERP Operations Case Study 2

Managing the
overall flow of
materials

Now let's take a look at Table 6.3, which shows you the highlights of the second case study in this chapter.

The largest plant of a major European car company produces all of the diesel engines for the company. More than 590,000 engines are assembled there every year. The company employs approximately 2,600 people and has sales of €1.86 billion annually.

Company	Austrian car engine plant
Existing Solutions	SAP R/3 for Financials, Controlling, HCM, Production Planning, Materials Management, Sales and Distribution, Quality Management, and Plant Maintenance
Challenge	To improve the recording of movement of goods, and to record on site rather than manually
SAP Solutions	SAP ERP Operations with mobile data entry (RFID) and warehouse management features
Benefits	Faster execution of production processes and fewer errors in warehousing

Table 6.3 SAP ERP Operations Case Study 2

The Challenges

The plant was aware of inefficiencies in the recording of goods movement. In addition, because data was not recorded on site, but instead was written and then entered into PCs, errors were being introduced in warehousing procedures.

Delays in recording goods information were causing slowdowns in production operations. The company needed a way to record information on the plant floor that would accelerate its operations and increase accuracy.

The SAP Solution

SAP ERP Operations allows integration of radio-frequency features via mobile devices equipped with scanners. This direct input of data helped to avoid errors that manual entry had introduced. These portable devices could be handheld or mounted on forklifts for ease of use.

Radio-frequency and mobile devices

The scanners were linked directly to SAP ERP Operations. Users quickly adopted the new system, and physical processes, such as shipping, engine assembly, and maintenance, occurred much faster and with a higher degree of accuracy. Lastly, because the system controls transport orders and organizes them in a logical way (to create the most efficient itineraries possible), all pick orders were triggered and sent out electronically.

The Benefits

SAP Console Because data is sent directly from the SAP system and integrated into SAP ERP Operations, it is available immediately for analysis or processing. The solution was also cost-effective because the mobile devices required no middleware to link to SAP ERP Operations via SAP Console.

Because the user interface is customizable for both look and language, users adopted the new system easily. The solution also made the company aware of new efficiencies that could be realized in change management, production control, and warehouse management. The company is already reworking its stock receipt process to incorporate mobile devices and SAP ERP Operations.

Conclusion

In this chapter, we looked at SAP ERP Operations, which makes your entire product chain more efficient. The three key pieces of SAP ERP Operations are

> Procurement and Logistics Execution
> Product Development and Manufacturing
> Sales and Service

Together, these areas of SAP ERP Operations provide features that allow you to handle your entire product lifecycle.

In Chapter 7, we'll look at SAP Customer Relationship Management (SAP CRM). Whereas SAP ERP Operations helps you produce your products, SAP CRM helps you take care of one of your most important assets, your customers.

7

SAP Customer Relationship Management

Without customers, most companies would be out of business. Gaining, servicing, and retaining customers are some of the most important activities any business can undertake. Managing customer relations begins when you market a product to them, continues through the entire sales cycle, and doesn't end when the sale is complete. If you're good at customer relationships and focus on supporting your customers after they buy, you can build relationships that will endure for years to come.

SAP Customer Relationship Management (SAP CRM) is part of the SAP Business Suite. This suite of products also includes SAP ERP, SAP Product Lifecycle Management (SAP PLM), SAP Supply Chain Management (SAP SCM), and SAP Supplier Relationship Management (SAP SRM).

SAP CRM allows for more efficient and effective interaction with customers, retailers, distributors, and others to help you support marketing, sales, and after-sales service.

In this chapter, we explain the role of SAP CRM in an enterprise and the specific features SAP CRM offers you. We also provide case studies of real world uses of SAP CRM.

How SAP CRM Fits in an Enterprise

SAP CRM is a very robust offering, and if you follow the levels of the solution map to their detailed level (see Appendix C, SAP Solution Maps), you will tally up perhaps a hundred or more features delivered by SAP products as well as partner products. In this section, we look at the solution map for SAP CRM and general capabilities in each of its six major areas:

> Marketing

> Sales

> Service

> Partner Channel Management

> Interaction Center

> Web Channel

These areas are outlined in the SAP CRM Solution Map.

SAP CRM Solution Map

The solution map for SAP CRM is a bit complex, so we'll tackle that first. In Figure 7.1, you can see that there are three main areas of CRM functionality:

> Marketing

> Sales

> Service

To the right of these categories on the map are three vertical categories: Web Channel, Interaction Center, and Partner Channel Management. Any of these three vertical categories might be used in any of the main categories, so they are considered cross-functional (and therefore listed vertically in the map). For example, you may sell via the web, but you might also use web commerce methods to market to customers or support them after a sale.

See appendix C, Solution Maps, for additional details

In addition, notice that at the far right of the solution map, Business Communication Management and Trade Promotion Management are listed vertically. Again, all of the three main areas of functionality may call on Trade Promotion Management features to analyze and report data about their activities or customers, and any of the three may use different Business Communication Management methods, such as handling customer inquiries via mobile devices.

Marketing		Partner Channel Management	Web Channel	Interaction Center	Asset Analytics and Performance Optimization	Segmentation and List Management	Campaign Management	Real-Time Offer Management	Lead Management	Loyalty Management	Trade Promotion Management	Business Communication Management
Sales					Sales Planning and Forecasting	Sales Performance Management	Territory Management	Accounts and Contacts	Opportunity Management	Quotation and Order Management	Pricing and Contracts	Incentive and Commission Management	Time and Travel		
Service					Service Sales and Marketing	Service Contracts and Agreements	Installations and Maintenance	Customer Service and Support	Field Service Management	Returns and Depot Repair	Warranty and Claims Management	Service Logistics and Finance	Service Collaboration, Analytics, and Optimization		

Figure 7.1 SAP CRM Solution Map

SAP CRM in an Enterprise

You may have heard the term *customer-centric*. Essentially this is a concept that many businesses use to drive their success. When you put the customer at the center of your business, you ensure that everything you do is an effort to gain and retain customer loyalty.

Customer-centric

When you think about it, the customer is at the heart of most of the activities that a business engages in, from designing and building products to promoting products, taking and fulfilling orders, and providing support. Customer relationship management focuses on the areas where you have the most direct contact with your customer — in the marketing/sales/service portion of your business.

Using SAP CRM, you can centralize customer data to ensure that everybody from your salesperson to your order picker has the same information. You can streamline processes such as telemarketing, sales account planning, and running customer interaction centers. You can set up customer self-service features to allow them to register products online or track shipments. This self-service frees up your customer service people for other tasks. For example, an online clothing store that implements customer self-service features saves its employees from answering routine questions about products or order status so they can spend time solving problems related to returns or cross-selling accessory products such as handbags or jewelry.

Customer self-service

SAP has built standard business processes into SAP CRM, including processes for handling customer complaints or product recalls, managing marketing campaigns, and tracking the results — even processing credit card payments and checking customer credit.

The following section provides details about many of the features included in SAP CRM, divided into six key areas.

A Closer Look at SAP CRM

Each of the areas of SAP CRM, such as Sales or Marketing, has its own set of capabilities. In this section, we look at these capabilities in detail, along with the types of business processes they help you manage.

SAP CRM Overview

Take a look at each of the major areas of SAP CRM listed in the solution map, each of which is discussed in more detail in the sections that follow. Table 7.1 outlines the key areas of CRM, based on SAP's solution map.

Category	Application
Marketing	Marketing Resource Management
	Segmentation & List Management
	Campaign Management
	Real-Time Offer Management
	Lead Management
	Loyalty Management
Sales	Sales Planning & Forecasting
	Sales Performance Management
	Territory Management
	Accounts & Contacts
	Opportunity Management
	Quotation & Order Management
	Pricing & Contracts
	Incentive & Commission Management
	Time & Travel

Table 7.1 SAP CRM Solution Map

Category	Application
Service	Service Sales & Marketing
	Service Contracts & Agreements
	Installations & Maintenance
	Customer Service & Support
	Field Service Management
	Returns & Depot Repair
	Warranty & Claims Management
	Service Logistics & Finance
	Service Collaboration, Analytics, Optimization
Web Channel	E-Marketing
	E-Commerce
	E-Service
Interaction Center	Telemarketing
	Telesales
	Customer Service
	IC Management
Partner Channel Management	Partner Management
	Channel Marketing
	Channel Sales
	Partner Order Management
	Channel Commerce

Table 7.1 SAP CRM Solution Map (Cont.)

The features in this solution map cover the entire lifecycle of customer relations, including the following:

> Marketing products and services to customers through a variety of campaign mechanisms

> Sales tools that help your salespeople plan, forecast, and follow through on sales efforts

> Services features that allow you to manage after-order service with service orders, service contracts, and repairs

> A range of tools for online selling and support

> Interaction tools to help you run your customer interaction operations with features for telemarketing and customer service

> Channel management to allow you to sell into specialized channels such as educational markets

We look at each of these in more detail in the sections that follow.

Marketing

First contact

Whatever business you're in, marketing your product or services to customers is sometimes the first contact you have with them. The presentation of your message through a variety of customer touch points and the professionalism of your marketing activities can make a great impression, or a poor one.

If you're involved in marketing, you're aware that it's a complex endeavor. You need sophisticated tools to plan, launch, and track campaigns. The ability to have current data, integrated systems and processes, and robust analytics is important to your work.

The marketing solution in SAP CRM provides a way to integrate your marketing data and activities. SAP CRM Marketing offers a central platform for a variety of marketing activities, including the following modules:

> **Marketing Resource Management**
Helps you in areas such as market research, planning and budgeting, cost and volume planning, brand awareness, and marketing project management.

> **Segment and List Management**
Involves managing and high-speed searching of customer and prospect information, generating predictive models, data mining, and list management and analysis.

> **Campaign Management**
Helps you to plan and simulate campaigns, creating a marketing calendar, doing campaign-specific pricing and real-time response tracking, and performing analysis of target groups and campaigns.

> **Real-Time Offer Management**
Takes current market conditions into consideration so that offers specifically meet your customers' needs. Also enables you to follow up on the effectiveness of those offers.

> **Lead Management**
> Helps you manage multiple interaction channels, automate quali-
> fication, dispatch leads, use web-based lead generation, and auto-
> matically initiate follow-up activities.

> **Loyalty Management**
> Helps you develop reward and membership programs and track
> retention of valued customers.

Sales

The area of sales has its own challenges, including managing sales   **Sales challenges**
territories, order tracking, and order processing. In a sales organization's world, timely data and the ability to stay on top of prospective
and existing customer activity are essential. Having accurate data and
analytical tools helps you break down current sales trends and forecast
future sales activity.

Tools, such as portals, that collect key sales data in one place (see Figure 7.2) save salespeople time because they don't have to hunt down
data that is relevant to their customers from a variety of sources; therefore, they can be more efficient and effective.

Sales features in SAP CRM include the following:

> **Sales Planning and Forecasting**
> Provides capabilities for strategic planning, forecasting, collabora-
> tion, and account planning.

> **Sales Performance Management**
> Tracks opportunities and sales against company forecasts and al-
> lows you to perform what-if scenarios to ensure you are on track
> for meeting your goals.

> **Territory Management**
> Allows you to manage market segmentation, assign and schedule
> territories, perform sales analyses by territory, and synchronize
> with your sales force via mobile devices.

> **Accounts and Contacts**
> Helps you plan sales visits, maintain an interaction history, use in-
> tegrated email and fax features, manage relationships, and control
> customer-specific pricing and analyses.

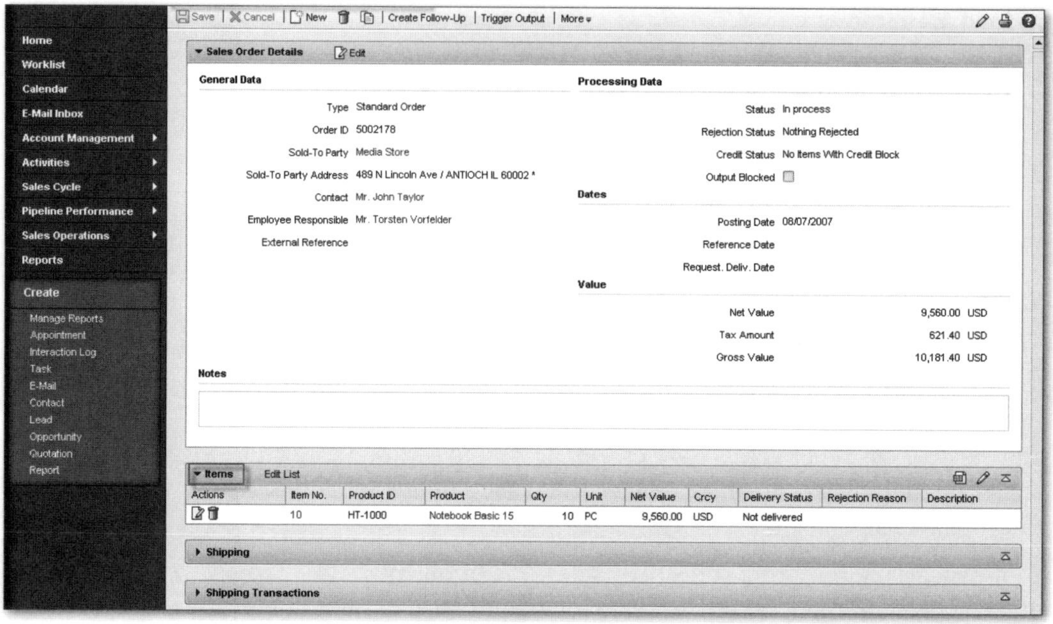

Figure 7.2 Creating a Sales Order Within SAP CRM

> **Opportunity Management**
> Helps you to manage team selling, organize competitive informa-
> tion, use account-specific sales processes, work with business part-
> ners, set pricing, and analyze and follow up on sales opportunities.

> **Quotation and Order Management**
> Provides the ability to handle quotations, track order status, vali-
> date orders, run credit checks, and process credit card payments
> and rebates.

> **Pricing and Contracts**
> Allows you to work with value and quantity contracts, sales agree-
> ments, contract negotiation, release order processing, and fulfill-
> ment synchronization.

> **Incentive and Commission Management**
> Includes direct and indirect sales compensation, incentive plan
> modeling, contracts and agreements handling, and commission
> simulation tools.

> **Time and Travel**
> Helps you to track salesperson activities, including features for time reporting, managing expense reports, cost assignment, and tracking receipts and mileage.

These sales tools provide information and streamlined processes, so that your sales force can spend more time selling and less time tracking data or filling out hardcopy expense forms.

Service

After you have connected with a customer and that customer has placed an order, you have to process that order and support your customer. That's where the Service area of SAP CRM comes in. Depending on your business, everything from managing in-house repairs of warrantied products to handling complaints and returns may come into play here.

SAP CRM Service includes the following areas:

> **Service Sales and Marketing**
> Covers service catalogs, service marketing and campaigns, service opportunity management, and service solution selling.

> **Service Contracts and Agreements**
> Includes managing service agreements, service contract processing, service plan processing, usage-based contract management, and service level management.

> **Installations and Maintenance**
> Tracks customers' installed base of equipments, configurations and locations for better insight and quicker problem resolutions.

> **Customer Service and Support**
> Handles service request processing, complaints processing, and case management (where all related records such as service orders and repair orders are bundled in a central repository).

> **Field Service Management**
> Includes service order management, service confirmation, and resource planning.

> **Returns and Depot Repair**
> Covers returns processing, loaner maintenance, in-house repair management, and quality management.

> **Warranty and Claims Management**
  Includes capabilities such as customer and vendor warranty, product and warranty registration, warranty claim processing, and recall management.

> **Service Logistics and Finance**
  Includes inventory, parts, and serial number management; financial integration; and billing.

> **Service Collaboration, Analytics, Optimization**
  Allows service delivery by multiple channels such as mobile devices and the web. Also includes service forecasting, planning, and analysis.

If your operation involves after-sales support and you manage that support in-house, this set of features within SAP CRM will help you track data and fulfill service contracts efficiently.

E-Commerce

E-commerce tools

Most companies have a web presence today. Customers have come to expect a range of e-commerce tools, including online ordering and order status checking, online catalogs, and the ability to pay online.

The Web Channel features of SAP CRM allow you to place your entire sales process online. You can provide easy-to-use sales tools and self-service features to customers that give them a personalized sales experience. You can also use features to streamline your backend fulfillment of online orders. Web Channel features are cost-effective for both business-to-business (B2B) and business-to-consumer (B2C) activities.

As you saw in Table 7.1, SAP ERP Web Channel breaks down into three main areas: E-Marketing, E-Commerce, and E-Service. The following are the specific features you can take advantage of in each of those areas.

E-Marketing

E-Marketing involves those aspects of your online store that promote your products or services. It consists of the following:

> **Catalog Management**
  Helps you create an electronic catalog of your products and describe their features and specifications.

> **Content Management**
  Allows you to create and manage content for your website that helps customers find what they need as they shop online.

> **Personalization**
> Allows you to create customer accounts and personalize their shopping experience.

> **Loyalty Management**
> Allows customers to enroll in loyalty programs, and accrue and redeem loyalty points.

> **Email and Web Campaigns**
> Enables you to promote your products online.

> **Store Locator**
> Helps online customers find the nearest store outlet. It's a feature that companies with brick-and-mortar stores usually build into their websites.

If gaining online customers is important to your organization, E-Marketing features will be valuable to your e-store presence.

E-Commerce pertains to actually pricing and selling via the Internet. This group of capabilities includes the following:

E-Commerce

> **Quotation and Order Management**
> Helps you set up a quotation system for products that are customized by product design or quantity discounts and process those orders.

> **Shopping Basket Management**
> This shopping cart feature helps you manage your online customers' checkout process.

> **Pricing and Contracts**
> Helps you manage how you price your products and offer discounts, as well as how you manage sales contracts for services or products.

> **Interactive Selling and Configuration**
> Allows you to set up live interaction between salespeople and online customers to help close the sale.

> **Web Auctions**
> Enables you to run an auction operation involving item postings, bidding procedures, and confirmations.

> **Selling via Partners**
> Provides tools for cross-selling through strategic sales partnerships.

If your company has online sales activities, SAP CRM E-Selling tools can provide a comprehensive solution to manage each aspect of your sales cycle.

E-Service Finally, *E-Service* has all of the tools required to manage orders and support customers:

> **Knowledge Management**
> Helps you to manage data about online sales and produce reports about trends helpful for planning and forecasting.

> **Service Order Management**
> Allows support of online sale service order processing.

> **Live Support**
> Contains tools for setting up live support for your customers so they can get answers to their problems in real time.

> **Installed Base**
> Helps you to measure the number of customers you have, as opposed to market share.

> **Complaints and Returns**
> Helps you handle customer issues efficiently to turn dissatisfied customers into satisfied ones.

> **Billing and Payment**
> Allows you to process invoices and payments for online sales.

> **Account Self Service**
> Gives customers the tools they need to get information without having to interact with a support person or salesperson.

E-Service tools round out the e-commerce capabilities of SAP CRM by taking your hard-won customer orders and handling them efficiently.

Interaction Center

Whether you call it your telemarketing group, customer service center, or telesales function, any area where you interact with customers is managed via the *Interaction Center (IC)* portion of SAP CRM.

Telemarketing and customer service IC covers activities such as telemarketing and customer support. If you have a customer interaction center, whether you use such centers to actively sell products or simply support customers after the sale, this SAP CRM feature will prove invaluable. Here are the various activities it supports in four areas: Telemarketing, Telesales, Customer Service, and IC Management.

Telemarketing helps you organize and manage outbound marketing campaigns, including the following:

Telemarketing

> **Campaign Execution**
> Plan your marketing and sales efforts.

> **Lead Management**
> Manage data about sales leads.

> **Personalization**
> Plan ways to connect sales efforts with potential customers in unique ways.

Telesales includes tools to help you manage the actual telemarketing effort where you're selling one-on-one to the customer:

Telesales

> **Accounts and Contacts**
> To manage contact information.

> **Activity Management**
> To track sales activity.

> **Quotation and Order Management**
> To enable your telesales force to provide quotes and place orders.

After you have obtained a customer's order, *Customer Service* helps you work with your customers in these areas:

Customer Service

> **Help Desk**
> Provides assistance with product features.

> **Customer Service and Support**
> Helps support your customers after an order is placed.

> **Complaint Management**
> Deals with customer issues regarding product problems or defects.

Lastly, *IC Management* is all about running your interaction center in these areas:

> **Knowledge Management**
> Controls data about your IC contacts.

> **Process Modeling**
> Helps you design efficient IC processes.

> **Communications Channels**
> Helps you set up efficient phone, online, and other communications methods.

If your company handles IC functions by itself, or even works with an outsourcing partner for a portion of them, these features will help you implement more efficient procedures and streamline your customer interactions.

Partner Channel Management

Managing partner relationships

What if you don't sell directly to customers? Many businesses work through partners to sell what they make. For example, companies such as jewelry manufacturers or book publishers primarily use retailers to sell their products. Other companies work with a franchise model or sell through third-party sales groups. How well these companies manage their partner relationships determines much of their business success.

Partner Channel Management

For example, Partner Channel Management allows you to manage your indirect sales channels; that is, your partners who sell for you. Tools for improved collaboration address sales, marketing, and service activities. In addition, analytics help you evaluate how your partners are performing.

Partner Channel Management covers the entire lifecycle of a channel relationship, from strategizing your partnerships to providing information to your partners about your products, managing pricing, managing orders, and even setting up collaborative showrooms.

The various areas of SAP CRM Partner Channel Management that support channel management include the following:

> **Partner Management**
> - Partner Lifecycle Management
> - Partner Training and Certification
> - Partner Planning and Forecasting
> - Partner Compensation
> - Partner Networking

> **Channel Marketing**
> - Partner Communication

- Catalog Management
- Campaign Management
- Lead Management
- Channel Marketing Funds
- Partner Locator

› **Channel Sales**

- Accounts and Contacts Management
- Activity Management
- Opportunity Management
- Pipeline Analysis
- Deal Registration

› **Partner Order Management**

- Quotation and Order Management
- Interactive Selling and Configuration
- Pricing and Contracts
- POS and Channel Inventory Tracking
- Collaborative Showroom
- Distributed Order Management

› **Channel Service**

- Knowledge Management
- Live Support
- Service Order Management
- Warranty and Claims Management
- Complaints and Returns Management

Many businesses today sell through multiple channels. SAP CRM provides features for keeping these vital channel relationships running efficiently.

Keeping vital channel relationships running

In the following section, we look at the technical underpinnings that enable SAP CRM to provide some of its functionality.

SAP CRM Technical Details

SAP CRM is supported by SAP NetWeaver, whose open architecture provides a web-based interface for accessing customer information.

SAP NetWeaver's open architecture

The SAP NetWeaver platform also enables interaction among various communication channels, such as telephone, email, chat, and short message system (SMS).

For example, if you want to set up a customer service operation, you will need a way to handle communication via telephone, email, and perhaps even a chat feature for real-time interaction with sales or service people and customers. These are all supported via SAP NetWeaver.

See Chapter 18 for more on SAP NetWeaver's support for SAP products

The analytics features of SAP NetWeaver are all about taking data and manipulating it to produce analyses, reports, and forecasts that provide consistent front- and back-office information. Integration services help users of SAP CRM connect with other SAP Business Suite solutions, such as SAP ERP, and with external systems. If, for example, you want to integrate your customer order process with your backend Financials, you can do that by using tools in SAP NetWeaver to integrate data from SAP CRM with SAP ERP Financials.

By now, you know that SAP CRM has a sound technical foundation and is packed with a long list of features, but you may be wondering how it works in the real world. The next section addresses this by beginning with a case study showing you how SAP CRM solved problems at one US company.

 Tip

> If you want to transition to SAP CRM faster, consider checking into the SAP CRM on-demand solution. This is a web-hosted solution that helps you switch to SAP CRM without having to implement the full solution in-house. These solutions are available in a subscription-based licensing model. You can expand your CRM features quickly and only as you need them. On-demand solutions from SAP use the same user interface as SAP CRM, so it's easy to shift the solution from a hosted one to a locally run, in-house solution down the road, if you want to make this transition without having to start from scratch.
>
> As of this writing, SAP Sales and SAP Marketing on-demand solutions are available, with a service solution planned in the future.

SAP CRM Case Study 1

Review Table 7.2 to get a quick snapshot of a case study regarding SAP CRM.

Company	US-based manufacturer of office equipment
Existing Solutions	SAP R/3, plus several third-party legacy systems
Challenge	To improve the access of customer service staffers to data about previous customer contact, to tie the online accessory store to the billing system, to centralize customer data and connect systems
SAP Solutions	SAP CRM and SAP Business Warehouse
Benefits	Better control of customer record management and centralization of data

Table 7.2 SAP CRM Case Study 1

SAP helped a US-based manufacturer of office equipment — including printers, faxes, and multifunction products — to implement a CRM solution. The company employs 1,100 people and is a subsidiary of a larger company based in Japan. This US-based manufacturer of office equipment sells its products through several channels, including mass merchandisers, dealers, distributors, retailers, and office superstores; however, all of its after-sales customer contact is handled in-house. Because this industry offers slim profit margins and has weak customer loyalty, differentiating itself via customer service was critical to the company's success.

Differentiation through customer service

The Challenges

The company faced several challenges regarding its customer relationships. Through its national service group, the company supports all customers and resellers, as well as parts distribution, returns, and customer contact centers. One of the key problems was that call-center staffers, who field almost 150,000 calls monthly, could not get records of previous calls. With a 20% repeat call rate, this caused huge problems, including a higher-than-industry-average rate of product returns.

The company's online accessory store was not tied into the main billing system. Orders were received via email and then entered into SAP R/3. Credit card checking was done after the receipt of the order. Decentralized customer data and disconnected systems were costing this company money, and worse, customers.

The SAP Solution

SAP worked with the company to phase in a solution that included SAP CRM working with SAP Business Warehouse (SAP BW). SAP CRM handled the customer contact processes, while SAP BW offered a method for centralizing customer data.

The solution was used across the organization, that is, in the customer service, technical support, parts distribution, and returns areas. Replacing disparate accounting, email, call center, and databases, the company integrated these into a single solution via SAP R/3, which the company had already implemented.

ASAP is an SAP rapid implementation methodology

The centralized data supported inventory and order-status data, call logging, retrieval of customer data, a solutions database to provide call center staff with consistent answers, up-selling and cross-selling, and a universal customer number system for order fulfillment and follow-up support.

The company took advantage of *ASAP*, an SAP rapid implementation methodology, to deploy SAP CRM and SAP BW. The Director of Parts Operations and MIS Directors headed the internal team, which implemented the following:

> Migrating data for 330,000 customers from SAP R/3 and other third-party and legacy systems to SAP CRM/SAP BW

> Deploying campaign management features and a solution database for internal use

> Adding capabilities for managing inbound email

> Automating four call centers in a phased rollout

The Benefits

The solution reduced returns and improved the company's business process efficiencies in dramatic ways. Their rate of returns dropped while the industry rates were rising. The company could now execute a campaign in hours, rather than days, and with fewer resources. It could generate reports that helped get better leads. The average cost of campaigns was lowered by $4,400.

By using a single customer database, data was more correct, providing for more consistent and accurate information throughout the customer support organization. SAP set up a system whereby customers could register their products online themselves, saving employee time. This data fed into SAP CRM for immediate access by company staff.

Time spent on customer support calls dropped, and the volume of calls themselves dropped. Interaction was shifted from phone to email and was handled through the centralized SAP R/3 database, resulting in significant savings. Standardized processes for complaint management ensured that grievances were handled better and customer satisfaction was higher.

One important benefit of the new system was reduced employee stress. When an employee interacting with a customer is more confident that the information he is accessing is accurate, stress is reduced considerably.

Looking Toward the Future

The company hopes to build on its efforts by deploying other SAP CRM features. The company plans to use Internet sales features in SAP CRM to replace its own online store. In addition, the company wants to take advantage of telemarketing and mobile sales features. The company will add Internet access for their dealers to receive leads and schedule sales appointments more efficiently.

Other important SAP CRM features

SAP CRM Case Study 2

Table 7.3 provides you with another quick overview of a case study before we explain it in more detail.

This Asian company deals in pulp and paper products, runs 14 manufacturing sites, and has various subsidiaries and partners. The company sells to customers around the world and has a workforce of more than 20,000.

Company	Asian paper mill products
Existing Solutions	SAP R/3 for critical business processes
Challenges	To obtain up-to-date customer information for customer inquiries, to ensure minimum disruption to operations and customer services
SAP Solutions	Upgrade to SAP ERP, SAP CRM, SAP NetWeaver Portal, SAP NetWeaver BW
Benefits	Increased process efficiency, higher productivity, reduced costs, and reduced time spent on financial calculations and IT maintenance

Table 7.3 SAP CRM Case Study 2

The Challenges

Salespeople and customer service people who had to work with customers of this large China-based company were not able to get the up-to-date customer information they needed to handle customer inquiries. Response times were not as fast as needed to keep customers satisfied.

The company had many self-designed forms and interfaces that had to be integrated or replaced all on a tight schedule. Moreover, the company had to ensure minimum disruption to operations and customer services.

The SAP Solution

1,000 users upgraded to SAP ERP at 14 sites

One thousand users were upgraded to SAP ERP at 14 sites. SAP worked with an internal team to perform the upgrade in 15 weeks with little downtime. Besides implementing SAP ERP, the team integrated SAP CRM so that salespeople and customer service people now have timely access to information through customized interfaces. Enhanced system performance also allows for faster response times.

In addition, SAP NetWeaver BW was implemented to improve the reporting available to managers for making key decisions about how to best serve customers and plan for the future.

The Benefits

Besides improvements in handling data, the company has realigned its processes for better customer service and increased productivity. The company's IT operation has less to do to maintain the system and make changes to it. The company's ability to more rapidly access and act on customer data has provided a competitive edge and laid the foundation for future growth.

Quickly access and act on customer data

Conclusion

In this chapter, we outlined the entire SAP CRM product and its many features for interacting with your customers, including the following:

> How SAP CRM fits into your enterprise

> The six key areas of SAP CRM, including both cross-industry (such as analytics) and SAP CRM-specific functionality in marketing, sales, service, interaction center, e-commerce, and channel management

> The technology on which SAP CRM rests

> How SAP CRM works in real-world settings

Setting the basis for serving your customers and collecting their orders is an important part of your business. But after you have those orders in-house, how do you ensure that you can fulfill them? In Chapter 8, we explore another useful tool that can help you to build your products and deliver them to your customers — SAP Supplier Relationship Management (SAP SRM).

SAP Supplier Relationship Management

We live in an age when people expect to be able to take charge of their interactions over the Internet, placing and tracking orders, updating their own account information, and so on. Companies that supply your enterprise with materials, products, or services need and expect the same access. *SAP Supplier Relationship Management* (SAP SRM) includes tools for enabling document exchange and electronic business transactions. It also includes features to help you identify sourcing opportunities, and qualify, negotiate, and contract with suppliers.

In addition, there are features that help you set up requisitioning and order systems, and manage receiving and financial settlements while enforcing internal and supplier compliance. All of these features, which we'll cover in this chapter, can result in dramatic cost savings for your enterprise and help you to service your own customers more efficiently.

How SAP SRM Fits into an Enterprise

Every company purchases something, whether that something is tons of steel to build cars, or just office supplies, computers, and telephones to run the business. SAP SRM helps any organization streamline its purchasing processes, which saves money and time in a multitude of ways.

Faced with the need to be profitable, companies of all sizes are looking to their sourcing and procurement procedures to find bottom-line savings. After all, regardless of the current economic climate, if you can reduce the cost of purchased goods and services without sacrificing quality, you can boost profitability without having to increase sales.

That's where SAP SRM tools come into play. SAP SRM automates processes between sourcing and procurement, both in the enterprise and across the supply base.

Purchasing Governance

Because we live in a global economy where many businesses are interconnected, public sector and government agencies are requiring companies to provide more detailed reports about the materials they purchase and the suppliers they use. This reporting can involve anything from having companies provide a list of their overseas vendors, to detailing how many green products they've purchased in the past year.

It becomes difficult to track these reports as the requirements change, especially if you have plants in multiple locations where you're required to comply with individual state and country regulations. For example, California may require that your fleet run on bio-fuel, and federal regulations may prohibit you from purchasing such materials from Cuba or Iraq.

This is where the Purchasing Governance solution can help you track and monitor purchasing requirements and regulations as they relate to your particular industry and purchasing needs.

Sourcing

Finding the right supplier

Choosing the right supplier, often referred to as *sourcing*, can have a great impact on your profitability. As a starting point, companies need to understand their spending and target the best categories and opportunities for sourcing. But getting the right price isn't the only thing you have to look for in a good supplier relationship. Finding the right supplier also means that you will work with organizations that deliver what they promise when they promise it, saving you costly delays or bottlenecks in your own business.

Finding that perfect supplier doesn't happen overnight. It requires that you analyze your own needs accurately by identifying the best candidates to meet your needs. Then you have to specify your requirements in a request for quotation or proposal. You can use tools in SAP SRM to help you locate, qualify, and negotiate with your suppliers in an organized, effective way.

 Tip

If you want to experience e-sourcing before committing to a long-term program, consider piloting a hosted version of the *SAP E-Sourcing On-Demand* solution as an inexpensive and low-risk first step.

Contract Management

When you locate a good partner, you have to negotiate the right terms to ensure that your contracts for products or services are complete, accurate, and keep you in compliance with any commerce regulations.

Negotiate the right terms

In many organizations, purchasing contracts are stored on hard drives or tucked away in filing cabinets, and nobody ever tracks or ensures compliance after the contracts are signed. There is often no way to know if suppliers are living up to their commitments, or even to quickly determine which categories of spending are covered by the contracts.

To manage purchasing contracts effectively, SAP SRM's *contract management* tools and the associated practices help you create the right purchasing agreements for each situation. Then, after the agreements are signed, SAP SRM helps you comply with your agreements and monitor supplier performance to make sure the supplier is delivering what it promised.

Contract management tools

Collaborative Procurement

After you've identified and contracted with suppliers, you can start to do business with them. Procurement is the part of supplier relationship management that involves actual purchasing processes. For example, when somebody in your organization submits a requisition to your purchasing department for a dozen new computers, it is the start of a process that involves placing the order, tracking the order, receiving the goods, and finally paying the supplier for what was delivered.

If your procurement processes are not efficient, employees who submit requisitions will become frustrated. Their productivity may suffer because they don't have what they need to do their jobs. If you are requisitioning the materials you use to build products, then delays can result in lost revenue for your company and disappointed customers.

SAP SRM's procurement tools are designed to streamline your purchasing processes and minimize the time it takes to receive goods or services.

Supplier Collaboration

Having the right suppliers and efficient processes for purchasing are two pieces of the puzzle. The third is putting tools in place that enable you and your suppliers to interact efficiently. In the past, you had to spend time calling your supplier to locate an order. They had to contact you to see if you were running low on a certain item. Phone tag and lost messages or documents inevitably resulted in mistakes. But with the advent of the Internet and more sophisticated software, you and your suppliers have the means to stay in touch and on top of your purchasing.

Ease of communication and access to data

Today, you can do everything from exchanging electronic documents to checking inventory and enabling electronic transactions online. This ease of communication and access to data can help make suppliers a more strategic part of your business.

SAP SRM provides the online interfaces that allow you to place orders and then receive advance notices of when the orders will ship. You can also use SAP SRM tools to check data such as inventory levels. Suppliers can even maintain and update electronic catalogs so your company always has current product information.

Supply Base Management

Many companies are running lean today and don't have the luxury of keeping extra inventory on hand. To ensure you have needed materials and supplies on hand, at just the time you need them, you have to maintain up-to-date information on your current suppliers, identify new suppliers, and evaluate supplier performance. Tools in Supply Base Management help you track your suppliers so that you can be proactive when changes occur.

A Closer Look at SAP SRM

SAP SRM offers several areas of functionality that take you from your early strategic planning to financial settlement with your chosen suppliers. In between, there are tools to handle everything from strategic sourcing, contracting, and requisitioning to receipt, ongoing supplier collaboration, and performance management.

Key Features and Functions

SAP SRM provides capabilities and benefits across all sourcing and procurement processes. Figure 8.1 shows SAP's SRM solution map and the types of activities and tools that fall within each main category.

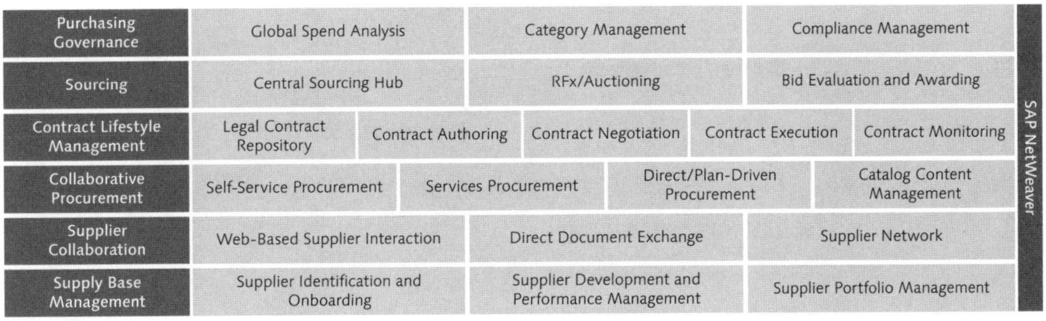

Purchasing Governance	Global Spend Analysis		Category Management		Compliance Management	
Sourcing	Central Sourcing Hub		RFx/Auctioning		Bid Evaluation and Awarding	
Contract Lifestyle Management	Legal Contract Repository	Contract Authoring	Contract Negotiation	Contract Execution	Contract Monitoring	
Collaborative Procurement	Self-Service Procurement	Services Procurement	Direct/Plan-Driven Procurement	Catalog Content Management		
Supplier Collaboration	Web-Based Supplier Interaction	Direct Document Exchange		Supplier Network		
Supply Base Management	Supplier Identification and Onboarding	Supplier Development and Performance Management		Supplier Portfolio Management		

(SAP NetWeaver)

Figure 8.1 SAP SRM Solution Map

Purchasing Governance

This area of SAP SRM includes the following tools:

> **Global Spend Analysis**
> As with many business processes, working with suppliers involves a lot of data. Being able to organize that data in a way that keeps it accurate and allows you to analyze it helps you plan for the future. Data on spending habits can be particularly challenging to

obtain and analyze, so SAP SRM provides a global spend analysis tool (see Figure 8.2) that helps you accurately categorize spending and cleanse the data periodically. This tool also provides reports that help you find opportunities for savings.

Figure 8.2 Analytics Provide Helpful Information in SAP SRM

Strategic sourcing processes

> **Category Management**
> This is a set of tools that allows procurement management to define best practices for employees to follow, including strategic sourcing processes. Category Management also provides a program management capability that helps you review your company's portfolio of procurement initiatives. This makes it easy to report on procurement team successes and make them visible throughout your organization.

> **Compliance Management**
> For you to have an overall picture of your procurement function, you need compliance management tools that provide information on the current state of your procurement operation, along with tools to help you define and enforce practices. These tools also support compliance with various national regulatory requirements.

After you have used these tools to plan and organize your procurement data, it's time to go shopping. You will need sourcing tools to find the right sources for the materials or products you need, as we'll explain next.

Sourcing

Historically, many steps in the strategic sourcing process have been handled manually, which took a lot of time. Without built-in best practices, many sourcing processes don't even lead to the best supplier decisions, but supplier collaboration technologies have streamlined sourcing.

SAP SRM provides an entire toolset for managing the sourcing process, including supplier identification, requests for information and proposals, auctioning procedures, bid evaluation, and awarding of contracts. With SAP SRM tools, you can also manage sourcing online, which can save money and provide for faster sourcing cycles and more competitive supplier bidding.

When you find the right source, the next logical step is to contract with that source. That's where contract management comes in.

Contract Management

Contract Management has its own set of tools for developing, executing, and monitoring contracts. You can create a contract document repository with clause libraries, templates, and rules that help you generate contracts and manage collaboration both inside and outside of your company.

Develop, execute, and monitor contracts

Revisions and renewals of contracts can often become chaotic, if you don't have a method of tracking changes and contracts that are becoming out of date. SAP SRM also helps you to efficiently distribute contracts and changes to contracts to help you monitor contract compliance.

Monitoring tools enable you to keep spending under control and be alerted to contracts that are about to expire so you can renegotiate them and avoid downtime.

After you have chosen and contracted with approved vendors, you need efficient procurement procedures, so that placing an order with those vendors is a seamless process.

Collaborative Procurement

Requisitioning and order management

SAP SRM includes tools for requisitioning and order management that help you put those procedures in place for all categories of spending, including indirect goods, direct materials, and services. SAP SRM supports four areas of collaborative procurement:

> **Self-service Procurement**
> The simplest way to avoid chaos in your company's spending is to ensure that all employees follow standard purchasing procedures. SAP SRM has features for desktop requisitioning that help to ensure consistent standards. Employees can create shopping carts full of catalog items, and also have the ability to add special order items. Each requisition is routed to the appropriate approvers or collaborators and then converted into a supplier order. After an order is placed, validation of contract terms, global trade directives, and calculation of taxes are automated. Then the order is tracked, and all order procedures, from sending out an advance shipping notice to documenting the receipt of goods, can be managed easily.

> **Services Procurement**
> Money spent on services typically makes up a large percentage of overall corporate spending, and yet, it is often the least well-managed type of purchase. When you spend money on services, it's not as simple as specifying a product code. Services may require upfront collaboration with the supplier to define job specifications. If you use recurring services such as janitorial maintenance, work may be performed without a purchase order, which can make invoice reconciliation a challenge. SAP SRM provides tools you can use to closely manage services spending and payment processes.

> **Direct/Plan-Driven Procurement**
> When purchasing requirements are created in systems outside of SAP SRM, such as from within SAP ERP or supply chain systems,

SAP SRM helps you manage associated purchase orders. This approach helps to centralize procurement through a single process that uses the supplier collaboration capabilities of SAP SRM.

> **Catalog Content Management**
> SAP SRM's Catalog Content Management tools let you make your products available to your customers in a catalog format online. As individual suppliers update their products, you can pull those products from their catalogs to update your own, or you can use collaboration tools within SAP SRM to have the supplier update your catalog directly. Your customers can then do online searches of your catalog to find just the product they need.

 Tip

If you work with international suppliers, you may want to consider using *SAP BusinessObjects Global Trade Services*. This service integrates easily with SAP SRM, helping you ensure that your purchasing procedures are in compliance with international requirements.

Collaborative capabilities within your company are one-half of the SAP SRM collaboration equation. You also need tools to enable you to collaborate with your suppliers, as you'll see in the next section.

Supplier Collaboration

The ability to work directly with suppliers online streamlines most procurement processes and helps all parties have the most up-to-date information. SAP SRM offers several capabilities to enable supplier collaboration, including web-based supplier portals (see Figure 8.3), where suppliers can exchange documents, receive POs, send shipping notices and invoices, manage inventory information, and so on.

Enabling supplier collaboration

Suppliers can also proactively manage their catalog content, so that your company always sees the latest available products and pricing.

Managing catalog content

When you have the right suppliers on board and have established collaborative procedures, you are ready to assess the performance of those suppliers to keep your relationships on track. That's where Supply Base Management comes in.

Figure 8.3 Work with Teams of Collaborators for Greater Efficiency

Supply Base Management

Many procurement decisions, such as awarding new business or deciding whether to renew an existing contract, rely on accurate data about supplier performance. It's a challenge for most procurement organizations to understand and manage their supplier portfolio and all of the related information about each supplier. From supplier self-registration and onboarding (i.e., bringing supply chain partners on board as part of your team) to ongoing profile management and performance management, these information management processes are a challenge. Yet, they are critical to the success of supply relationships.

Supplier data and performance information

SAP SRM offers centralized supplier data and performance information so that you can stay on top of things and take action if your suppliers are performing poorly. From a portfolio management perspective, your procurement organization can determine, at regular intervals, whether you need to expand or downsize the supply base in particular spending categories.

Now that we've covered all of the categories of functionality in SAP SRM, let's look at several case studies to see how this works in real-world companies.

SAP SRM Case Study 1

Table 8.1 gives you an overview of a case study that will show you how SAP SRM works in the real world.

Company	Motorcycle manufacturer
Existing Solutions	Legacy system with multiple products
Challenge	To improve communications with suppliers, to enable online interactions with suppliers and dealers, and to reduce on-hand inventory
SAP Solution	Self-service features of SAP SRM plus SAP CRM e-commerce features
Benefits	Faster ordering process, cost savings from streamlined inventory, less manual data entry (which cuts down on errors)

Table 8.1 SAP SRM Case Study 1

A large manufacturer of motorcycles based in India held a healthy market share. However, with a network of 350 component suppliers and more than 1,100 dealers and sales and service outlets, the company needed to streamline supplier processes to stay ahead in a competitive market.

Streamlined supplier processes to succeed in a competitive market

The Challenges

The company had three main goals: to improve communications with its suppliers and dealers, to enable both suppliers and dealers to perform transactions online, and to reduce on-hand inventory to save costs. The legacy system in place couldn't support any of these challenges, so the company had to find a solution that could build on its legacy system, while providing the necessary supplier support.

The SAP Solution

SAP Consulting helped with the implementation. As part of the SAP Services portfolio, SAP Consulting was able to provide a single point of access (SPoA) to a variety of services from SAP, including consulting, training, support, development, and hosting.

The SAP on-site consultants shared their project management expertise, coordinated resources, and kept the project moving forward. They used the proven ASAP project management methodology to keep the project on track and finished in just three months. In addition, the SAP consultants provided training for the manufacturer's implementation team, recommended use of best practices, and configured and tested the new system.

To enable online transactions by suppliers and dealers, the self-service features of SAP SRM were combined with e-commerce features available through SAP CRM. The ability to enter orders directly made the ordering process much faster and more efficient. In addition, inventory planning was improved, and costs were cut. Enabling suppliers and dealers to enter their own orders online cut down on manual entry in-house, which helped reduce data-entry mistakes.

Looking Toward the Future

The India-based manufacturer is planning to grow its use of SAP SRM features and to implement additional SAP products and functionality, including Financials integrated with SAP NetWeaver BW and SAP NetWeaver Portal.

SAP SRM Case Study 2

Table 8.2 is a snapshot of another case study that illustrates SAP SRM in action.

This producer of tobacco products has revenues of over €13.5 billion a year and employs more than 90,000 people in 180 countries. The company was experiencing out-of-control purchasing costs and needed a single system that would dovetail with its existing SAP system.

Company	Australian tobacco company
Existing Solutions	SAP ERP and multiple legacy systems
The Challenge	To improve policies regarding purchasing to save money, and to improve control by purchasing department on spending
SAP Solution	SAP SRM
Benefits	Procurement spending reduced by €292 million a year; improved visibility and analytics

Table 8.2 SAP SRM Case Study 2

The Challenge

This company had no policy in place regarding its procurement processes across the enterprise. In addition, its purchasing department was not involved in many purchasing transactions, leaving no control over spending.

Because of maverick buying habits by various groups, purchasing costs were extremely high. The company sought a solution that would fit with its existing SAP system and also support the entire procurement process.

The SAP Solution

SAP SRM was rolled out in 19 countries in the first phase, and then in another 31 countries in the second phase. The system was integrated seamlessly with existing SAP solutions. A country-based model provided both global consistencies and regional flexibility.

SAP SRM was configured in a single way for all users, providing a uniform supplier system across departments and countries.

The Benefits

With SAP SRM in place, the company reduced maverick buying habits and realized savings of €292 million annually. In addition, with consistent purchasing operations across the enterprise, the purchasing department was able to gain control of all procurement procedures.

The company was also able to gain visibility into its procurement data and generate analytics that helped make additional improvements to the company's processes.

SAP SRM Customer Fast Facts

Thousands of companies have gained value using SAP SRM solutions, but value isn't always easy to quantify. What kinds of bottom-line results might you expect to get?

Here are some quick examples of the types of savings companies have realized by using SAP SRM:

> A major global diversified manufacturer consolidated more than 10 million spend records to gain over 90% visibility into its spending and subsequently has put controls in place over that spending within sourcing and procurement.

> One of the largest international telecommunications companies successfully leveraged SAP SRM E-Sourcing to realize $12 billion in savings from merging processes. The company now has completely automated its sourcing processes.

> An $18 billion consumer goods company reduced the sourcing cycle time by 67% and implemented best practices in its newly defined and automated sourcing processes.

> One of the largest international pharmaceutical companies is managing thousands of RFx and auction events annually spending almost $10 billion. The company has reduced the timeline of each sourcing project by six weeks.

> A $20 billion international insurer built a comprehensive contracts repository, gained visibility into contract expirations and projects, and reduced its Sarbanes-Oxley reporting effort by 75%.

> One of the largest global office furniture makers automated its entire procurement process and reduced inventory by 60%, increased its automated invoice processing by 70%, and captured approximately 80% of its direct material spending.

> A major international conglomerate reduced its per purchase transaction cost from about $30 to only $2 by automating the process,

while gaining insight into spending habits and formulating more effective sourcing strategies.

> One of the world's leading consumer products companies increased contract compliance from 75% to 95% by turning its contracts into dynamically updated catalog content and ensuring that employees purchased from those catalogs.

> The world's leading supplier of mobile systems cut purchase cycle time by 80% and reduced the cost of order handling by 75%.

Every enterprise's results with SAP SRM will vary, but one thing is certain: Implementing efficient, consistent supplier relationship procedures will have a positive impact on your profitability.

Conclusion

In this chapter, you were introduced to the various features of SAP Supplier Relationship Management, which you can use to organize and streamline relationships with your suppliers. We covered the following topics:

> Sourcing to find the right vendors and partners

> Procurement to make your purchasing operations more efficient

> Contract management for dealing with supplier contracts

> Collaboration both inside and outside of your enterprise

Of course, now that you've spent all of this time procuring materials and components to build your products, you need to manage them. In Chapter 9, we'll move on to the next process — product lifecycle management. We'll explore the features and benefits of SAP Product Lifecycle Management (SAP PLM), which addresses the life of your products, from inception to execution.

SAP Product Lifecycle Management

Product Lifecycle Management (PLM) is the SAP solution that helps companies manage the entire lifecycle of creating a product, from the day the idea is conceived to the day the product is discontinued. During that time, SAP PLM provides support for managing projects, product development tasks, documents, and strategic relationships. In addition, important regulations and health and safety provisions become easier to handle with SAP PLM's Corporate Services.

In this chapter, we'll introduce you to the major features of SAP Product Lifecycle Management and provide examples of how it can fit into your enterprise.

How SAP PLM Fits in an Enterprise

Product lifecycle processes can be hard to get a handle on because they quite often cross various disciplines and groups in your organization. Management, designers, production, and sales, not to mention strategic external partners, need access to data about your product development processes.

Through four applications, SAP PLM offers tools to handle just about everything involved with product development. In addition, support from other SAP products can introduce features to handle related tasks, such as analytics or product launches. In this section, we will explore these tools and describe how they can support product lifecycles in your enterprise.

Support for Discrete and Process Industries

If you talk to SAP representatives, you'll hear how SAP PLM supports both discrete and process industries. But let's clarify the difference between these two industries before we proceed further.

Discrete Industries

Discrete industries (also referred to as *discrete manufacturing*) are often defined as those industries involving products that you can see, touch, or count. For example, if you manufacture electronic products such as radios, computers, medical equipment, cars, or furniture, you're in a discrete industry.

Process Industries

Process industries (also referred to as *process manufacturing*) are typically defined as those industries involving a chemical change. Good examples of this type of manufacturing include the petroleum industry, chemicals, food production, and textiles.

Of course, many companies have processes that touch on both of these types of industry. But the processes used in building tables and processing petroleum can differ, and SAP PLM offers tools to support both, as you'll see throughout the rest of this chapter as we delve into the features of SAP PLM.

SAP PLM Solution Map

The solution map for SAP PLM is shown in Figure 9.1. There are four areas of functionality:

> Product Management
> Product Development and Collaboration
> Product Data Management
> PLM Foundation

Each of these categories is discussed in more detail next.

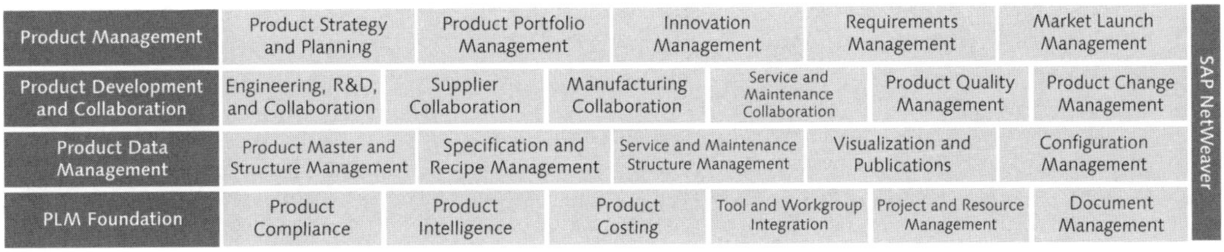

Product Management	Product Strategy and Planning	Product Portfolio Management	Innovation Management	Requirements Management	Market Launch Management	SAP NetWeaver
Product Development and Collaboration	Engineering, R&D, and Collaboration	Supplier Collaboration	Manufacturing Collaboration	Service and Maintenance Collaboration	Product Quality Management	Product Change Management
Product Data Management	Product Master and Structure Management	Specification and Recipe Management	Service and Maintenance Structure Management	Visualization and Publications	Configuration Management	
PLM Foundation	Product Compliance	Product Intelligence	Product Costing	Tool and Workgroup Integration	Project and Resource Management	Document Management

Figure 9.1 SAP PLM Solution Map

SAP PLM's Value in Your Enterprise

Being able to deliver new products quickly and efficiently has obvious benefits for any organization. SAP PLM allows you to explore market opportunities, reduce the costs of product development, manage your processes efficiently, integrate with suppliers and partners, and ensure product quality.

SAP PLM also helps you ensure that the data about your products is consistent across your organization. Everyone from your product designers to your sales force will be aware of new developments and designs. In addition, document tracking features help ensure that key data, such as engineering change orders, are handled with fewer errors.

Document tracking features

Integration with other SAP products, as well as MCAD and ECAD design tools, provide seamless process and information flow. With SAP PLM, you can develop prototypes and specifications to deliver to manufacturing partners, and ensure that your products meet the necessary product guidelines and safety regulations.

A Closer Look at SAP PLM

Each of the areas of SAP PLM provides a set of features to handle various aspects of product development. In this section, we look at these features and examine how they help you get from the concept to final product. Note that this is an overview; for each and every capability available, check out the detailed solution maps included in Appendix C, SAP Solution Maps.

Overview of SAP PLM

Take a look at each of the major areas of SAP PLM listed in the SAP PLM solution map, each of which is discussed in more detail in the sections that follow. Table 9.1 shows you the key areas of SAP PLM, based on SAP PLM's solution map.

Category	Features
Product Management	Product Strategy and Planning
	Product Portfolio Management
	Innovation Management
	Requirements Management
	Market Launch Management
Product Development and Collaboration	Engineering, R&D Collaboration
	Supplier Collaboration
	Manufacturing Collaboration
	Service and Maintenance Collaboration
	Product Quality Management
	Product Change Management
Product Data Management	Product Master and Structure Management
	Specification and Recipe Management
	Service and Maintenance Structure Management
	Visualization and Publications
	Configuration Management
PLM Foundation	Product Compliance
	Product Intelligence
	Product Costing
	Tool and Workgroup Integration
	Project and Resource Management
	Document Management

Table 9.1 SAP PLM Solution Map

> **➕ Tip**
>
> The *Collaboration Folders* (cFolders) application in SAP PLM allows for document collaboration during product development. You can share information with internal staff as well as external vendors using cFolders because it doesn't expose your backend system and therefore keeps confidential data secure. cFolders also works with the strategic sourcing features of SAP SRM.

Before we explore each of these categories in more detail, we'll discuss how they are all related to functionality in other SAP products.

SAP PLM and Its Relation to Other SAP Products

SAP PLM is supported by SAP NetWeaver, whose open architecture provides for a web-based interface for accessing product development information. You can establish outside partners and vendors involved in your product development and allow them to access your latest documents and data via the web, thereby streamlining your project teamwork.

The analytics processes supported by SAP NetWeaver Business Warehouse (SAP NetWeaver BW) and data warehousing allow you to have consistent product information, both across your business and with external partners or vendors. SAP NetWeaver integration functions help users of SAP PLM connect with other SAP Business Suite solutions, such as SAP Customer Relationship Management (SAP CRM), and with external systems.

See Chapter 18 for more on SAP NetWeaver

When you launch a new product, the integration of SAP PLM, and SAP CRM is also useful. With these two SAP applications in place, you can support market launches of new products, with automated delivery of the print materials that salespeople need, and seamless order processing.

SAP Supply Chain Management (SAP SCM) can also be called on to help with top-down and bottom-up demand planning. This, in turn, helps you forecast product need in the marketplace.

SAP SCM

In the following sections, we provide you with more detail about each of the major categories in the SAP PLM solution map.

Product Management

Product Management is where your product development project is defined and executed. This component would allow a software manufacturer, for example, to come up with the idea for a new game software, begin to plan the product development process, schedule the software engineers and other resources to work on the game, and strategize plans for this new product alongside other projects in the company.

Specifically, this module provides tools that help you brainstorm about your new product design and make your business case for your management to evaluate. Once underway, you can use Project Management tools to help schedule, manage resources, and track your costs. You can also use project-reporting tools to keep shareholders in the loop. If your company is managing several product development projects, the strategic and product portfolio tools will help you keep a broader view of all of your projects and products. The features in the Product Management area include:

> **Product Strategy and Planning**
Helps you align new product concepts with your overall business strategies and goals. With the new product roadmap, you allow collaboration across departments and resources as well as track risks and management of intellectual property associated with your new product.

Project Builder

> **Product Portfolio Management**
Allows you to evaluate, based on current market conditions, which new products warrant resources for development, which products need to be maintained at their current level, and which existing products need to be updated or retired.

> **Innovation Management**
Helps you to study market potential for ideas, evaluate technical constraints in producing the product, and measure the potential return on investment of the new product.

> **Requirements Management**
Captures all requirements — from business rules to functional and technical aspects — to ensure your products meet the needs of your customers.

> **Market Launch Management**
  Provides tools and strategies to help you successfully launch your new products in the market.

Product Management takes you through the product concept and planning stage. The next area of SAP PLM helps you deal with the product development phase.

Product Development and Collaboration

This area of SAP PLM offers different benefits depending on the type of industry you work for.

If yours is a discrete industry, you can use Product Development and Collaboration to move requirement structures through to concept structures and finally into product structures. Integration with authoring environments, such as CAD systems, helps you move through design to prototype. You can collaborate with external business partners in a secure web environment. If your concern is strategic sourcing, you can look to integration with SAP SRM.

Collaborate with external partners

A logical step in developing a new product is to create a product prototype. SAP PLM offers tools to ensure that you can procure the parts or supplies you need, produce the prototype, evaluate its design, and then move from prototype to final production.

When you have your final product defined, you can get configurations to sales so they can take the product to your consumers and provide equipment and technical asset structures to service and maintenance to support the product.

If your company is a process industry, you need to handle specifications and *recipes* (process definitions, such as how to process crude oil) at various levels. SAP PLM allows you to take enterprise-level recipes and implement them at the site and plant level. You can manage process trials that ensure that these recipes are foolproof before you send them on to production.

Quality management and product-costing capabilities are important features for all types of industries and underline the value of an integrated solution.

Product Development and Collaboration features include the following:

> **Engineering, R&D Collaboration**
> This is a business process that enables cross-department development essentially by providing centralized data storage.

> **Supplier Collaboration**
> These tools help you manage and evaluate the ability of your suppliers to provide the required parts and components within the established quality standards and desired time frame.

> **Manufacturing Collaboration**
> This helps you to define your recipes and process definitions prior to sending them on to your manufacturing group. In this context, a *recipe* can be thought of as the steps and materials needed to build a product. A process definition defines a process such as quality control.

> **Service and Maintenance Collaboration**
> This is where you establish product maintenance records, maintenance manuals, and warranty claims, as well as define the process for how your products are to be serviced.

> **Product Quality Management**
> This can be used with SAP ERP tools to define deliverables, quality measurements, and plan inspections for quality. The quality notification tool helps you to detect, define, and report on quality problems.

> **Product Change Management**
> This handles documents related to engineering change requests over the life of your products. These requests occur when things such as modifications to the original product are required to deal with market or product safety issues.

If your company made ice cream, the product development and collaboration phase is when you would test the recipes until the product met with your approval. After you've completed the Product Development and Collaboration set of tasks, the next area of SAP PLM, Product Data Management, will help you document your product specifications and create the specifications that will allow you to produce that great flavor in every batch you produce.

Product Data Management

Product Data Management is the paper-pusher of SAP PLM. This is the set of features that you use for handling documents throughout the life of your products, from planning and technical specifications to part management and bill of materials. Product Data Management includes the following tools:

> **Product Master and Structure Management**
> Involves the description of your product features in a product structure (a product structure describes how parts and components are assembled to create a product), as well as all of the data used in manufacturing processes.

> **Specification and Recipe Management**
> Involves managing the detailed product specifications and recipes (thorough descriptions of processes) for processes that connect the R&D function to product production.

> **Service and Maintenance Structure Management**
> Includes three processes: Phase-In Equipment, Corrective Maintenance, and Phase-Out Equipment. Essentially, you use this portion of SAP PLM to keep records over the life of various pieces of equipment used in your manufacturing process, including putting it into service, maintaining it, and retiring it from service.

> **Visualization and Publications**
> This is the process for issuing documents such as repair manuals, training manuals, and technical publications.

> **Configuration Management**
> Provides a history of all product changes made over the life of the product, including the management of parts catalogs and all documents detailing the individual components within your product.

Handle documents throughout the life of your products

SAP PLM Foundation

In business today, where there are products, there are often regulations. Some of these regulations pertain to product safety, some to waste disposal in the manufacturing process, and still others to employees' health and safety when working with these products. The PLM Foundation portion of SAP PLM is where you find the tools to manage product and process audits to ensure that you're meeting set criteria.

Regulations

The various areas of SAP PLM Foundation are as follows.

> **Product Compliance**
> The tools in this area of SAP PLM include Product Compliance, Audit Management, Product Safety, Hazardous Substance Management, Dangerous Goods Management, and Waste Management. These tools ensure that your products meet and comply with regulatory and government requirements for product and consumer safety, transportation and disposal of hazardous waste and dangerous goods, and proper labeling of products containing such things as cleaning agents or drugs.

> **Product Intelligence**
> Allows you to access and analyze all documents and information related to your products from all parts of your system, including SAP SCM and SAP CRM modules.

> **Product Costing**
> A set of tools that allows you to break down costs for products and services, including the costs incurred in each step of your production process. You can monitor orders and materials based on sales lots or individual sales documents.

> **Tools and Workgroup Integration**
> Provides for the integration of applications such as CAD/CAM into your system for product development.

> **Project and Resource Management**
> Contains all of the tools necessary for the management of this new product development process. You can manage the essential items such as the project scope, time, costs, resources, and milestones.

> **Document Management**
> Provides a way to integrate documents with your processes and make them available to you in a variety of formats, including graphics, CAD, and text.

Together, all of the tools provided in SAP PLM allow you to manage a product from its conception to its safe implementation in your workplace.

In the next two sections, you'll find case studies to help you better understand how companies have found benefits from implementing SAP PLM in their enterprises.

SAP PLM Case Study 1

Table 9.2 gives you an overview of the first case study in this chapter.

Company	German medical equipment manufacturer
Existing Solutions	SAP R/3 and other SAP products
Challenge	To continuously innovate and deliver products to market quickly
SAP Solutions	SAP PLM, SAP Easy Document Management, Windows Explorer integration, and link between SAP PLM and the CAD system
Benefits	Design and production collaborate more easily; incorporation of outside resources in product development processes; and consolidated, accurate data

Table 9.2 SAP PLM Case Study 1

A German medical equipment manufacturer needed to deliver innovative products to compete successfully in the marketplace. The company implemented SAP PLM to accelerate its product development and to manage documentation more efficiently.

Deliver innovative products

The Challenges

The company, one of the leading medical equipment companies in the world, specializes in surgical equipment. In the medical equipment field, it's necessary to develop innovative, cutting-edge products regularly if you want to stay in business. A full 30% of this company's income-generating products are less than five years old, highlighting the need for constant innovation with new products.

This company had to find ways to deliver new products faster and determine how to integrate its CAD data into its product development processes.

The SAP Solution

The company assigned four IT experts to a project team and implemented the solution in three phases. The first phase involved migrating development documentation for new products; the second phase connected SAP PLM with its CAD data and synchronized BOMs; the third phase addressed product change management to develop existing products. SAP Consulting helped with implementation and customization.

SAP R/3 to SAP PLM The parent company had been using SAP software solutions for many years and had used SAP R/3 since 1993. The company began to implement SAP PLM in 2002 to speed up its product development and deal with documentation challenges. The company had an existing digital archiving system in its back-office operations but needed to address document challenges in R&D. The company took advantage of SAP PLM's digital product documentation and centralized database. By assigning a unique number to each product-related project, the company could track all relevant documentation in a standardized project folder created using SAP PLM. Templates and checklists were put in place to guide the document-management process.

SAP Easy Document Management was implemented to provide an easy-to-use interface for employees to access documents and data. This SAP user interface is integrated into Windows Explorer so people could work in a familiar environment, thereby speeding up the adoption of the new system.

The company also linked SAP PLM to its CAD data. BOMs, 3D models, and drawings were made accessible through SAP PLM, linking the development and production processes.

The Benefits

Because of tighter integration, the two processes of design and production, which used to be divided, now work together. Project teams can collaborate more easily and have access to the same product data.

In addition, the new system allows the company to bring outside entities, such as doctors and hospitals, into the process to give its R&D team the input necessary to create the next great product.

Having both consolidated and accurate data helps the company know what its current product inventories are, what its current product costs are, and how changes in products affect sales.

Looking Toward the Future

The company focused its SAP PLM implementation in one location, where most of its medical equipment R&D takes place. In the future, the company plans to expand it to other departments and divisions throughout the parent company. After that, the company hopes that consistent data will be available to divisions around the world.

SAP PLM Case Study 2

Table 9.3 gives you a snapshot of the second case study we use in this chapter. You should review it before proceeding with the rest of this section.

Company	Specialty chemicals
Existing Solutions	Multiple local systems
Challenge	To implement one ERP solution and comply with chemical industry regulations
SAP Solutions	SAP ERP and SAP PLM
Benefits	Chemical laboratory integrated into supply chain, reduced costs, increased efficiency in product development

Table 9.3 SAP PLM Case Study 2

This German company generates annual revenues of over €5 billion and employs 22,500 people. The enterprise operates with more than 100 companies and has faced challenges in complying with health and safety management.

The Challenge

The company needed to streamline its multiple local systems with a centralized ERP solution. In addition, the company had to deal with multiple regulations for health, safety, and the environmental impact associated with its handling of chemicals.

The Solution

SAP ERP provided the centralized ERP system the company needed and included important quality management tools. The SAP PLM product integrated with SAP ERP easily and helped the company to meet legal requirements for health, safety, and environmental regulations efficiently.

The SAP solution also enabled the company to have faster access to master data in its operations around the world.

The Benefits

The company has achieved benefits in the area of lower costs, faster access to data for more immediate decision making, and increased efficiency. By implementing a single solution, the company has greatly reduced the complexity of its IT landscape. As a result of this unified solution, customer satisfaction has grown, and data transparency has helped the company adhere more closely to industry regulations.

Conclusion

In this chapter, we explored the four major areas of SAP Product Lifecycle Management that can help you handle products from concept to implementation:

> Product Management
> Product Development and Collaboration
> Product Data Management
> PLM Foundation

We went into detail for each of these areas to give you a deeper understanding of how SAP PLM works and to show how it can be implemented in your own company. The case studies helped put SAP PLM in a real-world context so you can fully understand the topic and the product.

In Chapter 10, we'll look at how SAP Supply Chain Management (SAP SCM) can help you manage your supplier and procurement processes, so you can get the materials you need to make the wonderful products you've planned with SAP PLM.

SAP Supply Chain Management

Supply chain management involves all of the business processes and coordination necessary to get a product or service from a supplier to a customer. This typically includes taking raw materials or various components and assembling them for delivery to the final user. In an enterprise, the supply chain process touches on several departments and often several companies, including those involved in planning and forecasting, sourcing (finding the right vendor), purchasing, inventorying, manufacturing, and distribution.

In this chapter, we'll explore the many features of *SAP Supply Chain Management* (SAP SCM) that help your enterprise automate and streamline your supply chain to save time and money, and deliver what your customers need when they need it.

How SAP SCM Fits in an Enterprise

The various features of SAP SCM connect the areas of supply, planning, manufacturing, and distribution in an enterprise in a way that enables everyone involved, both inside and outside of the company, to have access to vital information (what SAP calls *visibility*). This sharing of knowledge helps companies adapt their supply chain processes to an ever-changing competitive environment by helping them make decisions and execute them quickly. But to understand SAP SCM's approach to the supply chain process, you have to begin with the concept of an adaptive supply chain network.

The Adaptive Supply Chain

Shrinkage effect

In the past, supply chains were rigidly designed with processes, which were not easy to change because they were set up in a specific sequence. Given the ever-changing nature of businesses today, the old supply chain model doesn't work very well. Companies that stay with the older model can't make the quick changes that are necessary to stay competitive. In addition, the so-called *shrinkage effect* of today's tighter profit margins demands that the supply chain run as efficiently as possible to help make companies profitable.

Adaptive supply chain

The goal of SAP SCM is to make it possible for a company to transform its traditional supply chain from linear, sequential processes into an adaptive supply chain network. The idea behind an *adaptive supply chain* is that the companies involved in the supply chain network share information and resources in a way that helps them make adjustments quickly as market conditions change.

Furthermore, SAP SCM provides collaboration technology and easier access to data, which can help you reduce costs and improve your level of service.

Ex Example

Let's say that a large customer order for mobile computing devices comes in. In a linear model, you would contact one supplier for information, such as pricing and delivery times for parts to fulfill the order. Next, you would contact another supplier and then get back to the first supplier to see whether he can match the other price. You contact your salespeople and ask if another model or color would work for the customer. This linear approach is time consuming and inefficient. An adaptive model, however, allows you to contact your suppliers, manufacturers, distributors, and customers, and share information in a collaborative fashion. Suppliers can work together to get you what you need. Consequently, you can respond to shorter, unpredictable lifecycles.

SAP has identified five key phases that constitute an effective adaptive supply chain network:

> **Planning**
Involves planning and adapting to network-driven demand based on your enterprise business objectives.

> **Executing**
Means putting your supply chain into action based on available or anticipated supplies and resources.

> **Sensing**
Relates to being aware of variations based on internal or external events and alerting people to these issues.

> **Responding**
Involves collaborating on and responding to demands and deviations across your supply chain network.

> **Learning**
Relates to the previously mentioned four phases and means that you continually improve on your system from data generated in all of the phases.

The tools that SAP SCM makes available map to these phases, with features for planning and forecasting; analytics to help a company sense when changes are needed, how to respond to these changes, and how to improve processes; and tools for executing procurement, manufacturing, and distribution processes. Together, these features help an enterprise move toward an adaptive supply chain model.

Table 10.1, derived from SAP's white paper, *Adaptive Supply Chain Networks*, will help you distinguish a traditional supply chain from an adaptive supply chain.

Characteristic	Traditional Supply Chain	Adaptive Supply Chain
Information propagation	Sequential and slow	Parallel and dynamic
Planning horizon	Days/weeks	Hours/days
Planning characteristics	Batch	Dynamic
Response reaction	Days/hours	Hours/minutes

Table 10.1 Traditional Versus Adaptive Supply Chains

Characteristic	Traditional Supply Chain	Adaptive Supply Chain
Analytics	Historical	Real time
Supplier characteristics	Cost/delivery	Network capability
Control	Centralized	Distributed
Exception management	Centralized/manual	Distributed/automated
Integration	Standalone point solution	Intra- and inter-enterprise
Standards	Proprietary	Open

Table 10.1 Traditional Versus Adaptive Supply Chains (Cont.)

The next step to help you see how SAP SCM works in an organization is to examine the concept of visibility.

Visibility of Information

Lifecycle of a customer order

Consider the lifecycle of a customer order that is placed via your website. In the perfect adaptive network, the customer order information would be instantly available to suppliers across the supply chain. Inventory is checked and rechecked. Every department and vendor involved in fulfilling that order could observe the order flowing through every stage into the supply chain system and back out to the customer. That ability to view the current status of the order is the essence of *visibility*.

The challenge here is that in most companies today, all of that data resides in many separate systems. Plus, outside suppliers are often not integrated into your enterprise's system. By using tools in SAP SCM to increase visibility, you can handle that order faster, automate many tasks, and deal with exceptions as they arise.

Adding visibility to your systems is the first step. Once you have visibility in your supply chain process, the next step that you have to take is determining how quickly you can respond to what you see. That's where velocity of response comes in.

Velocity of Response

How quickly can your organization respond?

Put simply, *velocity of response*, the catch phrase in SAP SCM, means how quickly your organization can move in response to an event.

For example, how quickly can you respond to an order to move the information, the materials, and finally the products through your supply chain and deliver this order to your customer? Companies such as Dell Computer have won great competitive advantage by embracing velocity of response as a key goal. The planning tools in SAP SCM can be vital in ensuring that your organization can quickly respond and adjust plans to deal with change.

That being said, most companies can't respond quickly without the help of their business partners. Connecting with them efficiently is another key to effective supply chain management.

Sharing with Partners

It's now the nature of supply chain management that companies have to break down walls between them to enable partnerships. Few companies design, market, manufacture, sell, and deliver a product in a vacuum. They have materials or components suppliers. They outsource one piece of their manufacturing process or use an outside distribution company.

 Tip

Here's a good example of a specific process that SAP SCM can help you handle more efficiently. *Available to promise* is a concept related to how you use inventory to fulfill a customer order. Inventory can consist of items on hand, inventory you have placed on hold to fill back orders, and inventory you have placed in reserve. Available to promise inventory is the inventory you can use to fill a customer order.

When you receive an order, SAP SCM uses the collaboration request/promise architecture to send a request to every vendor who could fulfill it. This could include in-house and external partners anywhere in the world. The required delivery date is verified, and if the item isn't available, the customer is offered a substitute product.

Meanwhile, the transportation/planning engine routes requests delivery information to either your in-house or external transportation vendor to verify the ship date. The order-promising engine picks which vendor to use to fulfill the order, notifies the production-scheduling engine, and sends a confirmation to the customer.

SAP SCM can help you build in alerts to this system if exceptions arise and even handle customer requests for changes.

This shared responsibility to get services or products to market requires that there be a degree of information visibility that isn't snarled by firewalls or confidentiality policies. Having barriers among your partner systems means that your products don't get to your customers on time, and that much of your time is wasted on miscommunication or the mishandling of your collaborative efforts.

With challenges such as build-to-order and customization for the general customer population, being able to respond in a timely fashion demands a system that allows real-time information to flow freely through the entire supply chain. SAP SCM's collaborative tools enable this kind of interaction among departments, vendors, and customers.

Understanding the need for visibility, velocity of response, and integration with partners in the supply chain, you can now appreciate the tools that SAP SCM offers so you can achieve these goals.

SAP SCM Solution Map

Work in familiar Microsoft applications

The SAP SCM solution map is shown in Figure 10.1. There are 10 areas of functionality, including the use of SAP's Duet that allows users to work in familiar Microsoft applications such as Excel and Outlook to perform parts of the supply chain process.

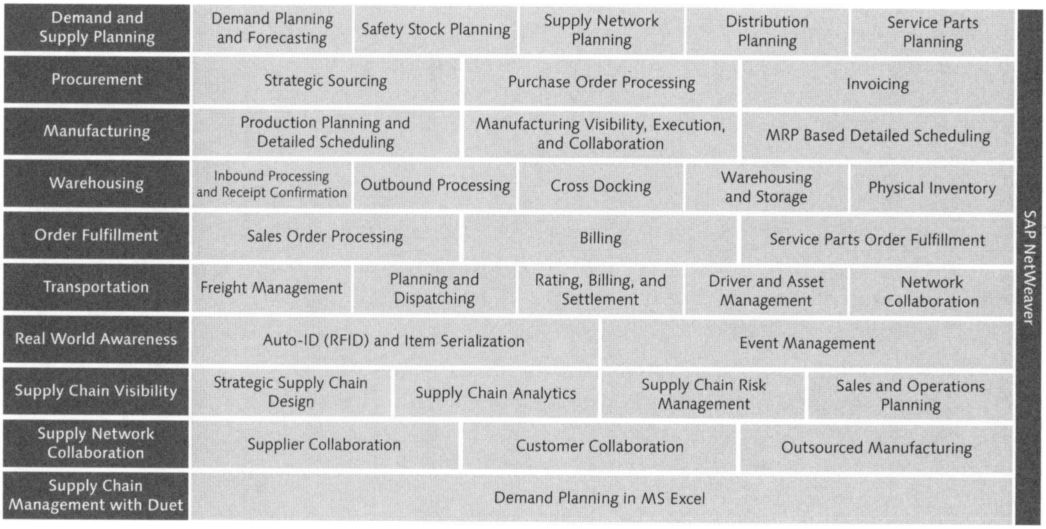

Demand and Supply Planning	Demand Planning and Forecasting	Safety Stock Planning	Supply Network Planning	Distribution Planning	Service Parts Planning
Procurement	Strategic Sourcing		Purchase Order Processing		Invoicing
Manufacturing	Production Planning and Detailed Scheduling		Manufacturing Visibility, Execution, and Collaboration		MRP Based Detailed Scheduling
Warehousing	Inbound Processing and Receipt Confirmation	Outbound Processing	Cross Docking	Warehousing and Storage	Physical Inventory
Order Fulfillment	Sales Order Processing		Billing		Service Parts Order Fulfillment
Transportation	Freight Management	Planning and Dispatching	Rating, Billing, and Settlement	Driver and Asset Management	Network Collaboration
Real World Awareness	Auto-ID (RFID) and Item Serialization			Event Management	
Supply Chain Visibility	Strategic Supply Chain Design	Supply Chain Analytics	Supply Chain Risk Management	Sales and Operations Planning	
Supply Network Collaboration	Supplier Collaboration		Customer Collaboration		Outsourced Manufacturing
Supply Chain Management with Duet	Demand Planning in MS Excel				

SAP NetWeaver

Figure 10.1 SAP Solution Map for SAP SCM

Note that two of the items on the solution map, Supply Chain Analytics and Supply Network Collaboration, are not part of the supply chain process itself but rather provide tools for designing supply chains and collaborating with others in the chain.

In the next section, you'll see the specific areas of SAP SCM and how they work to support your supply chain efficiency.

A Closer Look at SAP SCM

Each of the SAP SCM areas provides a set of features you can use to manage various aspects of the supply chain network. In this section, we'll examine these features and how they help you get from receiving a customer order to delivering a product or service. Note that this is an overview; for each and every capability available, see the detailed solution maps included in Appendix C, SAP Solution Maps.

Overview of SAP SCM

There are several major areas of SAP SCM listed in the SAP SCM solution map; we'll discuss each of them in more detail in the sections that follow. Table 10.2 outlines the most current listing of key areas of SAP SCM.

Category	Application
Demand & Supply Planning	Demand Planning & Forecasting
	Safety Stock Planning
	Supply Network Planning
	Distribution Planning
	Service Parts Planning
Procurement	Strategic Sourcing
	Purchase Order Processing
	Invoicing
Manufacturing	Production Planning & Detailed Scheduling
	Manufacturing Visibility & Execution & Collaboration
	MRP-Based Detailed Scheduling

Table 10.2 Key Areas of SAP SCM

Category	Application
Warehousing	Inbound Processing & Receipt Confirmation
	Outbound Processing
	Cross Docking
	Warehousing & Storage
	Physical Inventory
Order Fulfillment	Sales Order Processing
	Billing
	Service Parts Order Fulfillment
Transportation	Freight Management
	Planning & Dispatching
	Rating & Billing & Settlement
	Driver & Asset Management
	Network Collaboration
Real World Awareness	Auto-ID (RFID) & Item Serialization
	Event Management
Supply Chain Visibility	Strategic Supply Chain Design
	Supply Chain Analytics
	Supply Chain Risk Management
	Sales & Operations Planning
Supply Network Collaboration	Supplier Collaboration
	Customer Collaboration
	Customer Collaboration
	Outsourced Manufacturing
Supply Chain Management with Duet	Demand Planning in MS Excel

Table 10.2 Key Areas of SAP SCM (Cont.)

As you can see in Table 10.2, SAP SCM offers a robust set of tools; in fact, if you go to SAP's website and view the solution map, you'll find that each one of the feature sets in the right column of this table includes even more detailed features, which we don't have space to list in this chapter. However, in the sections that follow, we provide overviews of the major areas of functionality in SAP SCM.

Supply Chain Planning

This area of SAP SCM allows you to synchronize supply to demand using both push and pull network-planning processes. Simply put, *pull* happens when you request information from your system, and *push* happens without any request coming from the user. In a supply chain environment, you can make a request (pull) to replenish inventory and execute production; or, alternatively, an action could be initiated using a push, based on actual demand. Supply Chain Planning tools include the following:

> **Demand and Supply Planning**
  This set of tools in the Supply Chain Planning module enables decision makers within companies to perform strategic, tactical, and operational planning.

> **Demand Planning and Forecasting**
  This set of tools helps you to assess the anticipated customer demand (including promotional activities) on a finished product level.

> **Safety Stock Planning**
  This helps you to secure delivery (see Figure 10.2) and improve customer service by balancing the uncertainties in the area of supply and demand.

> **Supply Network Planning**
  This set of tools helps you manage and assign the best supply sources, distribute production over several plants (including subcontractors), select the best production resources in the plants, expand (drill down for more details) the bill of materials, and propose the procurement of components and raw materials.

> **Distribution Planning**
  This set of tools helps you deploy the available inventory over the network, balance stock levels in situations where you have excess inventory or shortages, and load transportation vehicles in the most efficient way.

> **Service Parts Planning**
  This delivers integrated planning capabilities to the service parts supply chain. While Service Parts Planning provides capabilities for handling the large parts volumes that are often a part of an aftermarket supply chain, it also delivers a tight integration of the end-to-end planning process with other processes, such as supply network collaboration, procurement, warehousing, and order fulfillment.

185

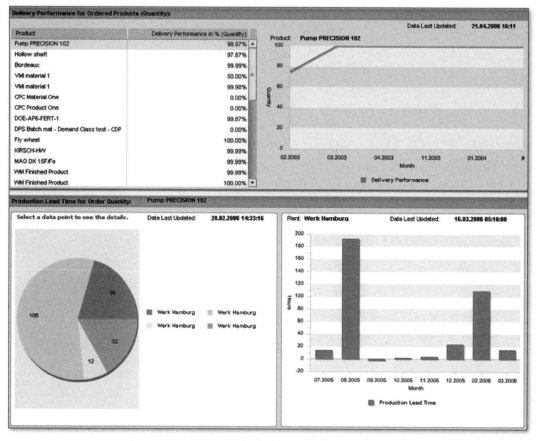

Figure 10.2 Keeping Track of Delivery Performance in Your Operation

> **Procurement**
> As you saw in Chapter 6, SAP Customer Relationship Management, procurement is all about ordering the materials or products you need to run your business. As you add more visibility to your operation, your suppliers will know to have the materials ready to process your orders at just the time you need them. Likewise, because SAP SCM links to SAP ERP Financials modules, your suppliers' invoices will be paid in a timely manner.

> **Supply Chain Visibility**
> This category of tools provides analytic, process management, and data maintenance features to facilitate the Sales and Operations

Planning (S&OP) process across your various departments. Processes such as Strategic Supply Chain Design, Supply Chain Analytics, and Supply Chain Risk Management feed into the S&OP process. This provides tools to help you analyze and adjust your plans to reflect the strategic goals of your organizations.

But planning is just the first piece of the supply chain operation. Building on good planning, you can then execute on supply chain demands with another set of SAP SCM tools.

Supply Chain Execution

SAP SCM helps companies and individuals sense and respond to change through an adaptive fulfillment network. In such a network, distribution, transportation, and logistics are all driven by and integrated with real-time planning processes. Supply Chain Execution features include the following:

Adaptive fulfillment network

> **Warehousing**
> This helps your company manage the end-to-end warehousing process, including inbound and outbound processing, facility management and storage, physical inventory (see Figure 10.3), and cross docking. You can also take advantage of new data collection technologies, such as RFID and voice recognition, and new workload balancing tools that can make your processes more efficient.

> **Order Fulfillment**
> This enables you to track and monitor the entire fulfillment process, including order entry, pricing, scheduling, and proof-of-delivery processes. The system can promise orders based on best availability of goods and components in distribution centers, production sites, storage locations, and availability of transportation resources.

> **Transportation**
> This enables your users to consolidate orders and handle shipments across your company most efficiently to optimize your transportation dollars. Companies can share information and combine orders directly with carriers and forwarders over the Internet, which helps you to keep better control of your processes and maintain control of your plans.

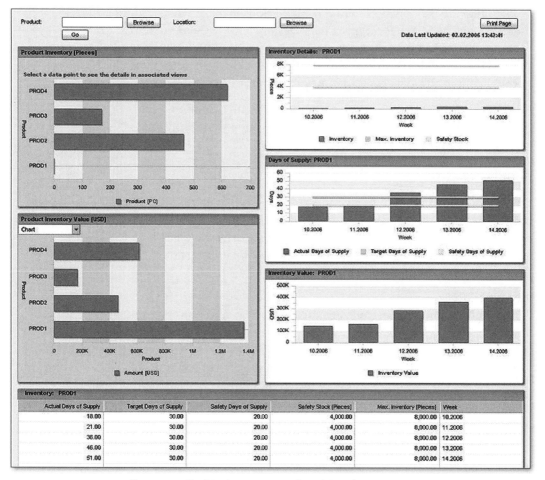

Figure 10.3 Tracking Inventory Levels and Trends

With this variety of features of SAP SCM, you can get tighter control over your supply chain execution. In addition, SAP SCM provides several tools that enhance your collaboration with suppliers, distributors, and others, as discussed in the next section.

Supply Network Collaboration, Design, and Analytics

There's an old saying that it takes two to tango. In this spirit, the supply chain world is a highly collaborative one. To help you create a supply chain that encourages cooperation and efficiency, SAP SCM enables network-wide visibility, collaboration, and analytics across your extended supply chain.

Your company can align and synchronize operations with suppliers, partners, and customers to manage supply chain events and monitor performance. Collaborative capabilities include the following:

> **Supplier Collaboration**
This helps your company connect to and collaborate with suppliers by providing third parties with easy and seamless access to your supply chain information. This capability also helps you to better synchronize supply with demand. Lastly, Supplier Collaboration offers support for your raw material, component, and contract-manufacturing suppliers.

> **Outsourced Manufacturing**
This is becoming commonplace in today's global business environment. This capability helps you connect to and collaborate with contract manufacturers by providing them with access to supply chain information, and extending the visibility and collaborative processes to their manufacturing processes.

> **Customer Collaboration**
This capability delivers an out-of-the-box menu-driven approach to collaboration that customers can use immediately. You can even tailor the way you deploy these capabilities based on each customer's level of sophistication.

Setting up these collaborative tools will make your organization much more responsive and flexible. One of the sources of data you can use in your collaborative efforts is a technology tool called RFID, which is covered in the next section.

Using RFID in SAP SCM

Radio Frequency Identification (RFID) technology is being used today across the supply chain to increase efficiency. Essentially, companies use RFID tags, thin labels that contain a silicon chip, which is something like the computer chip that drives your processor. When these labels are attached to items such as products, packaging boxes, or pallets, they provide a way to track items as they move through the supply chain.

Tags pass *read points* in the chain, and the item status is sent back to a centralized database. Think of the last time you tracked a package

Collaborative capabilities

RFID technology

from an overnight shipper and observed its whereabouts as it left the central facility, appeared at a regional distribution center, was loaded on a plane, or sent off in a truck to be delivered to you.

RFID can save companies money and ensure that their information is up to the minute. SAP SCM supports the use of RFID. SAP offers several preconfigured scenarios for RFID implementation and is building in real-world aware technologies into its business processes.

For more information on how SAP is working with RFID, visit *www.sap.com/solutions/business-suite/scm/rfid/index.epx.*

Now it's time to look at how many of the SAP SCM features work in real-world settings in the following two case studies.

SAP SCM Case Study 1

Table 10.3 gives you an overview of a case study that will make SAP SCM clearer for you to understand.

This European company produces not only packaging products but also several types of value-added services for the materials. As a result, it has five business units that must work with many intra-company requests. The company needed a way to support these transactions more efficiently.

Company	European product packaging and value-added services
Existing Solutions	A variety of solutions that differed among divisions and groups because of many acquisitions over time
Challenge	To make the shift from providing only products to adding services, and streamlining costs and response speed
SAP Solutions	SAP ERP and SAP SCM along with a paper machine management software from an SAP partner
Benefits	Consistent data and processes across the enterprise, and improved production planning and cost control

Table 10.3 SAP SCM Case Study 1

The Challenges

With a shift from simply providing products to providing services, the company had to deal with not just delivering a product but also meeting customer needs more efficiently. The company no longer simply delivered paper packaging. Now the company was trying to become a business partner that would deliver what a customer needed, in the time when it was needed, and in the amounts necessary to help its customers' own supply chain activities.

To add this kind of service, the company had to streamline costs and get its operations to move faster and more accurately. With many acquisitions over the years, however, the various units used different software products that were not very integrated. Furthermore, the company's supply chain operation in the paper packaging division was inefficient.

The SAP Solution

The company implemented SAP R/3 (whose functions are now available through SAP ERP) in all its business units. Then it implemented SAP SCM in its paper division, which supported the warehouse and quality control processes, as well as production planning and order promising.

SAP SCM was integrated with a software application from an SAP partner used to manage the use of its paper machines. The management system dealt with detailed planning and manufacturing tasks for the company's paper division. Using SAP SCM and SAP R/3 across the various units gave its users a single, consistent interface. SAP's ERP solution gave the company a holistic view of its financial processes and improved visibility and analytics.

Holistic view of financial processes

The Benefits

Using SAP R/3 software allowed the company to gain consistent finance, customer relationship management, sales, and distribution processes across units. In addition, SAP SCM and the third-party paper-machine management software helped the company instantly share paper-machine data via SAP SCM to keep the shop floor in touch with other areas of the business.

A well-connected business
The ability to view and analyze its financial information helped the company keep costs under control. In addition, SAP SCM helped the company make improvements in production planning, which increased its productivity, providing further cost savings.

The company gained better visibility into its operations and inventory to collaborate more effectively with its customers and minimize waste. SAP ERP software and SAP SCM created a single place for all business information, which increased the likelihood of having more accurate and consistent data on which to base decisions. The solution has had the following effects on the company's business:

> Delivery accuracy went from 70% to 98%.

> Stock rotation periods were reduced by six weeks.

> Working capital requirements were reduced by 30%.

> The total cost of ownership (TCO) of its IT department went from 0.9% to 0.6%.

> Higher levels of service are being produced, and there is less stock to maintain.

SAP helped the company change its from being purely about products to including enhanced services, which has kept the company competitive and successful. SAP SCM provided the tools the company needed to align its manufacturing and supply chain processes with its customers' needs.

SAP SCM Case Study 2

Table 10.4 gives you a snapshot of the second case study we use in this chapter. You should review it before proceeding with the rest of this chapter.

This US-based company sells its line of health and beauty products and small appliances around the world. In this industry, customers demand frequent introduction of new products, which makes the supply chain a key element in business success.

Company	US-based producer of health and beauty, as well as kitchen and appliance, products
Existing Solutions	A variety of supply network planning systems and non-integrated global operations
Challenge	To meet the demand for collaborative planning to handle smaller orders with faster turnaround and direct shipments
SAP Solutions	SAP SCM
Benefits	Fewer canceled orders, freight cost savings, improved inventory returns, elimination of chargebacks from customers due to non-delivery of products

Table 10.4 Table 10.4 SAP SCM Case Study 2

The Challenges

Eighty percent of the company's orders currently arrive via electronic data interchange (EDI) or by fax, with the majority of orders coming through Europe.

Because customers today are placing smaller orders and expecting faster turnaround, this company, which sources products from contract manufacturers, needed a way to improve collaboration with its partners. The company had to reduce the time to get products on the shelves and incorporate direct shipments to do so.

Furthermore, the company needed the ability to perform accurate forecasts in collaboration with manufacturing partners to help streamline inventory and cut down on returned products or orders that did not get fulfilled on time, resulting in canceled orders.

Accurate forecasting

The SAP Solution

SAP SCM is now integrated with the SAP Business Suite, so that, in addition to supply chain issues, the company can track pricing, credit, and delivery. The company first rolled out SAP SCM in Canada, and then in five continental European subsidiaries. In the near future, they'll implement it in the United Kingdom and the United States.

SAP SCM has provided a way for the company to integrate all of its operations and partners around the world to improve supply chain performance and adjust it to match market demand. The company gained visibility into forecasts, inventory, and production, and made significant improvement in collaboration with manufacturers to ensure that supply will meet demand.

Each company sales unit worldwide now uses SCM to create a monthly forecast, and these forecasts are folded into a worldwide supply chain planning document. The system has also been set up to issue alerts if a vendor has not received a shipment on time.

The Benefits

This international company is now experiencing some key benefits from its SAP SCM solution. The company has reduced the amount of obsolete inventory on hand and improved its ability to stock items that are in demand. The company is also noticing an improvement in customer satisfaction levels, in addition to cost savings from reduced cancellations, penalty charges, and shipment inefficiencies.

Conclusion

In this chapter, we explored the many benefits of SAP Supply Chain Management, which addresses an enterprise's need for more efficient relationships with partners and suppliers, including the following:

> The ability to take advantage of an adaptive supply chain
> Increase in visibility and velocity of response
> Improved collaboration with partners
> Improved supply chain planning and execution
> Enhanced collaboration

Collaborative capabilities offered by SAP SCM help you respond to customers faster, find the best prices and suppliers for your needs, and improve cooperation across entire supply networks.

In Chapter 11, SAP's Strategy for Small to Midsize Enterprises, we'll look at some exciting new directions for SAP, with a recent ramp-up of SAP's focus on small and midsize company products, including SAP Business One, SAP Business All-in-One fast start programs, and SAP Business ByDesign.

11

The SAP Strategy for Small to Midsize Enterprises

Until recently, SAP products were thought of as primarily for Fortune 500 companies, despite the fact that about 65% of all SAP customers were actually small to midsize (SME) companies. But with the new products SAP has developed for the SME market, SAP is becoming better known as the choice for any size business.

The truth is, all companies face the same issues: optimizing operations, increasing efficiency, cutting costs, and building lasting relationships with customers, so they all need quality solutions. If you are part of a small to midsize company, you can now find an SAP solution that will fit your unique requirements and offer you the robust business management and business intelligence (BI), and performance management functionality you need to power your business from end-to-end, streamline your operations, and improve visibility into your business information for better decision making.

SAP offers a complete portfolio of solutions, including SAP Business One, a single, integrated application to manage your entire small business, SAP Business All-in-One, a comprehensive, integrated industry solution to power your business end-to-end, and SAP Business

ByDesign™, the best of SAP, delivered on-demand as a software-as-a service (SaaS). In addition, SAP now offers SAP BusinessObjects Edge Business Intelligence (BI) as a core part of the solution portfolio specifically engineered, priced, and packaged to address customer's business intelligence and performance management requirements.

In this chapter, we will explore SAP's strategy to address the small to midsize market, and discuss the functionality of and value delivered by each of the solutions offered in the SAP SME Portfolio.

SAP's Support of the Small Business and Midsize Company Market

Enterprise-wide solution

SAP has had the reputation of working mainly with larger companies, and in its early years, most adopters were large. That was a logical first tier market because it's the larger enterprises that are geographically diverse and have many departments and divisions. So for these companies, enterprise software was essential to helping them centralize processes, increase visibility of information, and enhance communications. In addition, in the past, implementing an enterprise-wide solution with the required customization was often beyond the budget and capabilities of many smaller companies.

However, there are only so many large companies in the world, and it was inevitable as SAP gained many of them as customers, and as enterprise computing grew more user friendly, that SAP would focus on gaining a larger presence in the SME market — a $29 billion opportunity. Where the large enterprise market offers 20,000 potential customers, the SME markets add up to well over 50 million companies.

The Challenges Facing Small to Midsize Companies

Smaller companies have many opportunities larger companies don't simply because they are small and more nimble, and have plenty of room to grow. But these small companies also face challenges such as stiff competition and fewer resources. So an efficient IT infrastructure can help them make the most of their assets and overcome some challenges.

For example, with a more global economy, a greater number of smaller companies are competing against each other. However, with a bigger customer universe, they are also finding greater opportunities. These greater opportunities of the global economy do bring new challenges though in terms of complying with regulations, taxes, and currencies, so these companies need help managing these issues. And to grow, these companies have to run their operations as efficiently as possible so they can attract resources, gain additional capital, and stay competitive. For these and other reasons, small and midsize companies require solid IT tools and systems, which is where SAP solutions can help, as we'll demonstrate in the rest of this chapter.

Bringing Enterprise Computing to Smaller Companies

Advances in enterprise computing now make addressing the needs of this market easier than ever. SAP's 35 years of gathering knowledge of back-office and front-office best practices is integral to their success with smaller businesses. In addition, SAP brings several technical features to the table:

> Preconfigured templates (*Best Practices*)

> Tools to accelerate the implementation of industry-specific solutions

> The SAP NetWeaver platform to support integration

> Easy-to-use interfaces

> A network of partners with proven industry expertise

SAP is a big believer that to make the best business decisions for your company, you need to have as much information as you can get from all possible sources. To address this, SAP continually makes improvements to their solutions, and so as we mentioned earlier, they now include SAP BusinessObjects Edge™ BI in the offerings for small to midsize companies.

SAP BusinessObjects Edge BI lets you perform interactive, *ad-hoc* exploration of data that resides in Microsoft, Oracle, PeopleSoft, and Siebel systems. You can generate highly formatted reports that can be accessed through familiar interfaces such as a web browser, Microsoft Office, a PDF document or Microsoft SharePoint. Monitor key perfor-

Generate highly formatted reports

mance indicators at a glance with visual dashboards that provide drill down into details that explain the root causes of trends and variances. And model scenarios to resolve problems or capitalize on opportunities by adjusting graphical controls.

But there have been many other changes and adjustments to the SAP midsize strategy, most notably back in 2007, when SAP committed its resources, and even launched a new business model that included a retooling of its own internal processes, to deliver solutions to a larger customer base further down in the mid-market. In future years, SAP will use innovative methods for delivering its products and services, including a "try-run-adapt" model that allows customers to try out products via Internet-hosted services before they actually buy them. So let's have a look at the SAP SME portfolio.

The SAP SME Portfolio

SAP SME Portfolio

Beyond the financial opportunities of the small to midsize market, SAP recognizes that the market is unique in its requirements. Small to midsize companies vary a lot in their structure, systems, and needs. Far from being simpler than larger companies, their needs are often just as complex; however, they are much less risk-tolerant because of their often tight profit margins and niche markets.

Consequently, SAP offers the small to midsize market a portfolio of solutions mentioned earlier: SAP Business One, SAP Business All-in-One, SAP Business ByDesign for Business Management, and SAP BusinessObjects Edge BI for Business Intelligence. Figure 11.1 summarizes the Business Management offerings.

> **SAP Business One**
> SAP Business One application is designed specifically for small businesses. It integrates the entire business across financials, sales, customer relationships, e-commerce, inventory, and operations. An important feature of SAP Business One is that it gives you access to SAP's extensive partner ecosystem, allowing you to extend the core functionality with over 550 add-on solutions that can help you meet your unique business and industry-specific needs. SAP Business One is the best fit for small businesses that have outgrown accounting-only solutions and are looking to streamline business operations with an integrated, on-premises solution.

Business Management Solutions			
	SAP Business One	**SAP Business ByDesign**	**SAP Business All-in-One**
What It Is	A single, integrated solution to manage your entire business	The best of SAP, delivered on demand	A comprehensive, integrated industry solution to power your business end to end
Best For...	Small businesses that have outgrown their packaged accounting-only solutions	Companies that need business software but don't want to support a large IT backbone	Midsize companies with industry needs that want a scalable foundation
Number of Employees	Up to 100	100 - 500	100 - 2,500
Industry	Primarily used in wholesale, retail, professional services, and light manufacturing	Primarily used in manufacturing, professional services, and distribution	Used in all major industries
Key Functionality	General business management functionality* and over 550 add-on solutions, many of them industry-specific	General business management functionality*	General business management functionality* and over 700 industry-specific solutions
Deployment	On premises	On demand	On premises
Implementation	6 - 8 Weeks	4 - 8 Weeks	8 - 16 Weeks
How to Buy	Traditional licensing	Monthly subscription	Traditional licensing

* General business management functionality typically includes financials, purchasing, inventory, operations, production, sales, and customer relationship

Figure 11.1 SAP Business Management Solutions

> **SAP Business All-in-One**

The SAP Business All-in-One solution is the best fit for mid-size companies with sophisticated business processes and industry-specific needs. This solution provides a comprehensive and flexible business management option that has support for industry-specific best practices built in. So it helps you manage everything from financials, human resources, inventory, manufacturing, logistics, and product development to customer service, sales, and marketing in one configurable solution. It's available from SAP and over 1,100 SAP partners in 50+ countries, and it can be readily configured to meet the business requirements of midsize companies in any industry.

> **SAP Business ByDesign**

SAP Business ByDesign™ is the best fit for companies that want the benefits of a large-scale business management solution without the large IT infrastructure. It is delivered on demand and fully managed by SAP. And because it is an on-demand solution, there are no upgrades to manage, no maintenance, and no up-front capital costs. SAP experts in worldclass hosted data centers managed, monitor, and maintain it, so you don't have to invest time and money in any additional IT resources to build or support it.

In addition, the portfolio now includes the Business Intelligence solutions of Crystal Reports®, Xcelsius®, and SAP BusinessObjects Edge.

> **SAP BusinessObjects Edge**

SAP BusinessObjects Edge is also ideal for midsize companies. It consists of three elements: BI for improved business insight; Planning and Consolidation for more efficient budgeting, planning, and forecasting; and Strategy Management, which includes a scorecard feature to help you check your actual results against strategic goals. The BI element of BusinessObjects Edge is offered in a standard version, or versions with added data integration and data management tools, which we will cover later in the chapter.

> **Note**
>
> Also included in the Business Intelligence solutions are Crystal Reports and Xcelsius, but these will be covered in detail in Chapter 12 on the SAP BusinessObjects Portfolio.

In the next sections, we'll provide a primer on each of these products and review their key product features to help you determine which product will meet your specific needs.

How SAP Business One Works for Smaller Businesses

Integrates with Microsoft Outlook, Word, and Excel

SAP Business One is designed to be used in businesses with between 10 and 100 employees, and minimal system requirements. The single-system design of SAP Business One keeps total cost of ownership (TCO) low and makes administration and system maintenance straightforward and simple.

The really great thing about SAP Business One is that it is quick to install, simple to maintain, and most important, easy to use. And because it works on any Microsoft Windows based PC, it integrates with Microsoft Outlook, Word, and Microsoft Excel. The Outlook integration allows you to synchronize calendar appointments, contacts, and tasks between SAP Business One and Microsoft Outlook. And you can connect to SAP Business One from Word and then save a Word document as an activity in SAP Business One. You can also do this with Excel, enabling you to exchange and share data to keep all parties up to date about account developments and business opportunities.

SAP Business One has customers in a wide variety of industries but does especially well in the macro-verticals of wholesale, distribution, retail, light manufacturing, and professional services. And thanks to SAP's extensive partner ecosystem, you can extend the software's core functionality with over 550 add-on solutions to meet your unique business and industry-specific needs. SAP Business One has 40+ country versions and tens of thousands of customers. It is sold and implemented exclusively by its network of 1000 certified channel partners.

Macro-verticals

> ### ▶ Note
>
> SAP is planning the release of BusinessOne 8.8 in 2010. Planned changes include removing eCommerce functionality and Web CRM. In addition, Crystal Reports will be added. Version 8.8 will also add a remote support platform, data archiving, support for local best practices, and a single code base to support 40 countries. There are other new functions being added, so be sure to check with your SAP resource to get the latest details when the new version is released.

The current version of SAP Business One includes several areas of functionality useful to a variety of industries.

The SAP Business One Solution Map

The SAP Business One solution map shown in Figure 11.2 organizes the features of the software into seven categories, four that address core business areas and three that deal with implementing and customizing the product. Together, these features help small businesses manage all of their core business functions, such as manufacturing, distribution, sales, and customer relationships.

Manage core functions

SAP Business One Key Functionality				
Accounting and Financials	**Sales and Customers**	**E-Commerce and Web Store**	**Purchasing and Operations**	**Inventory and Distribution**
• General ledger and journal entries • Cost accounting • Budget and project management • Banking and statements • Payment processing and reconciliation • Financial statement and reporting • Sales tax and VAT • Multicurrency support	• Opportunities and pipeline management • Customer and prospect contact and activity management • Sales quotations and orders • Sales and pipeline forecast • Web-based customer relationship management • Service contact management • Service call management entry and tracking	• Online products catalogs • Web store integrated with inventory • Online shopping card • Email and promotional campaigns • Payment, tax, shipping, and handling	• Purchase proposals • Purchase orders and deliveries • Goods receipts and returns • A/P invoice and credit notes • Bills of material (BOMs) • Production orders • Forecasting and material requirements planning (MRP)	• Items management and items queries • Receipt to stock, release from stock, and stock transactions • Warehouse transfer and serial numbers • Inventory revaluation • Customer and vendor catalog • Price lists and special pricing • Batch management • Pick and pack

Reporting and Administration
• Microsoft Excel-based reporting • Data migration workbench, user-defined fields, application programming interface (API), and SAP Business One Software Development Kit • Payroll Accounting • Employee directory and administration, employee time

Figure 11.2 SAP Business One Solution Map

➕ **Tip**

> SAP Business One also includes e-commerce functionality that helps you set up an online store. E-commerce operations are fully integrated with inventory and financials, and have tools for online catalog, shopping cart, order processing and notification, customer configuration, and online customer service.

The following sections break down the features of SAP Business One into core business areas, including Accounting and Financials, Customer Resource Management, Operations and Distribution, and Administration and Reporting. Let's start with Accounting and Financials.

Managing Accounting and Financials

Manage all parts of your financial operations

Financials is where SAP started when it delivered its first enterprise resource planning software product many years ago. There's a good reason for that. Financials are at the heart of every kind of business, and managing them efficiently gives businesses of every size what they need to start up, operate, and succeed. Some of the functionality that SAP Business One provides in this area includes the following:

> **Financial Accounting**
Perform all kinds of financial transactions, including general ledger, journal entries, budgeting, and accounts payable and receivable.

> **Accounting Postings**
Automate real-time accounting postings in response to relevant business events.

> **Banking**
Track all of your banking payments and reconciliations, including check, cash, and credit cards.

> **Financial Reporting**
Automate financial reporting for items such as profit and loss, cash flow, balance sheets, and aging reports.

> **Taxes**
Automate calculations and reporting, including sales, use, and value-added tax. See chart of accounts for SAP Business One in Figure 11.3.

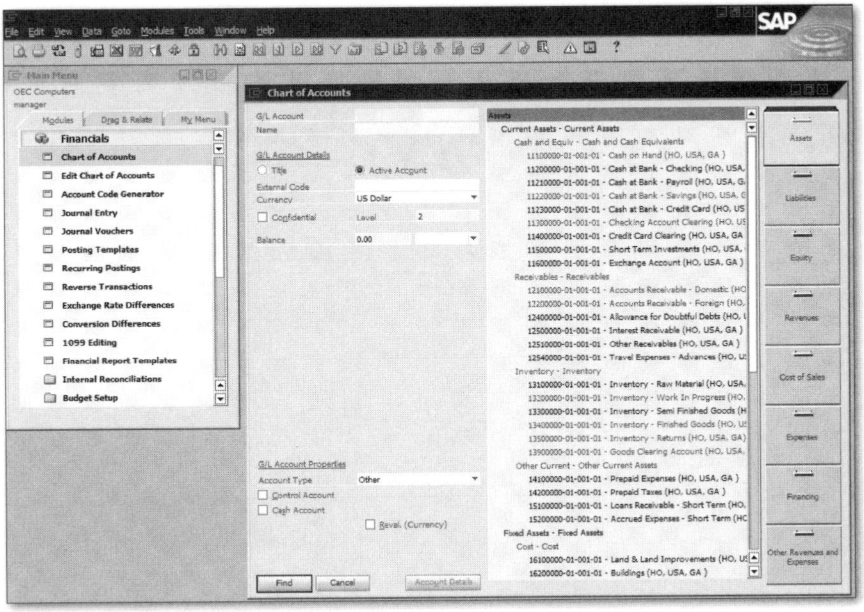

Figure 11.3 Chart of Accounts in SAP Business One

After you have your Financials in place, you can focus on your customers.

Connecting with Customers

Keep your customers satisfied

Customers are the lifeblood of any operation, and regardless of the size of your company, if you don't set up your processes to acquire and retain customers, you'll regret it. SAP Business One provides functionality that helps you keep customers satisfied and ensures that those who serve them are well equipped to do so:

Use dashboards to analyze sales

> **Sales Opportunity Management**
  The typical sales process moves through several stages. You can use SAP Business One to track sales opportunities from your first contact to the sales close. You can create quotes, enter orders, and provide better customer service from the office or online. And your sales manager can use SAP Business One to forecast revenue potential. User-friendly dashboards allow you to monitor and analyze sales opportunities and generate all kinds of sales reports (see Figure 11.4).

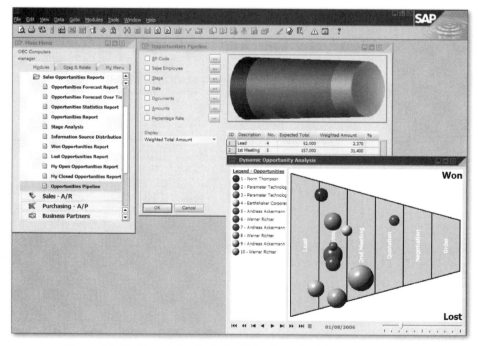

Figure 11.4 Dashboards for Analyzing Sales Opportunities

> **Web CRM**
Currently these features are available on a limited basis and will likely be removed in the next release. But as they exist now, they allow you to provide secure access to customer data over the web when your sales force is on the road. You also get a web-based interface so your customers can submit inquiries and check their order status in real time. And you can access customer and sales information over the Web.

> **Microsoft Outlook Integration**
You can manage and maintain customer contacts by synchronizing customer data from SAP Business One into Microsoft Outlook contacts or calendar, resulting in increased sales effectiveness and stronger customer relationships.

> **Marketing Campaigns**
Use tools to initiate and execute marketing campaigns by using templates for mass e-mails.

> **Customer Service and Support**
The customer service folks in your organization can use these tools to administer customer warranties and service contracts, manage service calls, and track all kinds of customer interactions.

> **Business Partner Management**
Manage your master data for resellers and channel partners and allow resellers, partners, and customers to access relevant data over the web.

Then once you have a customer order, you need to fill their orders and deliver the goods using the Operations and Distribution features of SAP Business One.

Purchasing and Operations

SAP Business One offers a systematic approach to managing the procurement process, from creating purchase orders to paying vendors. You'll find all the tools you need to manage the complete order-to-pay cycle, including receipts, invoices, and returns. You can also plan material requirements for production, control bills of material, and replenish inventory automatically. In this area you will find these features:

Managing customer orders

> **Purchasing**
Use these features to set up and manage vendor contracts and all

kinds of vendor-related transactions, such as sending out purchase orders, making updates to stock quantities, and handling returns and credits. You can also generate automatic production and inventory replenishment orders.

> **Production Planning**
> With this feature, your users can work with a simple-to-use process to manage your production material requirements; control BOMs, including product descriptions, warehouse location, composition, and quantities; and work with MRP features.

Inventory and Distribution

Effective inventory management tools

SAP Business One also lets you manage your inventory and operations, including quotes, sales orders, shipping, and billing. You can perform inventory counts, monitor stock, and track transfers in real time and across multiple warehouses.

> **Sales and Delivery**
> When a customer expresses interest in your product or service, you can generate price quotes, and then when they are ready to buy, you can enter their orders (see Figure 11.5), set up deliveries, and manage all billing and accounts receivables activities.

Streamline pick-and-pack processes

> **Inventory Management**
> You can use these tools to manage inventory levels with inventory counts, stock tracking, and transfers between warehouses by serial number, lots, or bin location. And you can provide real-time inventory updates, inventory valuation, availability checks, and pick-and-pack processes. There are even features to streamline your pick-and-pack process.

There are, of course, some processes that exist not to get products to customers, but to support your administrative processes or help you develop your overall business strategy, which brings us to the last area of SAP Business One — Administration and Reporting.

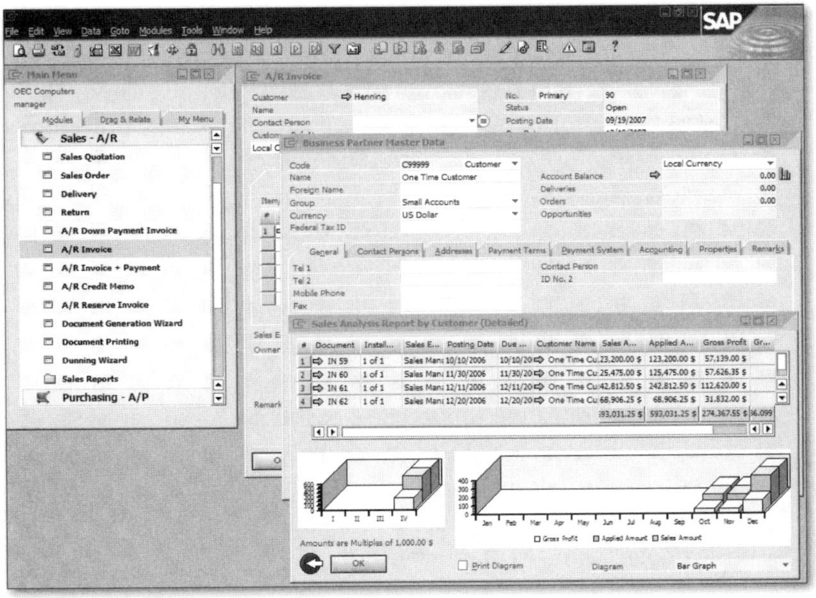

Figure 11.5 Sales Opportunity Reporting

Streamlining Reporting and Administration

There are certain tools that cut across your organization that everyone from the CEO on down can benefit from such as efficient procedures, easy-to-use software interfaces, and useful reports with up-to-date information instantly. And that's what the administrative and reporting tools provide:

> **Human Resources**
These features help you organize a centralized place for maintaining and managing employee records and data, such as home contact information, time and attendance records, and training history.

➕ Tip

The Drag & Relate feature in SAP Business One is handy for using all of your business data; it puts information into easy-to-understand formats. In addition, you can easily drill down to deeper levels of detail in your company's data.

207

Initiate credit checks and manage exceptions to workflow processes

> **Automatic Alerts**
Workflow-based alerts allow you to monitor, notify, and take action based on certain business alerts. You can define custom alerts and workflow processes by setting up approvals and procedures that make sense for your business. And you can manage exceptions to have SAP Business One detect, log, and report on them. You can even determine the steps that should automatically take place when a specified event happens. For example, you could set up an alert so that whenever a customer order exceeds a certain amount, a credit check is initiated.

> **Dashboards and Reports**
You can create your own reports and dashboards for various areas of your business, such as sales, bookkeeping, inventory, financial statements, and customer interactions. You can also generate Microsoft Excel-based reports that allow you to drill down to deeper levels of detail using XL Reporter.

> **Note**

Dashboards are user interfaces that provide a control center for working with data, such as a salesperson might use to check all relevant facts about a customer in one place.

Enabling E-Commerce and Web Stores

Finally, you can use SAP Business One tools to create an online presence that will help you level the playing field against larger competitors by allowing you to reach more customers. You can design, build, and configure online stores get your e-commerce activities organized. E-commerce tools in SAP Business One include the following:

> **Design Tools**
Use customizable templates and various tools to help you design, create, and configure your online store.

> **Online Catalogs**
Create and manage online catalogs and build in negotiated, customer-specific pricing.

> **E-Commerce Selling Tools**
Incorporate special promotions and coupons, or build in suggested

selling techniques (such as indications of when customers who bought one product also bought another product).

> **Synchronize E-Commerce**
Automate the synchronization of all online orders with the SAP Business One database.

 Note

SAP is considering removing some e-commerce features in version 8.8, so please check with your SAP source if this is something your company needs.

SAP Business One is the packaged solution ideal for much smaller businesses. If your organization is in the midsize category, however, there are two other solutions you can consider: *SAP Business All-in-One* and *SAP Business ByDesign.*

SAP Business All-In-One

The SAP Business All-in-One solution is a comprehensive and flexible business management software with support for best practices built in, plus updated messaging on the SAP website. It's for your company if you're looking for a comprehensive, integrated industry solution to power your business end to end.

Integrated solution to meet business needs end to end

Benefits of Using Business All-in-One

Unlike other business solutions in the market, SAP Business All-in-One helps you manage everything from financials, human resources, procurement, inventory, manufacturing, logistics, product development, and corporate services to customer service, sales, and marketing – in one configurable solution. So let's look at each of these benefits.

Improve Financial Management
SAP Business All-in-One enables you to accelerate financial closes, increase the accuracy of financial reporting, and maintain superior cash management. You can improve your ability to maintain a set of balanced books reflecting any business dimension. Support for international and local accounting standards also helps you reduce your risk of noncompliance.

Maintain Operational Excellence

With SAP Business All-in-One, you can improve your efficiency and effectiveness by streamlining business processes, enhancing service levels, and cutting costs and errors. The solution helps you shorten cycle times, increase order accuracy, reduce the volume of customer calls, decrease billing disputes, and lower inventory costs with better order-to-cash processes. And you can resolve issues faster and boost customer satisfaction with low-cost interaction channels such as Web-based self-service.

Enhance Agility

SAP Business All-in-One allows you to respond more quickly to change, enhance customer experiences, and differentiate your company from your competitors. You can respond quickly to changing market conditions and customer demands by adapting your business processes. You can quickly launch new initiatives to speed time to market. And you can align your channels with your customers' interaction needs and preferences to provide consistency and convenience across all customer touch points. This customer insight in turn can help you can drive innovation to set your products and services apart.

Unify and Simplify

All the functionality is integrated to simplify your business and IT landscape across functions, regions, and teams. By supporting streamlined business processes it enables you to complete a process from beginning to end. You might, for example, create an opportunity using CRM functionality, convert it directly into a quote, and then later convert it into a sales order – complete with product, pricing, billing, and delivery – using ERP functionality. And business intelligence functionality gives you real-time visibility into your sales performance throughout the entire process. In addition, centralized data and business intelligence help ensure that you have a "single version of the truth," providing a 360-degree view of your operations, employees, and customers.

Drive Adoption and Improve Productivity

Additional advantages include faster adoption working with SAP's partner network, increased productivity, and fewer errors. The integrated software and common desktop environment help your employees learn how to use the software quickly, and the integration eliminates manual data re-entry between different functional areas, which can save time and reduce the risk of mistakes.

SAP Business All-in-One is Powered by SAP NetWeaver

And because SAP Business All-in-One is powered by SAP NetWeaver, you can quickly and cost-effectively add on to your existing solution as your business grows and your needs change with the help of SAP partners. SAP NetWeaver is also the ideal technology platform to integrate SAP and non-SAP software, reducing total cost of ownership across the entire IT landscape.

Service-oriented architecture (SOA)

SAP Business All-in-One features a user experience designed for maximum productivity and ease of use, including the following:

> **User-friendly design** – Intuitive Web-like features and online tutorials help accelerate adoption and reduce the need for formal training.

> **Automated workflows** – By automating manual processes you'll save time and money by, for example, generating an automatic alert on all contracts that are up for renewal or on customers with overdue payments. You can also escalate service requests for your most important customers and automatically route tasks between groups and departments.

> **Intuitive navigation** – Role-based navigation, screen personalization, quick links to key data, snapshots of recent records, key reminders and alerts, and an advanced search help users perform daily tasks more efficiently.

> **Groupware integration** – Integration with desktop tools such as IBM Lotus Notes and Microsoft Office allows users to manage their activities and communications more effectively– any time, any place. Users can synchronize tasks, appointments, and e-mails and export customer and opportunity lists.

Work with IBM Lotus Notes or Microsoft Office and synchronize easily with SAP Business All-in-One

In addition, SAP Business All-in-One solutions offer the following integrated functionalities:

> **Enterprise Resource Planning**
The ERP functionality in SAP Business All-in-One is based on the SAP ERP application, and includes comprehensive functionality to

manage all aspects of your operations. It also delivers role-based access to business application data and analytical tools.

> **Business intelligence**
  Gain insight and improve decision making with tools for financial and operational reporting and analysis. SAP Business All-in-One offers best-practice reports, analytics, and tools to help satisfy the rigorous reporting requirements for financial accounting, logistics, customer relationship management, and more – all preconfigured by business role and business scenario.

> **Customer Relationship Management**
  The customer relationship management (CRM) functionality in SAP Business All-in-One is based on the SAP CRM application, so with the CRM functionality in SAP Business All-in-One, you can boost marketing results with targeted messaging, close more deals with sales tools that improve effectiveness, and increase revenue and customer loyalty with superior service. Effectively manage all aspects of your customer relationships, from generating leads to closing a deal, including follow-up support and add-on sales.

> **Best practices**

Best practices by industry and function

  The SAP Best Practices package provides proven methods and tools for organizations to implement best business practices in key functional areas in a range of industries. SAP Best Practices are based on 35 years of experience in more than 24 industries worldwide. The result is rapid yet reliable solution deployment, which translates into less time, lower costs, and reduced project risk.

In addition to the overall SAP Business One solution there is also the SAP Business All-in-One *Fast-Start program*. This solution, which SAP partners can help you implement, brings the more robust features of SAP's ERP, CRM, and BI functionality to the table for midsize companies with a smaller investment and faster ramp-up.

What Is SAP Business All-In-One Fast-start Program?

Fast-Start program requires a smaller investment and offers a faster ramp-up

The SAP Business All-in-One fast-start program is designed for manufacturing, wholesale distribution, and service companies seeking industry-specific functionality at a low cost of ownership and low risk. The fast-start program gives you a preconfigured, pretested software stack that includes SAP Business All-in-One, the low-cost SAP MaxDB database, and Novell SUSE Linux Enterprise Server operating system. In addition, SAP and select hardware partners, such as HP , IBM, Intel, and Fujitsu, have combined their latest innovations to deliver this software stack preinstalled on optimized hardware. As a result, you get a joint hardware and software solution.

With this program, you can improve the entire software acquisition process, shortening implementation times, speeding up your time to value, and reducing overall solution TCO. And, with this solution you choose the functional building blocks that will determine your estimated solution scope and cost and then work with an SAP consultant to determine the next steps. A personalized demo will be created with your data, showing end-to-end scenarios to give you the full picture of what SAP Business All-in-One can deliver for you.

The SAP Business All-in One fast-start program offers your company:

> **Simplicity** – The pretested, preconfigured software is configured to select hardware, which simplifies the buying process.

> **Time savings** – With preinstalled SAP software, it takes less time to get up and running, delivering rapid time to value.

> **Affordability** – You get a lower TCO based on complete, pretested software.

> **Best practices** – You receive the SAP Best Practices package for your industry, which includes templates and methodologies for rapid implementation, as well as documentation and preconfigured support for business process scenarios.

The fast-start program is easy to use and provides a fast path to improving user productivity. Users work with a simplified computing environment that has a user-friendly interface and role-based navigation. This ease of use provides employees with easy access to information.

Because the fast-start program is based on the SAP Business Suite, it can be configured and customized to adapt to special needs of an industry or business. You can look to the SAP partner community to help you implement the fast-start program and also use vertical market partner solutions and third-party applications, which can be integrated with the solution. SAP has also enlisted hundreds of partners that will help you with their own add-ons for specialized applications.

Fast-start program can be configured and customized to any industry or business

In some countries, you can configure the fast-start program on the web. You can see the configurator in Figure 11.6

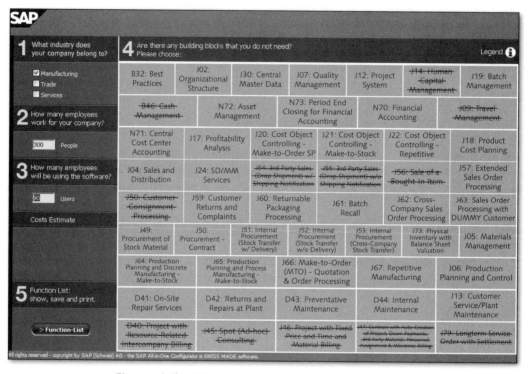

Figure 11.6 The SAP Business All-in-One Fast-Start Program Can Be Configured on the Web

Later in this chapter, we provide case studies of both the SAP Business One and SAP Business All-in-One fast-start program solutions so that you can see and compare them in action. For now, let's move on to the final SME offering — SAP Business ByDesign.

SAP Business ByDesign

The SAP Business ByDesign solution is the most complete on-demand business solution for midsize companies. It addresses the needs of your entire organization, is adaptable, and allows you to react quickly whenever your business needs change. In addition, it is personalized to improve productivity with a role-based user experience, built-in learning and support environment, analytics, and collaboration.

SAP Business ByDesign is the newest mid-market solution and was launched by SAP in September 2007. It continued to be introduced in stages into 2009 for the following countries: China, France, Germany, India, the United Kingdom, and the United States.

SAP Business ByDesign (see Figure 11.7) is an on-demand solution that adds to the existing SME Portfolio, rather than replacing any existing products. Because it's an on-demand solution, there are no upgrades to manage, no maintenance, and no up-front capital costs. It's managed, monitored, and maintained by SAP experts in world class hosted data centers, which means you don't have to invest time and money in any additional IT resources to build or support it.

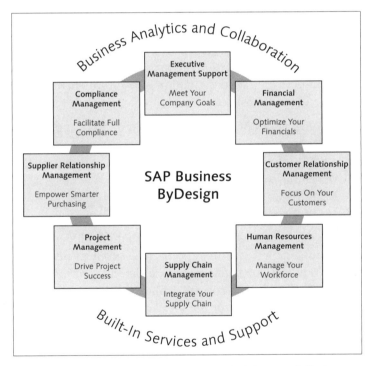

Figure 11.7 The Complete Business System — SAP Business ByDesign

An Adaptable Suite of Functionality

SAP Business ByDesign offers a complete integrated suite of functionality — it supports Financials, Customer Relationship Management, Human Resources Management, Supply Chain Management, Project

Management, Supplier Relationship Management, Compliance Management, and Executive Management Support, and includes useful features such as analytics. All functionality is delivered through services, so external integration interfaces to web shops or supplier portals is easy.

However, rather than configuring a system with a team of consultants or by using sets of best practices, the idea behind Business ByDesign is that the system is simply adapted to the needs of a particular organization (something SAP calls "configurable and extensible"). This adaptation takes various forms and can be easily modified along the way. Companies can choose the functionality and try it out to make sure it satisfies their needs. If not, they can adapt it until it does.

SAP Business ByDesign adoption catalog

SAP Business ByDesign also offers an adoption catalog. You can configure your custom system by making choices from this catalog and responding to some specific questions about your business. This process should make both initial configuration and future changes and additions easier and more cost-effective.

In addition, customer service capabilities are built into the application and automated through a global service backbone. If your company expands globally, SAP Business ByDesign supports your growth with built-in compliance for countries around the world.

Underlying Technology

Model-based development techniques

Business ByDesign is a product built entirely with model-based development techniques. The result of this approach is a product that offers sets of application process components (e.g., order entry or invoicing) that you can combine to meet a particular business requirement. You can get these benefits on demand through a subscription fee.

Another difference is that SAP Business ByDesign uses a form of cloud computing, in that SAP hosts the applications you're using, and you access the functionality online through a *software as a service* (SaaS) model. This is a plus for you because by not having these applications onsite, your IT staff can focus more on your critical IT needs instead of having to implement, maintain, and upgrade these applications. Also, by having these applications hosted elsewhere, especially in today's economy, you may reduce or eliminate the need to purchase additional hardware such as servers and disk storage. Instead, because SAP

Business ByDesign is an on-demand solution, customers pay only for the pieces and user licenses they need on a subscription basis, which can be more cost effective. Because of the hosted nature of the product, SAP expects to get an enhanced and faster feedback model from users, which it can use to make future improvements.

Although you can configure the software to meet most of your needs, you can't modify the code as you can with SAP ERP or the SAP Business All-in-One fast-start program system. However, because it is based on services, there are open interfaces that allow you to make interface changes to the system as necessary. SAP Business ByDesign is based on the SAP NetWeaver platform, and, as such, offers functionality that is useful to a wide variety of industries.

SAP Business ByDesign Integrated Functionality

With SAP Business ByDesign, you get a fully integrated solution that covers all of your core business needs.

> **Management Empowerment:** Gives managers an overall view of business performance and access to the organizational information they need. Management dashboards provide real-time, customized analytics and allow you to accurately track the most important aspects of your business.

> **Financial Insight:** Provides a single, up-to-date view of your financial condition through the integration of core business processes and financials. You can keep track of payables and receivables, payment and liquidity, inventory and fixed assets, taxes and expenses, and compliance and reporting, and more.

> **Customer Relationship Management:** Provides comprehensive, flexible support for customer relationship management processes that span marketing, sales, and service activities to help you find the right opportunities and maximize customer satisfaction and revenue.

> **HR Resources:** Helps ensure efficient HR operations and maximize the potential of your employees. Use employee and manager self-service features to streamline execution of daily tasks. And adapt HR services to changing business needs by adding, enhancing, and automating processes, including workloads, personnel, and payroll.

> **Supply Chain Management**: Helps you build an efficient supply chain so you can respond quickly to changing markets. Optimize

Fully integrated solution to meet all business requirements

material flow by managing demand and supply, and design, set up, and execute flexible warehouse and manufacturing processes to fit your products and business models.

> **Project Management**: Plan and track projects using graphical tools such as Gantt charts and network diagrams. Share information among team members with workflow-driven task management, and provide up-to-the-minute project data for easy tracking of costs, purchases, and employee and contractor hours.

> **Supplier Relationship Management**: Strengthen your relationships with suppliers and improve your procurement processes to reduce costs and turn suppliers into a competitive advantage. Identify and manage the best suppliers for materials and services. Gain insight into order management, supplier invoicing, and purchase requests.

> **Compliance Management**: Keep up-to-date and compliant with changing laws and regulations using preconfigured tools for your company's accounting practices, applicable tax structures, and relevant labor legislation. Frequent and automatic updates help ensure your financial books and government reporting meet regulatory standards.

Easy access to support

> **Simplify IT**: Use built-in IT services, automated maintenance and support, and a quality-assured service model. Work with SAP experts to monitor and maintain your on-demand system. Take advantage of built-in learning and help provide easy access to resources.

➕ **Tip**

> Business ByDesign uses a concept called a *mashup*. A mashup is a website or a software application that uses content from several sources and integrates it into a single user experience.

This wraps up our discussion of the three SME Business Management offerings from SAP. Now let's look at the newest Business Intelligence offering, SAP BusinessObjects Edge Business Intelligence (BI).

Midsize BI solution – SAP BusinessObjects Edge

SAP BusinessObjects Edge BI

SAP now offers SAP BusinessObjects Edge Business Intelligence to meet the BI and performance management needs of the SME market. It is designed to help midsize companies improve business processes, discover new opportunities, and gain a competitive advantage. It offers solutions that address any business intelligence requirement – from flexible ad hoc reporting and analysis, to dashboards and visualization, to powerful data integration and quality as well as prepackaged data mart solutions:

> **SAP BusinessObjects Edge Business Intelligence (BI):** This application brings together the simplicity and speed of search with the trust and analytical power of BI to provide immediate answers to your business questions. Your users can leverage familiar keyword searches to find information hidden in data sources, then navigate and explore directly on data – without the need for existing reports or metrics. This solution is available in three versions:

> 3 versions available

- *SAP BusinessObjects Edge BI standard package*, which can provide enterprise and ad hoc reporting as well as world-class visualization

- *SAP BusinessObjects Edge BI with data integration*, which can deliver the ability to combine data from multiple sources; populate a data warehouse expediently; and leverage ad hoc, advanced, and drilldown analysis

- *SAP BusinessObjects Edge BI with data management*, which can enable data parsing, cleansing, and address synching

> **SAP BusinessObjects Edge Planning and Consolidation**: This application can help you simplify and streamline the budgeting, planning and forecasting process, enabling all stakeholders to collaboratively participate in the process of allocating resources.

> **SAP BusinessObjects Edge Strategy Management**: This helps companies respond to and execute necessary strategy changes with agility. It allows everyone from executives to front-line workers communicate plans clearly and translate them into priorities and tasks, and then monitor and report on progress to any level of detail. The solution is built on the three pillars of strategy management: goals, initiatives, and key performance indicators (KPI).

In addition, Crystal Reports and Xcelsius are part of the BI offerings, but as mentioned earlier, we will cover these in Chapter 12, The SAP BusinessObjects Portfolio. So this concludes the review of the SAP

SME Business Intelligence offerings. Hopefully you got a good overview of the great options available and you understand which solution could work for your company or your clients. So now let's take a look at what the small and midsize products, SAP Business One and SAP Business All-in-One fast-start program, might look like when implemented at a company.

Small Business and Midsize Company Case Studies

The following two case studies help you understand the strengths of each product and may help you determine which solution is the best fit for you.

The SAP Business One solution excelled in easy implementation and user acceptance for a small Chinese company, whereas the vertical solution and prepackaged Best Practices packages used to configure an SAP Business All-in-One solution delivered through the fast-start program made it a perfect fit for a midsize US company.

SAP Business One Case Study 1

Table 11.1 gives you a quick snapshot of a Chinese fishing equipment company's experience with SAP Business One.

Company	Chinese fishing equipment manufacturer and wholesaler
Existing Solutions	Non-SAP software
Challenge	To stay competitive in a strong market, to track sales and purchase orders, to monitor back orders dealing with a large number of SKUs, and to support multiple price tables
	Previous system incorrectly read bar codes and provided inaccurate month-end closings
SAP Solutions	SAP Business One
Benefits	Fast implementation, easy user acceptance, easy access to real-time information, better credit controls, visibility into inventory, reduction in order time and stock levels, improved customer service

Table 11.1 SAP Business One Case Study 1

As a leading maker, distributor, and retailer of sports fishing equipment, this company sells more than 3,000 products. The company employs a total of 30 people but broadens its reach through 36 international distributors. The company was using an off-the-shelf software package for accounting, sales, and distribution, which used a batch method, rather than working with real-time data. The old system could no longer support the company's growing business.

In addition, the company was facing tough competition in key markets. The company looked at 15 possible vendors and chose to implement SAP Business One to improve the efficiency of its financial systems, reporting, and other key business processes. The company especially liked SAP's scalability, ease of use, and features.

Tracking invoices and payments

The company worked with an SAP implementation partner and found the implementation of SAP Business One to be very smooth — it took only two months to implement it. SAP Business One enabled the company to provide updated information in real time. The ability to track invoices and payments was much improved, which resulted in tighter credit control. The company found they could close out end-of-month books in half the time it used to take. Inventory management was also improved because employees could view stock availability easily. The order cycle time was reduced by 30%. The enablement of automatically generated bar codes and support for multiple price tables helped to support the 15,000 SKUs used by the business.

Reducing order cycle time

Employees found SAP Business One easy to learn and use. Furthermore, it provided all employees with customer and order information as needed. Management found real-time reports useful in helping them monitor current business and forecast future trends. In the future, the company hopes to integrate SAP Business One with its website for online ordering, and integrate its systems with retail operations to provide access to real-time stock availability information.

SAP Business All-In-One Fast-Start Program Case Study 2

Table 11.2 introduces you to another case study for a small business, a Hawaii-based sun care product manufacturer with 155 employees that manufactures and distributes its line of products internationally. This time, the focus is on the SAP Business All-In-One fast-start program.

Company	North American manufacturer and distributor of sun care products
Existing Solutions	Non-SAP software
Challenge	To maintain a competitive position and integrate and optimize supply chain management with partners; and to improve inventory management, coordinate production schedules, and improve customer satisfaction
SAP Solutions	Vertical SAP Business All-in-One fast-start program solution for the consumer packaged goods industry with features for inventory management, production planning, and customer relationship management
Benefits	More flexibility and efficiency in product distribution, resulting in a more competitive company with higher customer satisfaction, and efficient supply chain management, including production plans and inventory management

Table 11.2 SAP Business All-in-One Fast-Start Program Case Study 2

The company had challenges in managing inventory, coordinating production schedules, and maintaining a high level of customer satisfaction. The company worked with an SAP vertical solutions reseller to implement an SAP Business All-in-One solution delivered thorough the fast-start program .

Inventory management, schedule coordination, and maintaining customer satisfaction

Added flexibility and efficiency in the distribution of its products, along with a better match to customer requirements, helped to improve customer satisfaction and competitive position. The company streamlined its supply chain management, improved inventory management, and generated better production plans and forecasts.

Conclusion

In this chapter, you've learned about the various products that SAP offers small and midsize enterprises, and SAP's approach to the needs of those markets. SAP, once perceived as being a solution for only large companies, has now moved beyond that image with solutions for smaller businesses and midsize companies. These solutions, for which we provided an overview, are:

> SAP Business One for smaller enterprises

> SAP Business All-in-One program for midsize enterprises

> SAP Business ByDesign for midsize enterprises with a hosted solution

> SAP BusinessObjects Edge Business Intelligence

Next, we will provide an overview of the data tools and reporting applications, specifically SAP Business Intelligence and Reporting, in Chapter 12, SAP BusinessObjects Portfolio.

12

The SAP BusinessObjects Portfolio

SAP has had a strong business intelligence solution, but to address today's volatile markets and increasing regulations, SAP purchased BusinessObjects in 2008.

Both companies had a track record in software for business users, and their combined strengths allowed SAP to address the growing market for business performance optimization focused on business intelligence. Where SAP BEx (SAP Business Explorer) had traditionally focused on analysis, BusinessObjects included emphasis on reporting and ease of use that perfectly addressed changes in approach to business performance optimization in the marketplace. With this acquisition, SAP became a key industry leader in business intelligence.

SAP purchased BusinessObjects to further strengthen its BI offerings

The next generation of business performance optimization tools from SAP is likely to blur the lines between analysis and reporting further through tighter integration. SAP BEx Report Designer is also likely to be phased out and replaced by BusinessObjects premium offerings.

BI and enterprise performance management, as well as information management and governance, risk, and compliance have been separate disciplines in the past. Their convergence into a single, complete, and integrated solution addresses business users' demands for broader insight from multiple sources, aligned strategic decision making across teams, optimized operational decisions, and flawless execution across operational systems. This shift delivers a new ability to manage and track integrated performance and risk indicators.

In the next section, we'll examine the four core areas of components that comprise these solutions: SAP BusinessObjects business intelligence (BI), SAP BusinessObjects information management (IM), SAP BusinessObjects enterprise performance management (EPM), and SAP BusinessObjects governance, risk, and compliance (GRC) (Figure 12.1).

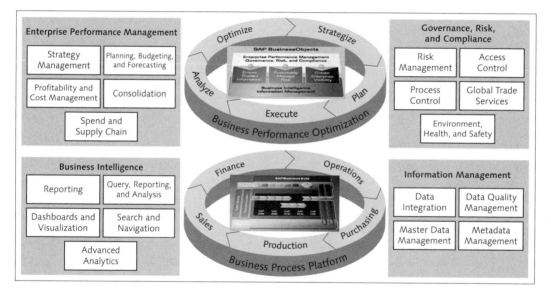

Figure 12.1 SAP BusinessObjects Portfolio

What Is Business Intelligence?

As today's global economy shows, what happens to a company or an industry in one part of the world can have a ripple effect on organizations in many other parts of the world. Take, for example, the auto industry. As sales began to drop, the auto industry was slow to react. Huge inventories remained on car lots, and several key companies went bankrupt. As auto-manufacturing plants shut down for extended periods, other industries and companies that supplied parts and materials to the auto industry were forced to lay off employees and face closure themselves.

In response to this economic volatility, additional laws and regulations were enacted to monitor how companies do business and to prevent some of the widespread business failures from reoccurring. As a result, companies find that to stay competitive and in compliance, they need to quickly access and analyze their company data, and then rapidly make business decisions that could impact the future of their business.

Information and knowing what to do with it are the keys to making your business successful. Not only do you need to have access to all of the relevant data within your organization, but you also need to know what is happening with your competitors, your suppliers, and the general market trends affecting your industry. Taking days to research these items is no longer an option; you now need information (business intelligence) at the "speed of thought" to take advantage of new opportunities and to avoid the pitfalls that may be lurking.

Information makes the world go round

In most organizations, data comes in many different formats and is stored on multiple databases and servers. So, when a situation comes up where you need to make a critical decision, it's very difficult to pull all of the information you need together quickly. One of the essential tools you need for generating business intelligence is business warehousing. Business warehousing provides a central repository for your company's data, which comes from both SAP and non-SAP sources, and then makes it available to you in real-time when you need it for those important business decisions.

An organized repository for your data

Understanding Business Intelligence Tools

Although having all of your data in one central repository is a good start, you still don't have all you need to make the best decisions. This is where SAP BusinessObjects business intelligence (BI) tools come into play. Now that you have readily accessible data, these tools help ensure the quality and reliability of the information and then display and report it to you in a way that best helps you extract what you need to make those informed decisions. In this section, we'll look at SAP BusinessObjects BI tools that ensure data integrity and quality.

SAP BusinessObjects BI tools empower you and your employees to make better strategic decisions and narrow the gap between concept and execution. By bringing the information you need from all sources within your organization, allowing you to analyze the data in different formats, enabling you to manipulate different variables within that data to achieve maximum results, and then finally reporting those results, your company will be poised to achieve its goals.

Before we look at each of the SAP BusinessObjects BI tools, we need to talk about the SAP BusinessObjects Explorer.

SAP BusinessObjects Explorer

The SAP BusinessObjects Explorer software, the accelerated version for SAP NetWeaver Business Warehouse (SAP NetWeaver BW), uses intuitive information search and exploration functionality that allows you to make BI available throughout your company. And with immediate insights into your data, users can "explore business at the speed of thought – and improve their ability to make sound, timely decisions," according to SAP.

Users can find what they need, when they need it, without having to involve your IT staff. And with the feel of common search sites such as Google and Yahoo!, little training is required (see Figure 12.2).

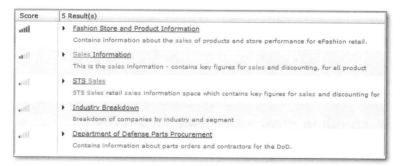

Figure 12.2 SAP BusinessObjects Explorer Search Results

SAP BusinessObjects Explorer delivers a lot of useful functionality including:

> **Search across data fields and metadata:** Users can enter a few keywords to find the most relevant information instantly from across all data sources.

> **Intuitive exploration of data and charts:** Results are complemented with contextually relevant details as is common with Internet search engines.

> **Automated relevancy and chart generation:** The most relevant search results are presented first and a chart that best represents the information is automatically generated.

> **High performance and scalability:** The combined software and hardware solution delivers the high performance and scalability needed to get immediate results when browsing very large data sets – up to billions of data records.

As you can see, SAP BusinessObjects Explorer is an integral part of the overall BusinessObjects BI solution. So now let's have a look at the SAP BusinessObjects BI tools that enhance data analysis and analytical reporting within your organization.

SAP BusinessObjects BI Advanced Analytics

Using your data to maximize the potential of your organization requires in-depth analysis and examination of all possible scenarios. SAP's new advanced OLAP (online analytical processing) tool currently called Pioneer, due to launch in 2010, will provide a robust means to query information in your data warehouse. The OLAP processor in Pioneer allows you to drill-up or down through data, get a slice of data by adding or removing specific elements, look at just the exceptions by setting minimum and maximum thresholds on the results, or look at selected data within a hierarchical structure. Your queries can then be saved and reused or modified to give you the exact information you need. Pioneer will be offered in a Microsoft Office version and a web-based version.

SAP BusinessObjects Web Intelligence Manages Information

SAP BusinessObjects Web Intelligence provides a self-service approach through the use of ad-hoc queries to display and report data. An easy-to-use series of screens lets you create an initial query into your data warehouse. A panel lets you view the results from that query, and you can then drag and drop the parameters you want to use for your output result and select any appropriate filters to be applied to the data (see Figure 12.3).

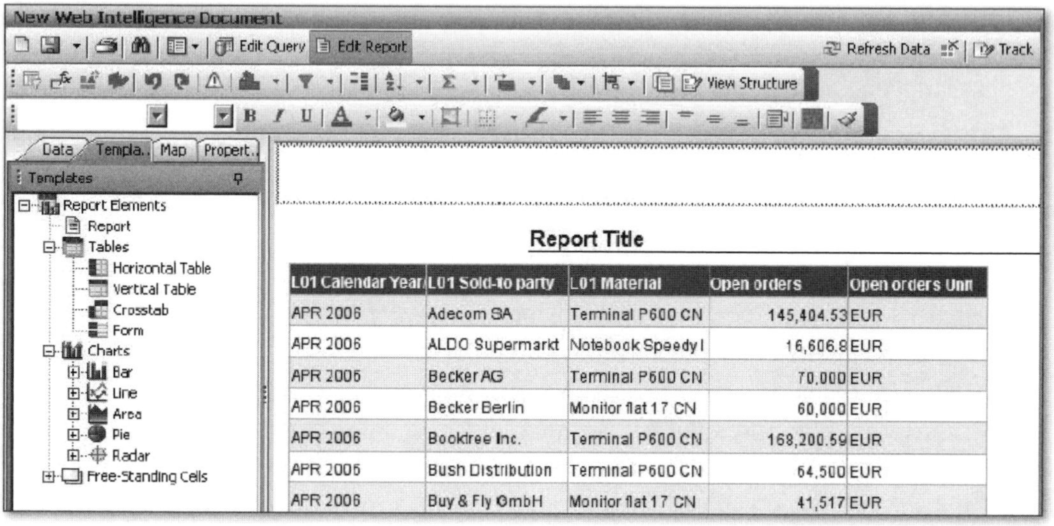

Figure 12.3 SAP BusinessObjects Web Intelligence Query Panel

Your results can then be displayed in a format that best suits your needs, such as a table, form, bar graph, line graph, or pie chart (see Figure 12.4). The report results can also be integrated into Xcelsius, mobile devices, Office applications, and Adobe PDFs.

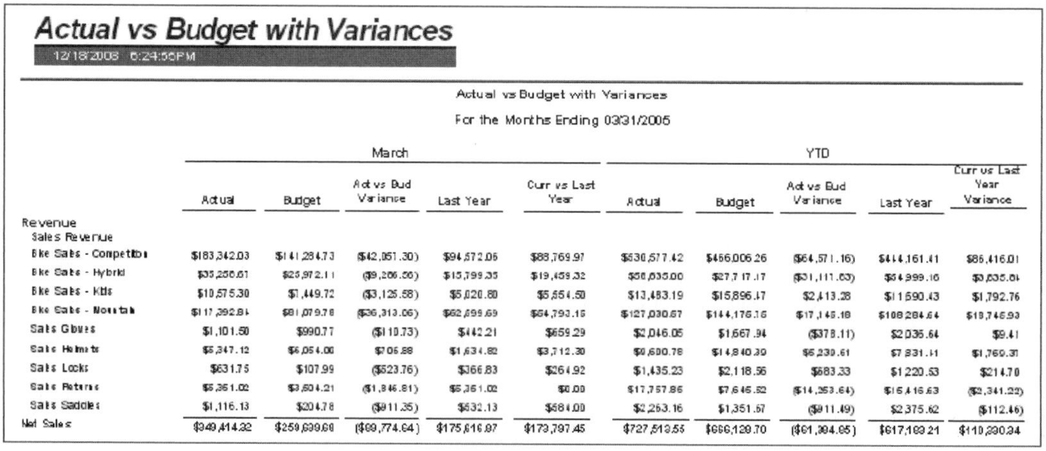

Actual vs Budget with Variances

12/18/2008 6:24:55PM

Actual vs Budget with Variances

For the Months Ending 03/31/2006

	March					YTD				
	Actual	Budget	Act vs Bud Variance	Last Year	Curr vs Last Year	Actual	Budget	Act vs Bud Variance	Last Year	Curr vs Last Year Variance
Revenue										
Sales Revenue										
Bike Sales - Competition	$183,342.03	$141,284.73	($42,057.30)	$94,572.06	$88,769.97	$530,577.42	$466,006.26	($64,571.16)	$444,161.41	$86,416.01
Bike Sales - Hybrid	$35,256.61	$25,972.11	($9,286.56)	$15,799.35	$19,459.32	$58,835.00	$27,717.17	($31,111.83)	$54,999.16	$3,835.84
Bike Sales - Kids	$10,575.30	$7,449.72	($3,125.58)	$5,020.80	$5,554.50	$13,483.19	$15,896.47	$2,413.28	$11,690.43	$1,792.76
Bike Sales - Mountain	$117,392.84	$81,079.78	($36,313.06)	$62,599.69	$54,793.15	$127,030.67	$144,176.16	$17,145.18	$108,284.64	$18,746.93
Sales Gloves	$1,101.50	$990.77	($110.73)	$442.21	$659.29	$2,046.05	$1,667.94	($378.11)	$2,036.64	$9.41
Sales Helmets	$5,347.12	$6,054.00	$706.88	$1,634.82	$3,712.30	$9,600.78	$14,840.39	$5,239.61	$7,831.41	$1,769.37
Sales Locks	$631.75	$107.99	($523.76)	$366.83	$264.92	$1,435.23	$2,118.56	$683.33	$1,220.53	$214.70
Sales Returns	$5,351.02	$3,504.21	($1,846.81)	$5,351.02	$0.00	$17,757.86	$7,646.52	($14,253.64)	$15,416.63	($2,341.22)
Sales Saddles	$1,116.13	$204.78	($911.35)	$532.13	$584.00	$2,263.16	$1,351.67	($911.49)	$2,375.62	($112.46)
Net Sales	$349,414.32	$259,639.60	($89,774.64)	$175,616.87	$173,797.45	$727,513.55	$666,128.70	($61,384.85)	$617,183.21	$110,330.34

Figure 12.4 SAP BusinessObjects Web Intelligence Report in Table Format

Crystal Reports

Another tool used for reporting the results of your data warehouse queries is Crystal Reports. Crystal Reports provide precision reporting of information from your data cubes and allow you to control the fonts, layouts, positioning, pagination, and sorting of the data to be displayed (see Figure 12.5).

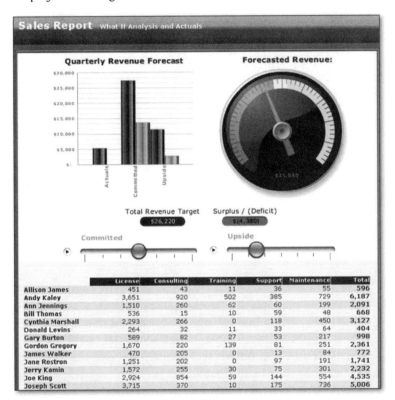

Figure 12.5 Budget Analysis in Crystal Reports

Another feature of Crystal Reports is *dynamic bursting*, which allows you to send personalized report content to individual recipients. If you're going to use your Crystal Report for analytical purposes, Xcelsius is embedded into Crystal Reports so that you can create interactive "what-if" scenario dashboards (Figure 12.6). These reports can be sent via e-mail, be delivered via the web, or be embedded into your enterprise applications.

Dynamic bursting

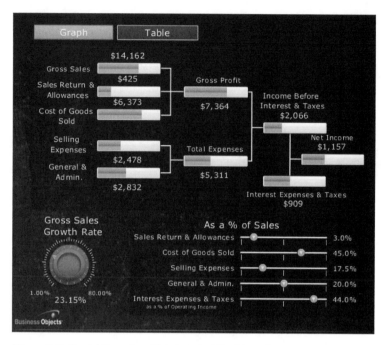

Figure 12.6 Crystal Reports with Integrated Dashboard

Xcelsius

The ability to get a visual representation of your information or query better helps you understand its nuances and interrelationships. The SAP BusinessObjects BI tool in this area is Xcelsius. Xcelsius provides a holistic view of key metrics and information with dashboards that are easy to create and use. Dashboards with dropdown menus and sliders allow you to change data variables to create what-if scenarios so you can see exactly where business opportunities are and how risks can be minimized. Because these dashboards are intuitive and easy to create, you can quickly capture historical data to analyze trends and free your IT people from having to create custom tools each time you need a visual representation of your data. Xcelsius dashboards can be integrated in a secure manner into Microsoft SharePoint sites or Microsoft applications such as Word, Outlook, and PowerPoint (see Figure 12.7). They can also be embedded into Adobe PDF and Crystal Reports.

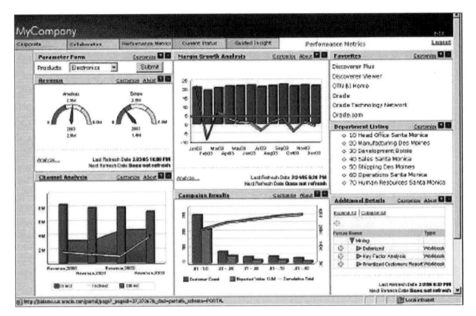

Figure 12.7 Xcelsius Interactive Dashboard Inserted in a PowerPoint Presentation

As these tools show, having the best and most accurate information is the key to sustaining your business during lean times. As an example, of how these reporting tools can be used, we'll look at what SAP has done to help organizations manage stimulus funds from the government, using the Public Sector solutions.

SAP for Public Sector Solutions to Manage Stimulus Funds

Many public sector organizations have received stimulus funds from the government to help them during difficult economic times. In return for this money, strict requirements are in place for these organizations to report back and show their accountability to the government and the public regarding how this money is spent and the measurable results of their efforts.

SAP's new economic funds reporting and management solutions, based on its SAP BusinessObjects portfolio, help these public sector organizations meet these obligations by providing tools that show transparency into and accountability for the projects being funded by

Monitoring and reporting on how stimulus money is used

233

the stimulus money. With these applications, reports measuring the project's performance against established benchmarks show whether the public can regain its trust and confidence in this organization.

Here are some of the items that can be tracked and reported on by the SAP for Public Sector solutions.

> **Efficiency**
> The projects developed with stimulus funds are expected to operate efficiently with lower costs and elimination of waste and redundancy.

> **Improve business performance**
> These projects need to demonstrate that they are viable projects that will improve business processes and business sustainability and not add unnecessary levels of bureaucracy.

> **Long-term outcomes**
> Viable and quantifiable long-term results should be the end results from the projects developed with stimulus money. People need to see tangible results from their investment.

> **Reacting to change**
> The inability to react quickly to changes in the economy and regulation led to many organizations needing these bailouts to survive. Legislation and regulations continue to change rapidly, and these organizations need to prove that they are able to react to these changes and stay in compliance.

Accountability SAP technology quickly reacted to conditions in the public sector and provided a means for organizations to monitor the effectiveness of their efforts, as well as meet their obligations to the government and the public for accountability of these funds.

In the next section, we take a look at how SAP BusinessObjects information management (IM) solutions allow companies to take further control of their information.

SAP BusinessObjects Information Management Solutions

Being able to access your data from all sources and have it displayed in an easy-to-understand format is critical to helping you make informed decisions. With the right tools you can deliver integrated, accurate, and timely data – both structured and unstructured – across your enterprise. These tools will help ensure that your data is reliable for all of your important initiatives, such as business transaction processing, business intelligence, data warehousing, data migration, and master data management.

Open Hub Services and Data Broadcasting

Open hub services distribute the data from the business warehouse, via web services, to applications that you use daily within your business. By dispersing your information in this way, you can ensure that the same version of information reaches all people even if they are in different departments or working on different applications.

Information or data broadcasting allows you to take large amounts of business intelligence data and distribute it securely via e-mail or an enterprise portal to large groups of people. The data that is sent can be from different sources, such as SAP BusinessObjects BI web applications or dashboards, and in different formats, such as HTML or Zip files. With data broadcasting, your information can flow immediately into web collaboration rooms on your enterprise portal, or it can be sent to people at scheduled intervals depending on its criticality.

Data can flow as you need it

Within SAP BusinessObjects Information Management there are a number of specific solutions you can use, so let's look at each briefly.

> **SAP BusinessObjects Data Federator**
> SAP BusinessObjects Data Federator helps you integrate data from various sources and pulls it together to make it look like it came from one single source, all with real-time speed.

> **SAP BusinessObjects Data Insight**
> SAP BusinessObjects Data Insight lets you monitor, analyze, and report on your data to maintain its integrity and quality. With these tools, alerts can be programmed to notify you if data falls below a certain quality level. Other functions let you monitor and analyze your information for new data relationships and business rules that can be added to your business data projects.

> **SAP BusinessObjects Data Integrator**
> SAP BusinessObjects Data Integrator allows you to explore, extract, transform, and deliver data anywhere and provides the foundation

for your data. These tools help you build in rules that filter out unwanted data and preserve its quality, and let you monitor the impact to your data when the data source changes (Figure 12.8).

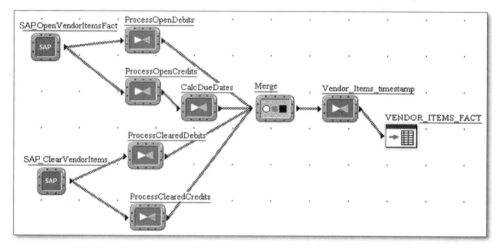

Figure 12.8 SAP BusinessObjects Data Integrator

> **SAP BusinessObjects Data Quality Management**

SAP BusinessObjects Data Quality Management software helps you verify that your data is complete, standardized, and accurate. Because compliance regulations require you to deliver reports that are truthful and that can be verified during an audit, these tools have features that monitor your data against government lists to prevent questionable transactions. Other functions ensure your data is current, and monitor it for duplicate information (see Figure 12.9).

The proposed merger between Mega, Inc. and CNA Systems, Incorporated, has been postponed, Mega CEO Joe Smith said in an analyst call. "CNA's 1st quarter revenue dropped by 32%, and they lost 23 million dollars," Smith explained. CNA Systems sources blame weak sales in China. CNA shares (CNAI) fell 47 percent to $9.84 on May 12, the first trading day after the announcement.

Company	Mega, Inc., CNA Systems, Incorporated
Date	May 12
Person	Joe Smith
Person Position	Mega CEO
Currency	23 million dollars, $9.84
Measurement	32%, 47 percent
Country	China
Concept	proposed merger, analyst call, 1st quarter revenue weak sales, first trading day
Event: M&A	The proposed merger between Mega, Inc. and CNA Systems, Inc. has been postponed

Figure 12.9 Protect Your Data at the Point of Entry

236

> **SAP BusinessObjects Text Analysis**

SAP BusinessObjects Text Analysis lets you retrieve information from such unstructured sources as e-mails, blogs, documents, notes, and the web. Uncover "hidden" information about customer sentiments, market trends, industry buzz, and product and service issues so you can support corporate initiatives, including voice of the customer, root cause analysis, win/loss analysis, employee satisfaction, competitive intelligence, and customer retention. You now have the complete sphere of information from both traditional and alternative sources to help you in the decision-making process.

> **SAP BusinessObjects Metadata Management**

SAP BusinessObjects Metadata Management software combines and integrates metadata (data about data) from all sources into a relational repository. A metapedia takes metadata and associates it with common terms, phrases, and business concepts for your business. When this is done, everyone within your business is on the same page as to the meaning of these terms, and multiple definitions are eliminated. Your employees see one unified look, yet have access to all of the data they need.

Now we'll move on to look at Enterprise Performance Management.

Understanding Enterprise Performance Management

Performance management is a business process and as such is a true ERP function. SAP BusinessObjects offers several performance optimization applications such as corporate performance management, strategic enterprise management (SEM), enterprise performance management (EPM), financial performance management (FPM), and operational performance management (OPM).

Where a BI platform is generic and as such can serve a wide variety of self-service needs or be custom developed into an analytic application, SAP BusinessObjects EPM focuses on process support.

Planning in SAP NetWeaver BW Integrated Planning is an example of this, because it offers a function and feature of the platform versus the planning process support that can be built in SAP BusinessObjects Planning and Consolidation.

The performance management offerings in SAP BusinessObjects include:

> **SAP BusinessObjects Strategy Management**
> This solution helps you set goals and determine strategies. You can also monitor and manage performance tracking for both high-level objectives and operational deliverables.

> **SAP BusinessObjects Planning and Consolidation**
> You can use this application to increase accuracy in planning, which helps you reduce budget cycles and costs. And you can improve both financial and management reporting and support better decision making.

> **SAP BusinessObjects Financial Consolidation**
> This application helps you complete financial consolidation and reporting cycles more quickly.

> **SAP BusinessObjects XBRL Publishing application by UBMatrix**
> Simplify and speed up the preparation of XBRL (eXtensible Business Reporting Language) documents that help you communicate financial and business information.

> **SAP BusinessObjects Financial Information Management**
> Use these tools for connectivity, mapping, and loading functionality to better manage your financial information.

> **SAP BusinessObjects Intercompany**
> This tool helps you speed up close activities by allowing your people to reconcile balances directly without costly delays at corporate and divisional levels.

> **SAP BusinessObjects Profitability and Cost Management**
> This application helps you identify the reasons for underperformance. You can then take action to control costs and ensure greater profitability across various activities.

> **SAP BusinessObjects Spend Performance Management**
> SAP BusinessObjects Spend Performance Management allows you to realize cost savings and reduce risks in dealing with suppliers by providing constant visibility into spending patterns, potential savings, and factors determined by external markets.

> **SAP BusinessObjects Supply Chain Performance Management**
> Use this application to improve supply chain efficiency. You can

emphasize actionable, operational process factors that have an impact on your supply chain performance.

The next component of SAP BusinessObjects is Governance, Risk, and Compliance (GRC).

The Current Need for GRC

Even within corporations that have a serious need to deal with complex regulations and compliance, there is some uncertainty about what GRC means and what it involves. In fact, the three areas (i.e., governance, risk, and compliance) have a logical relationship (see Figure 12.10), although they are often treated separately. In the following sections, we'll discuss each of these areas in greater detail.

GRC: What does it mean?

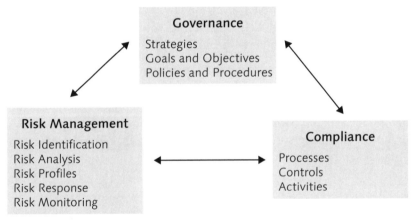

Figure 12.10 Interrelationship of Governance, Risk Management, and Compliance Management

Governance

Governance involves those in your company who are entrusted with the strategic directives for your enterprise. Governance is focused on the people "at the top" of your organization, and the way they specify your enterprise goals and measure your accomplishments against those goals.

If you think of this in terms of your corporate policies and procedures, and setting corporate strategy, you'll begin to see how they could relate to effective implementation of risk management and compliance.

Risk Management

Risk management looks at potential exposures to internal or external events and the positive or negative impact of that exposure. Companies must anticipate any risk associated with a business initiative or process, and then monitor and control that risk. Examples of such risks would be a political shift in a country where you market your products, or a new regulation that might cause you to have to modify your strategy.

In the area of risk management, you work to identify, measure, and report potential risks that could expose your governance goals.

Compliance

Compliance essentially involves the processes you use to comply with rules and regulations. This is crossing your t's and dotting your i's to ensure that you meet the letter of the law. Compliance means taking notice of the various rules that pertain to your enterprise and setting up your systems to comply with those rules.

Non-compliance can be costly

An important part of compliance is the ability to *show* that you are in compliance, which may require you to produce a variety of reports, financial statements, or verification of data by top management. Non-compliance can be costly, with penalties that can be detrimental to an organization, or personally damaging to top managers who have not enforced compliance.

The Role of GRC in an Enterprise

Many companies scramble to deal with each regulatory demand separately, with no centralized GRC policy in place across the enterprise. That fragmentation can be costly. There are literally hundreds of laws, trade agreements, and documentation requirements, some industry- or country-specific. Could anyone possibly handle such demands without a comprehensive strategy?

These types of challenges are largely responsible for the attitude toward GRC in today's world.

The Need for an Integrated Approach

In many companies, there is a *"putting fires out"* mentality about GRC. They focus on the latest risk as it arises and address each individual regulatory mandate separately, often in isolation from other GRC-related efforts in the organization. Consequently, companies end up using different standards and methods within their enterprise to measure and comply with regulations.

 Tip

The Sarbanes-Oxley (SOX) Act is a U.S. federal law passed in 2002 that came about in response to several U.S. company accounting scandals such as Enron and WorldCom. Essentially, the law seeks to control corporate accounting abuses.

Compliance with SOX is critical to many enterprises, and non-compliance can be costly. For example, a large software company recently invested a great deal of energy to stay SOX-compliant. But a compliance committee that reported to the CFO and CIO worked on this initiative failed to take into account new sales commission plans. Aligning commission payments with their overall performance meant that they had to delay the reporting of their yearly financial results.

For more about SOX, go to *www.sarbanes-oxley.com*. You'll also find a toolkit with compliance checklists at *www.sarbanes-oxley-forum.com*

Costs of Compliance

This state of affairs can be costly to a company in many ways. Companies that haven't adopted an integrated GRC strategy are probably throwing people at the problems. AMR Research estimates that "approximately two-thirds of the cost of compliance is in people — specifically headcount and services." Inefficient manual GRC enforcement is tantamount to throwing money away. In addition, delayed or canceled initiatives (i.e., due to the amount of time people have to spend dealing with GRC), as well as the inability to focus on core responsibilities, can have an impact on the bottom line.

Impact on the bottom line

Benefits of Integrated GRC

To help resolve the fragmented approach to GRC at many companies (see Figure 12.11), SAP offered the first integrated, comprehensive GRC software solution. This integrated approach to governance, risk management, and compliance is new to many managers. But the need for this approach makes sense because integrating these efforts helps your employees avoid spending time on tasks that are fragmented and result in a costly duplication of effort. For example, if your company has one person in each of your plants trying to keep up with employee

Integrated GRC

safety compliance, doesn't it make sense to consolidate your plants' efforts so they have a centralized way to ensure consistent compliance across the organization?

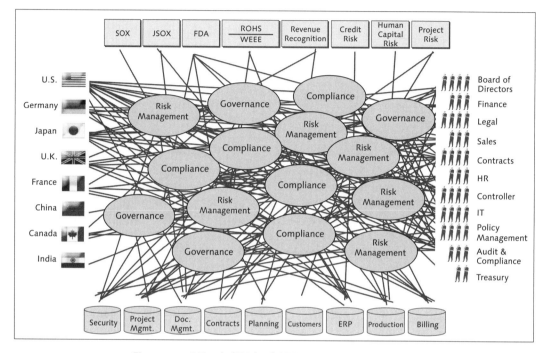

Figure 12.11 A Tangled Web of GRC Issues Exists at Many Organizations

SAP BusinessObjects Solutions for GRC

SAP BusinessObjects governance, risk, and compliance solutions offer several benefits to an enterprise. With the SAP BusinessObjects GRC solutions in place, you can standardize components and automate operations across your business processes with both industry-specific and cross-industry solutions. SAP has developed its GRC framework by working with what it calls its "ecosystem of partners," which means SAP has used its alliances with key customers and consultants to determine what GRC issues to address and how to address them in a business setting.

Four Levels of the SAP BusinessObjects GRC Solution

Business processes can involve several steps and cross many departments, or even shift outside of your organization. For that reason, SAP doesn't take a single layer approach to something as complex as GRC. Rather, there are four levels to the solution that helps ensure that nothing falls between your corporate cracks. The four levels of the SAP BusinessObjects GRC solution are:

> **Level One: Common Software Foundation**
> SAP provides a foundation that gives you an enterprise-wide methodology, vocabulary, and way of measuring your GRC efforts. You can incorporate existing information into this new GRC system so you don't lose the work you've done.

> **Level Two: Embedded Horizontal and Vertical GRC**
> Horizontal areas include financial reporting, security, privacy, records retention, supply chain import-export support, environmental standards, occupational health and safety, and risk management. These are issues most businesses have to deal with. Vertical mandates are the ones that are specific to a wide variety of industries. Using SAP BusinessObjects GRC, day-to-day activities take GRC issues into account, even down to the industry-specific level. Take note of the following:
>
> – This doesn't require your employees to do anything special in addition to their own work; instead, the software makes compliance and risk-aware practices part of their daily tasks. All GRC elements such as policies, processes, risks, controls, and so on are located in the SAP BusinessObjects Repository.

> GRC elements

>
> – This repository can ensure consistency in the way your entire organization deals with regulations and policies. You can also use the repository to help rationalize the number of controls because you can replace lower level controls with higher level controls. A control documentation and monitoring application is included, providing a global organizational view of all controls in place.

> SAP BusinessObjects Repository

> **Level Three: Business and Risk Management**
> SAP software provides a risk registry as part of the business and risk management layer. This registry is constantly monitored by objects, processes, and projects throughout your enterprise. A risk map

> Risk registry

offers an overview of all risk management issues, which can help you identify shifting risk profiles over time (see Figure 12.12).

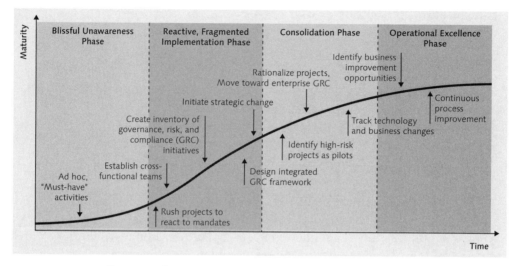

Figure 12.12 SAP's Integrated Approach to GRC

> **Level Four: Measurement and Collaboration**
>
> Data in the GRC applications is used to generate business alerts that are pushed to the right decision maker. Analytical tools such as risk balance sheets help your company make decisions about its strategy and potential conflicts.

Next, we'll explore the horizontal and vertical solutions that SAP offers in more detail.

The Horizontal and Vertical Compliance Solutions

The horizontal solutions in SAP BusinessObjects GRC provide a foundation for all enterprise applications and cross industry boundaries.

SAP BusinessObjects Access Control

These solutions help you comply with regulations regarding how you segregate your resources with proper access and authorization (Figure 12.13). The software includes monitoring, testing, and enforcement tools. You can use SAP BusinessObjects Access Control to comply with SOX and identify risks and avoid violations. SAP BusinessObjects Access Control has two components: a cross-enterprise library of SoD rules (a database of segregation of duties rules that provides the ability to create custom rules); and access management tools, which include enterprise role management, compliant user provisioning, and super-user privilege management. In addition, SAP BusinessObjects Access Control enables access audits to periodically review user access and compliance with business policies.

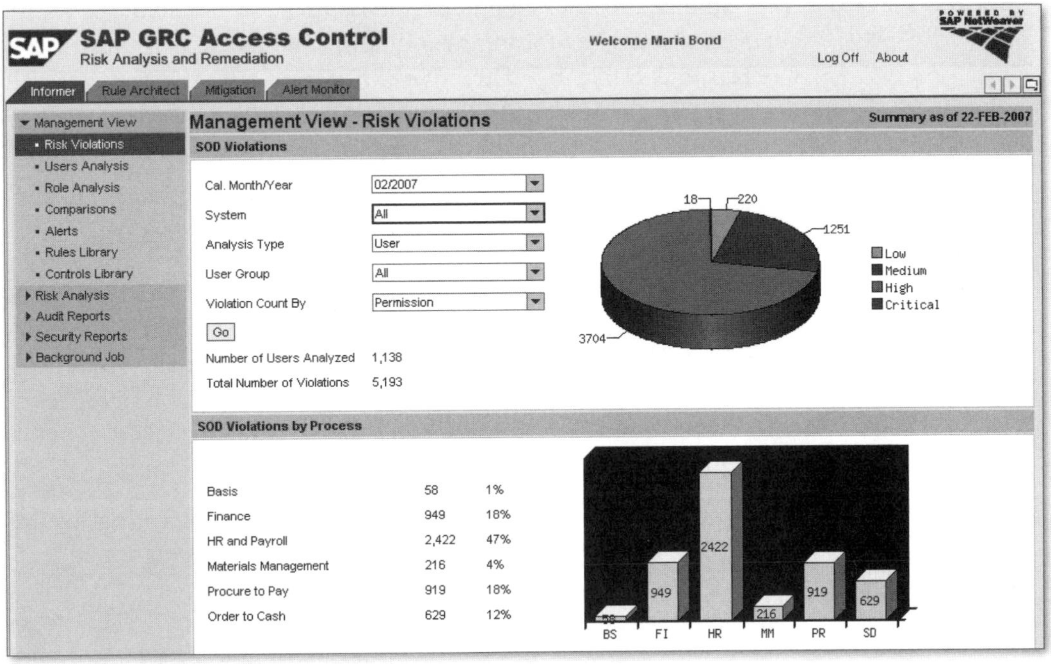

Figure 12.13 SAP's BusinessObjects GRC Access Control Monitors Risk Violations

SAP BusinessObjects Global Trade Services

This application gives you control over cross-border shipments, which can involve compliance with any of 600 laws and 500 trade agreements, and filing of multiple documents. Using this solution, you can automate import and export processes and verify that you are in compliance with regulations. The SAP BusinessObjects Global Trade Services application helps expedite customs clearance to get your products delivered faster, while also reducing the risk of violations. The solution helps you manage data related to trade such as duties, denied party lists, and tariff codes. Tools include export management, import management, trade preference management, and restitution management.

600 laws and 500 trade agreements

SAP Environment, Health, and Safety Management

This solution includes occupational health, industrial hygiene and safety, hazardous substance, dangerous goods, product safety, and waste management tools. There are features that integrate into any company's business processes and vertical environmental solutions, such as SAP xApp Emissions Management (SAP xEM).

Deal with specific issues

These applications deal with specific issues such as chemicals safety and occupational healthcare. In addition, compliance with Restriction of Hazardous Substance Directive (RoHS) and Waste Electrical and Electronic Equipment (WEEE) works through an ecosystem of GRC partners, including TechniData Compliance for Products and SI Recycling Administration (REA).

SAP Risk and Sustainability

This solution is achieved by increased transparency for your processes and better business insight through sophisticated analytics. This information helps you make better decisions about potentially risky projects and compare the risk against the potential return on investment (ROI). Also, automation, analytics, and alerts help your business avoid compliance problems.

SAP BusinessObjects Repository

Finally, as part of the control documentation and monitoring feature set, the SAP BusinessObjects Repository contains information regarding a huge range of governance, risk, and compliance data, which is available across enterprise systems.

Vertical solutions exist for a variety of industries. With complex processes, such as supply chain management and environmental requirements that vary by industry, there is a need for industry-specific solutions to supplement the horizontal solution set. Solutions exist for industries such as banking, automotive, chemicals, high-tech, utilities, life sciences, oil and gas, and consumer products.

Both horizontal and vertical solutions are embedded at the business process level to ensure that employees are using them to stay in compliance. In addition, they support various enterprise software systems, such as SAP, Oracle, PeopleSoft, and legacy systems.

Understanding the solutions offered is the first step. The next step is to understand *exactly* where your company is (i.e., at the moment) in relation to GRC excellence, so you can begin to devise a strategy to get where you should be in accordance with governance, risk, and compliance. This concludes the review of the SAP BusinessObjects portfolio. Let's wrap up this chapter with a look at how it is being used today.

SAP BusinessObjects Case Study 1

Table 12.1 gives you a snapshot of the case study that we will discuss in detail in this section. Review the table before you go on to read the rest of the case study.

Company	International liquor distributor
Existing Solutions	SAP ERP on SAP NetWeaver, Oracle database, IBM hardware, Microsoft Windows
Challenge	To achieve SOX Compliance Certification, to monitor segregation of duties (SoD)
SAP Solutions	SAP BusinessObjects Access Control to test and enforce SoD, SAP BusinessObjects Access Control integrated with Oracle database and IBM hardware, embedded SAP BusinessObjects Access Control into existing SAP system
Benefits	Detection of SoD violations and resolution of problems and exceptions, fast implementation with no need for separate system, ease of use, changes in procedures easier to implement, ability of management to set strategic directions for compliance

Table 12.1 SAP BusinessObjects GRC Case Study 1

A worldwide liquor distributor with revenues in excess of $3 billion and 6,000 employees had SAP ERP software in place on the SAP NetWeaver platform. As a privately held company, it did not have to comply with SOX. Still, to help control its business processes and align itself with financial institution procedures in case it ever did want to go public, the company chose to comply. To do so, the company had to get certified, which took a year of documented compliant operations. Monitoring SoD was the last step for this company in becoming compliant in time for the next year's audit.

SAP's Solution

SAP NetWeaver and SOX

The SAP BusinessObjects Access Control application allowed the company to test and enforce SoD across its global manufacturing, supply chain, and procurement processes in just three weeks. This allowed the company to detect SoD violations, and provided information about what needed to be done to resolve problems and exceptions. Analyses of changes in user access and authorizations helped prevent new risks.

SAP BusinessObjects Access Control

The company was able to integrate the SAP BusinessObjects Access Control with its Oracle database and IBM hardware, operating on Microsoft Windows. SAP BusinessObjects Access Control was embedded directly into the company's existing SAP system, helping with a fast implementation and saving the company from having to add on a separate system. The company could use the product for two weeks under a demo license to ensure that it was right for the job, and then purchase it.

The Solution in Place

Once in place, the application monitored 300 users in 30 to 40 roles involving more than 50 business processes. End users reported that the solution was easy to use, helping the IT department to run a check for conflict whenever a user requested a change to his function. In this way, conflicts such as the ability of customer service to create a customer and process the customer's order, which could permit an employee to modify a customer address and ship an order to a different address, could be easily spotted.

Checking for conflicts

When conflicts are noted, changes in procedures help to correct the problem. Segregation of tasks is often the answer to such conflicts. Also, the so-called "transparency" of roles helps management identify issues that can influence their strategic direction in relation to governance. This helps the company to be proactive about GRC, rather than reactive.

SAP BusinessObjects GRC Case Study 2

Now we'll examine another case study. First review the snapshot of this case study in Table 12.2.

This U.S.-based manufacturer of storage devices faced multiple regulations for international exports. The company produces chips, add-in cards, and network storage devices, and sells to many businesses, countries, and agencies. With international sales representing half of its income, compliance with global regulations with an environment of tight national security became a key focus of the organization.

Company	Manufacturer of high-tech storage devices
Existing Solutions	SAP R/3
Challenge	To consolidate and make improvements to global trade compliance processes, and to automate compliance
SAP Solutions	SAP BusinessObjects Global Trade Services
Benefits	Better identification of denied parties, standardized compliance policies in place, audit trail and accountability, integration with entire supply chain

Table 12.2 SAP BusinessObjects GRC Case Study 2

The Challenge

The company needed to consolidate its compliance efforts to save wasted effort and redundancy. The company had three different home-grown systems to deal with import and export functions.

In addition, the company needed to automate its compliance efforts to save time and money. Part of this effort involved screening potential business partners to ensure that they were not on any restricted party lists published by various governments. Data entry was labor intensive, and the current systems hampered any growth through acquisition.

Compliance efforts

SAP's Solution

In implementing a solution, the focus was on denied party list screening to ensure that partners are not restricted by any government and export control checks to verify any embargoes and license requirements.

SAP BusinessObjects Global Trade Services provided the features required to check all relevant information against shipments with accurate electronic files. An audit trail was generated automatically, helping the company to meet reporting requirements.

SAP R/3   SAP BusinessObjects Global Trade Services was integrated with the existing SAP R/3 system so the company could easily upgrade both products to stay current. The SAP BusinessObjects Global Trade Services solution was in line with revenue generating and supply chain systems. In addition, the SAP BusinessObjects Global Trade Services system included a standard interface for screening denied parties.

The Benefits

There are obvious benefits to staying in compliance with regulations regarding denied parties in terms of both company reputation and costly penalties. In addition, the company can feel confident about having standardized processes for compliance across the organization, and enjoy the benefits of an automatically generated audit trail if questions are ever asked about the company's procedures.

The electronic records generated by SAP BusinessObjects Global Trade Services are simple to access, so the company can do the required last-minute checks for every shipment without causing delays to its shipping operation.

Finally, integrating its compliance with its larger operations system provides additional security so that no activities stray outside the lines of compliance requirements.

Conclusion

As you saw throughout this chapter, SAP BusinessObjects covers four core areas: business intelligence (BI), SAP BusinessObjects information management (IM), SAP BusinessObjects enterprise performance management (EPM), and SAP BusinessObjects governance, risk, and compliance (GRC). We looked at each of these in detail beginning with the Business Intelligence tools which help ensure the quality and reliability of your information and then help you display and report on it in various ways that help you extract what you need to make better informed decisions. These tools ensure that your information is reliable, consistent, and complete without your employees having to know data modeling or coding, so your IT team can focus on more critical projects, and you can have real-time access to information when and where you want it to stay on top of changes in the business world. From there you learned about how the SAP economic funds reporting and management solutions for the Public Sector help these organizations meet their obligations by providing tools that show transparency into and accountability for the projects being funded by the stimulus money. This solution shows how quickly SAP can help you react, monitor, and report on changing conditions and regulations.

Then we transitioned to a discussion of the SAP BusinessObjects Information Management solution that helps you access your data from all sources and display it in an easy-to-understand format is critical to helping you make informed decisions. With these tools will help ensure that your data is reliable for all of your important initiatives, such as business transaction processing, business intelligence, data warehousing, data migration, and master data management.

We also learned about enterprise performance management with BusinessObjects EPM, which offers several performance optimization applications such as corporate performance management, strategic enterprise management (SEM), enterprise performance management (EPM), financial performance management (FPM), and operational performance management (OPM). All of these applications are focused on process support. And because the BI platform is generic and can therefore serve a wide variety of self-service needs or be custom developed into an analytic application, SAP BusinessObjects EPM focuses on process support.

We wrapped up the chapter by providing an overview of all the GRC tools that SAP offers to keep your enterprise on the straight and narrow regarding regulations and laws. And although GRC activities can be costly and time-consuming, they are mandatory, so SAP Business Objects GRC provides the means for you to keep cost and time to a minimum while ensuring that you stay in compliance across the board.

Next we'll move on to Part III, Essential SAP Tools.

PART III
Essential SAP Tools

Understanding SAP Composite Applications

A hundred or so years ago, companies built all the parts of the products they made. But over the years, companies have turned to a manufacturing model in which they purchase and then assemble pieces and components made by others to create their own final products. Composite applications and SAP's version of them, called SAP composite applications, are akin to the software version of that manufacturing model. With composite applications, you take functionality from several different sources and use it to build solutions.

This chapter explains how that process works and describes the SAP composite applications that are available to help your business run more efficiently.

Understanding Composite Applications

Composite applications are based on a service-oriented architecture, so they are built by combining services. For example, you might take several financial services to build a composite application that comprises a customer ordering process.

Composite applications, services, and architecture

We introduced the concept of services in Chapter 2, The SAP Approach to Enterprise Software, and you can get more in-depth information about services and service-oriented architecture in Chapter 17, Service-Oriented Architecture. In the meantime, here are some useful definitions to help you out before we dive into composite applications:

> A *service* is a discretely defined piece of business or technical functionality (e.g., the calculation of shipping charges).

> *Service-oriented architecture* (SOA) is the concept of designing software as loosely coupled services that support business processes.

> SAP uses SOA as a blueprint for implementing the integration of technologies, applications, and business semantics throughout an enterprise.

So, within that SOA context, we'll move on to the specifics of what constitutes a composite application.

What Is a Composite Application?

WSDL — Web Services Description Language

A composite application draws on functions and data from existing applications and integrates them into one program. Web services are integral to helping those applications communicate by using a standardized way of describing their functionality called Web Services Description Language (WSDL). With composite applications, you can fold web services into workflows, dashboards, and all kinds of business processes.

Building composite applications

Within SAP, there are several elements that support composite applications. First, there is the SAP blueprint for SOA that shows you the products and services from SAP that help you implement SOA. Next is SAP NetWeaver, the technology platform you can use to build composite applications (covered in detail in Chapter 18, SAP NetWeaver as a Technology Platform); third is the SAP NetWeaver Composition Environment, which is a development environment to help you in creating composite applications by describing functionality rather than writing lines of code.

With SAP, you get the application that coordinates functionality to run a process, but you'll also need to have the supporting elements in place so the composite application can call on that functionality, which can come from SAP or another company's programs.

But exactly how are composite applications created? That's what we'll explain in the following section.

Where Do Composite Applications Come From?

SAP and its partners have built composite applications based on the SAP NetWeaver platform. These applications are built to reuse pieces of business functionality and address common business processes, such as SAP Merger and Acquisitions or SAP Product Definitions.

Composite applications are built on the SAP NetWeaver CE using CAF

SAP and its partners have used *SAP Composite Application Framework* (CAF) capabilities in the SAP NetWeaver CE composition environment to build composite applications, and your own company could even use SAP CAF to build its own tailored composite applications or add functionality to those SAP offers.

SAP CAF uses an industry standard programming approach called *model driven architecture*, also referred to as simply *modeling*. For example, you might build an xApp that calls on functionality contained in SAP NetWeaver Business Warehouse (SAP NetWeaver BW), SAP ERP, and SAP NetWeaver Process Integration (SAP NetWeaver PI). In modeling, you also reuse applications and enterprise services to build a new application.

Model driven architecture

To put modeling in simple terms, you describe to the modeling system (such as SAP CAF) what you want an application to do, and it provides an application that does just that.

Developers can use either role-based or process-based modeling, focused either on the person performing the process, or the process details, depending on the business need. With role-based modeling, for example, you might focus on the user interface for a role-based dashboard.

 Note

Role-based composition involves the use of guided procedures, which can use services created in SAP CAF.

You should note that composite applications don't replace existing applications; they reuse the functionality of existing applications to address different needs as they arise. The way in which composite applications are built provides tremendous benefits to an enterprise, as you'll learn in the following section.

Composite Application Benefits

Because composite applications reuse functionality, you don't have to start from scratch every time you need an application to address a business process. This provides tremendous cost savings in your IT budget and gives you the means to create or acquire innovative new solutions that you can put to work quickly. In addition, SAP composite applications leverage your existing IT investment by using services you already have in place to build functionality.

These applications can help your business in a variety of ways. They can provide portals that are accessed on user desktops or from mobile devices and improve access to data or collaborative tools that allow you to share data. Because they are built on SAP NetWeaver, you can integrate them across your various systems and applications. This allows users to use the applications and interfaces they are most comfortable with to access them.

Often composite applications fill a gap in a business process that is making your organization less efficient. For example, the *SAP Sales and Operations Planning* application (SAP SOP) helps finance, sales, purchasing, and production collect, analyze, and track sales and operations data. Many businesses can benefit from this functionality, and now it's available out of the box in the form of an SAP composite application, saving you the trouble of buying or creating an application of your own.

Now let's take a look at these applications and provide a sampling of the specific functionality they have to offer.

SAP Composite Applications

Because a composite application draws on functions from existing applications, SAP Business Suite, including SAP ERP applications, provides a huge treasure trove of functionality for SAP composite applications to draw on.

In the following sections, we'll discuss some specific composite applications to help you understand just how useful they can be in a business setting.

SAP Resource and Portfolio Management

The *SAP Resource and Portfolio Management* (SAP RPM) composite application provides functionality in the area of R&D and your IT strategy. You get features to help manage your project portfolio, streamline the execution of projects, and improve the way you allocate resources on projects. SAP RPM includes the following features:

Functionality for R&D and IT strategy

> **Portfolio Management**
> Bring various portfolios (projects, programs, services, etc.) in line with your corporate strategies.

> **Resource Capacity Management**
> Get projections of your near-term demands for resources. Choose resources to assign to projects and programs in your enterprise's structure and approval process.

> **Portfolio Performance and Program Monitoring**
> Integrate with SAP and non-SAP systems to gain a comprehensive view of information about each program across your operation, including actual project costs, forecasts, baselines, and other key performance indicators (KPIs).

> **Portfolio Simulation and What-If Analyses**
> Simulate a variety of scenarios and observe how they affect your budgets, resources, and schedules.

> **Expertise Management**
> Your organization can keep current information about your employees' skills and experience. This helps managers to find the right match of expertise for projects and for hiring purposes, and it also acts as an incentive for your employees to build on their abilities in order to advance their careers.

> **Governance**
> Built-in templates and workflows help you enforce corporate, IT, and other policies throughout your organization in a consistent way.

> **Implementation Methodology Support**
> Manage the differences between your portfolios, regardless of which method or model you use. You can also manage all human and financial resources involved in your various portfolios, either in resource pools or across your enterprise.

SAP RPM helps you execute and track projects and improve your decision making regarding your overall portfolio of projects or programs.

SAP Sales and Operations Planning

Accuracy of sales projections

The *SAP Sales and Operations Planning* (SAP SOP) composite application supports sales and operations to help you get a handle on tasks such as making accurate sales projections and determining the capacity of your production operation. SAP SOP includes the following features:

> **Consolidation of Business Planning**
> Your managers can use this feature to review and keep high-level plans for sales and operations current. In addition, managers can shift business strategies as needed to reflect the sales and operations realities.

> **Data Aggregation**
> People in your company can tap into the most important information about products, marketing, manufacturing, and sales territories. Automated alerts help keep people apprised of variations from your plan.

> **Planning Integration**
> You can use the integration capabilities of SAP NetWeaver along with this composite application to access data from non-SAP applications and combine SAP and non-SAP applications to consolidate planning data such as supply and demand.

> **Milestone and Process Management**
> You can deal with planning for multiple programs, specify task and resource assignments, and track your planning in a way that allows you to easily provide information about your program or project as needed.

> **Generation of Analytical Reports**
> Closely analyze the reports that help everybody stay informed and

observe both trends and the progress that is being made in sales and operations.

You can use the tools in SAP SOP to create a single plan to help drive your sales and operations and share information about key projects with others.

SAP Product Definition

The *SAP Product Definition* composite application tackles product development processes such as developing ideas for new products, defining and designing products, and evaluating new product ideas. This xApp also helps to facilitate collaboration during product design phases. SAP Product Definition enables you to do the following:

> Gather ideas from many people, and then group those ideas into classifications using idea management tools.

> Integrate concept development with market research data from several sources. Perform feasibility assessments with a *stage-gate process* (a process used by many companies that provides a roadmap for product development).

> Adapt to different development requirements thanks to easy-to-configure process templates with a straightforward interface.

> Gather all data on your product into a single, centralized repository, and use that data to draw on historical ideas for inspiration.

In short, SAP Product Definition helps you maximize your good ideas, develop products in a timely way, and make sound decisions about bringing products to market.

New products

SAP Product Definition helps you turn your good ideas into reality

SAP Cost and Quotation Management

The *SAP Cost and Quotation Management* (SAP CQM) composite application helps your business turn quotes into profits. Quoting too low can cost you profits; quoting too high can cost you a job. SAP CQM includes the following features:

Quotes into profits

> **Opportunity Screening**
Qualify incoming requests for quotation (RFQs) based on the type of quote, likelihood of receiving the contract, expected turnaround time, and estimated revenue, profit, and risk.

> **Data Cleansing**
> Match incoming customer part numbers with internal part numbers and supplier numbers.

> **Flexible Cost Assignment**
> Assemble quotes based on a configurable set of cost categories, including material costs, variable costs, assembly costs, and nonrecurring engineering costs.

> **Retrieval of Prices from Multiple Sources**
> Access price information from virtually any application — including data on contracts, purchase orders, supplier quotes, previous quotes, and standard prices — because SAP CQM leverages the SAP NetWeaver platform.

> **Sourcing with Suppliers**
> Get pricing information from your supply chain. SAP CQM considers approved vendor lists for given components, supports offline sourcing, and incorporates incoming supplier quotes.

> **Team Management**
> Support teams collaborating on quotations. You get workflow integration and software support for five key roles: account manager, quote team lead, data manager, quote team member, and reviewer.

> **Attachments Handling and Storage**
> Keep relevant supporting material with your quotation. You can store attachments such as bills of materials, approved vendor part number listings, and design documents.

In short, SAP CQM helps you estimate your internal and external costs so you can generate quotes that can win you profitable business.

SAP Composite Applications for Mobile Business

Cross-industry applications help you connect your global teams easily

Though there are many more composite applications, we'll finish our sampling with a composite application for mobile business, one of the cross-industry applications. With these applications, you can help people who are in different locations connect. SAP composite applications for mobile business include the following:

> **SAP Mobile Sales**
> Enables salespeople on the road to tap into sales opportunities and accelerate the sales cycle.

> **SAP Mobile Service**
> Provides field service engineers with quick access to service orders and customer information and enables managers to coordinate your many field service activities.

> **SAP Mobile Asset Management (SAP MAM)**
> Provides service engineers with access to work orders and information about equipment from various backend applications while on the road.

> **SAP Mobile Time and Travel (SAP MTT)**
> Enables service employees to report their time and expenses offline and then upload them when they return to the office; also improves the timeliness and quality of reporting.

As you can see, SAP composite applications can be used in real-world business settings to provide ready-to-use functionality in a variety of business processes.

Conclusion

In this chapter, we defined composite applications and described how they can benefit your business. We also introduced you to several SAP composite applications that provide pieces of business processes right out of the box. After developing an understanding for how composite applications can help you in your business, you can more closely examine those applications that best meet your needs and requirements.

In Chapter 14, User Friendly SAP — Duet™, Alloy™, and Adobe® Interactive Forms, we'll introduce you to some tools that will help your employees get their work done, including a tool that allows you to use Microsoft Office products in your SAP environment, and integrated SAP Adobe Interactive Forms technology to help you on your way toward that ideal paperless office.

14

User-Friendly SAP —
Duet™, Alloy™, and Adobe®
Interactive Forms

Enterprise computing software is constantly being upgraded with new features, easier-to-use interfaces, and more sophisticated capabilities. Although these features provide a wonderful jumping off point, there are several ways you might want to make many of the tools that SAP offers more accessible to your employees.

For instance, you can encourage employees to use SAP tools and save time and money on training by allowing them to leverage the software programs and functionality to which they're accustomed. That's what Duet and Alloy are all about: providing a way for Microsoft Office and Lotus Notes users to interface with SAP Business Suite functionality from their familiar Office and Notes environments.

In addition, you can replace paper-based forms with HTML-based SAP Interactive Forms software by Adobe, which can be viewed by anybody. SAP Interactive Forms make entering data easier and also allow you to capture form data electronically. Implementing such forms inside or outside of your organization can make your employees' and customers' lives much easier and save you time and money.

Microsoft Office, Lotus Notes, and Adobe Interactive Forms interfacing with SAP Business Suite

Let's begin the review of these three practical tools with an overview of Duet and how it brings familiar interfaces to SAP functionality.

Duet: Providing Information Workers with What They Need

Microsoft and SAP Duet is a joint offering of SAP and Microsoft that can work with many of the SAP applications, including SAP Customer Relationship Management (SAP CRM), SAP ERP 6.0, SAP Supply Chain Management (SAP SCM), and SAP Supplier Relationship Management (SAP SRM). Although Microsoft and SAP have collaborated in various ways over the past 15 years to provide customized solutions to customers and support each other's standards, this is the first time they have jointly created and marketed a product.

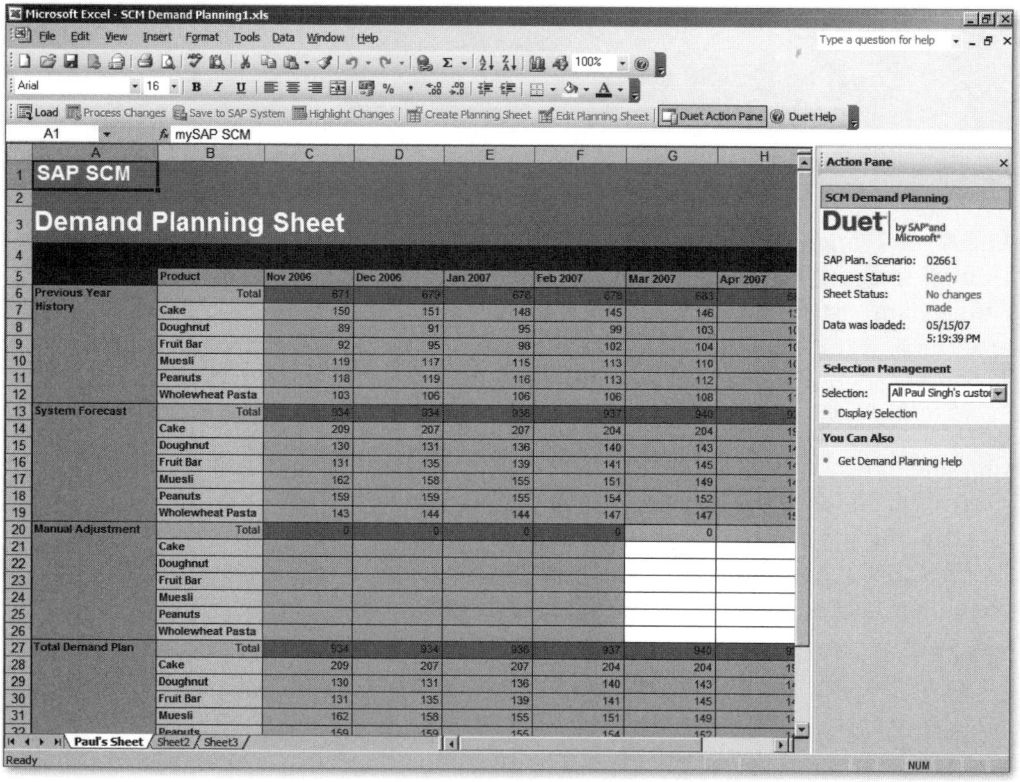

Figure 14.1 Microsoft Office Excel Provides an Interface to SAP Functionality Through Duet

Essentially, Duet allows office workers to take full advantage of SAP business processes and business intelligence through the Microsoft Office environment (see Figure 14.1). Workers can use features such as analytics delivered through Microsoft Excel or scheduling tools via Microsoft Outlook. These functions are synchronized between Microsoft Exchange and SAP.

By allowing workers to use the software they are familiar with, you cut down on training time and help people feel comfortable participating in new enterprise processes that you introduce. As a result, you can increase corporate policy compliance, improve decision making, and save time and money.

Key Functions and Features

The initial release of Duet software includes four scenarios for self-service functionality that you can access through Microsoft Office applications:

Duet scenarios

> Time Management allows you to schedule, record time spent, and review project work and billable hours via Outlook's calendar feature (see Figure 14.2). This data is then automatically updated in the SAP ERP system.

> Budget Monitoring provides access to financial information that you use to create and monitor budgets, as well as alerts for budget variances and postings, transfers of budgets, and posting adjustments. This data can all be integrated with SAP ERP Financials.

> Team Management allows users to update human resource records to which they have access and perform activities such as searching for open positions in the organization or entering management approvals through Outlook.

> Leave Management enables users to submit leave requests with the Outlook calendar that can then be integrated with approval guidelines and HR processes in the SAP system.

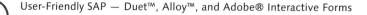
Figure 14.2 Keeping Track of Your Schedule in Outlook

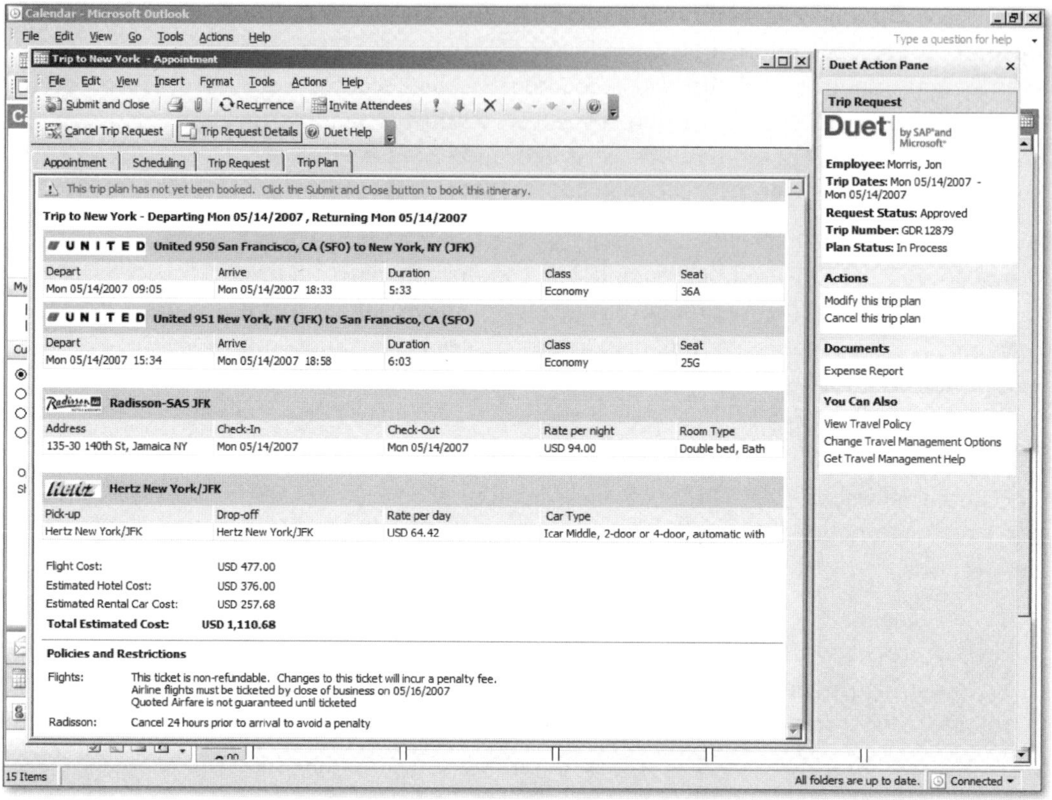

Duet 1.5 scenarios

Additional scenarios were implemented in Duet 1.5 (working with both Office 2003 and Office 2007):

> Travel Management allows employees to make travel arrangements for air, hotel, and car rentals using Outlook, ensuring compliance with company travel policies via SAP.

> Sales Management helps you manage sales activities, including making sales appointments, updating sales contacts, and obtaining pricing approvals through Outlook. You can access sales analytics from SAP CRM as well, and even use Microsoft Word to generate purchase agreements (see Figure 14.3).

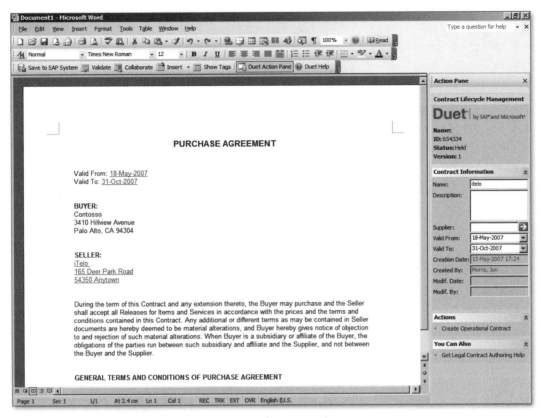

Figure 14.3 Working with Word Documents as Part of Your Everyday Business Processes

> Purchasing Management works through Excel, enabling you to handle purchase order processes and supply chain planning in the familiar spreadsheet interface. Analyze supplier performance data via SAP SRM.

> Reporting and Analytics allows you to request one time only reports and scheduled reports, and look at SAP analytics through Outlook or Excel. SAP BusinessObjects Live Office is a plug-in for the Office environment that allows the user to use the BI client tools inside Excel, Word, PowerPoint, and Outlook for reporting and analytics.

> Demand Planning involves the use of Excel to create planning sheets and analyze demand data you obtain from SAP SCM.

Reporting and Analytics

> ❭ Recruitment Management lets managers and HR staff view open positions, schedule interviews, and provide candidate feedback.

> ❭ Workflow Approval enables managers to approve such things as invoices, new hires, marketing promotions, and merit increases through Outlook.

These business process-focused tasks, which often involve a great deal of data entry and retrieval of data, are a good match for the capabilities of Office applications. Performing these activities in a familiar interface requires little, if any, training. Moreover, the data is automatically integrated with SAP enterprise products, thereby avoiding the need for rekeying and any resulting errors.

How Duet Works

Duet components

So how exactly does Duet work? Essentially, it uses the web services architecture of SAP NetWeaver to allow direct calls from a client to a web service. Microsoft Exchange Server is used to route messages in the Duet system. For the technically minded among you, here are the details of Duet:

> ❭ A client add-on module for the Office environment includes a runtime engine, secure cache storage for data, and an output queue.

> ❭ An SAP add-on for the backend SAP ERP software provides an engine to bundle service requests to SAP Business Suite applications, configuration tools, and a metadata (data about data) repository.

> ❭ The Duet software server enables deployment of Duet and allows communication between the Microsoft and SAP components. This server includes a runtime metadata repository, an element that formats and routes information in the Microsoft Exchange Server, and a module that sends updates to client systems.

This architecture offers several layers of security that come from both Windows and SAP. This security is easy for employees to live with because it's available in a single sign-on (SSO), role-based system. When a user signs on, he is authenticated at the desktop, but Duet then maps the user token to the user profile in SAP. Then, depending on the user's role in the organization, he is granted certain access privileges.

➕ Tip

Duet allows offline web service calls because the client add-on offers secured caching functionality, which stores sets of data to be used both offline and online. That means a worker on the road can access information such as a contact form offline. If a user enters data while offline, it is automatically updated in SAP the next time the user logs on to the system. In addition, for the sake of security and privacy, you can designate sensitive information to only be available through online access.

Configuring Duet is relatively simple. There are several preconfigured templates, such as those for typical employee leave requests. When you install Duet, your administrator can simply choose the types of built-in requests to use for your organization.

Preconfigured templates

Examples of Duet in Action

Imagine Outlook as a window on a wide variety of activities, not just an email tool and a contact database. For example, if you work in a sales organization, your typical day using Duet in the Outlook interface might be something like the following.

You make a morning sales call in a nearby town. In trying to close a big deal with the client, you decide to request approval from your boss to offer special pricing. Within minutes of entering the request as an Outlook task, you get approval.

A typical day with Duet

On the short flight home, you track your time offline. When you get back to the office and log on to the system, your hours are automatically delivered to the SAP system where billable hours are tracked.

Before you go into your sales appointment, you check your contact database through Outlook to be sure you have all of the necessary background information about your customer (i.e., spouse's name, interests, and past order-related issues that help you connect during the sales call).

Back at the office, contract in hand, you request a report on your customer's payment history, which you receive via an email in your inbox. If you want to see more detail, you can drill down through levels of data stored in SAP from within Outlook. You can even export the report to Excel and modify and update it there.

Drilling through levels of data in SAP from Outlook

You spend some time scheduling meetings and appointments for the following week, and they are synchronized. Next, you have to make travel arrangements for next week's sales calls, so you submit travel requests via Outlook. The system automatically suggests itineraries that are in compliance with company travel policies for you to approve. In addition to the tools just outlined, you can use Outlook with Duet to approve employee requests, request and approve leave time, access budget data, authorize bonuses or vacation, and more.

Microsoft isn't the only company that has found synergies with SAP. IBM has also found a way to integrate SAP into its products through a new application called Alloy, which we'll discuss next.

Alloy: Joining SAP and Lotus® Notes®

IBM and SAP

For more than 35 years, SAP and IBM have teamed together to enhance the user experience of their joint clientele. For companies using Lotus Notes, SAP has teamed with IBM to create a new application called Alloy. Alloy, like Duet, allows your employees to continue using the tools they are already familiar with — in this case, Lotus Notes — while providing access to data within the SAP Business Suite (see Figure 14.4). Workers also have greater flexibility to view reports (online and offline), obtain procurement data, and use analytics through the integration of SAP Business Suite information into Lotus Notes. Your workers are more productive because all of the information they need to make an accurate and timely decision is immediately available to them.

Alloy's Key Features

Alloy 1.0 features

The first release of Alloy provides access to the following SAP functions through Lotus Notes:

> Reports Management allows you to personalize, schedule, and access reports from SAP Business Suite applications via Lotus Notes while maintaining data security. Reports can then be shared with and viewed (both online and offline) by coworkers without violating security.

> Leave Management and Travel Management permit you to submit and approve leave and travel requests (see Figure 14.5) through Lotus Notes.

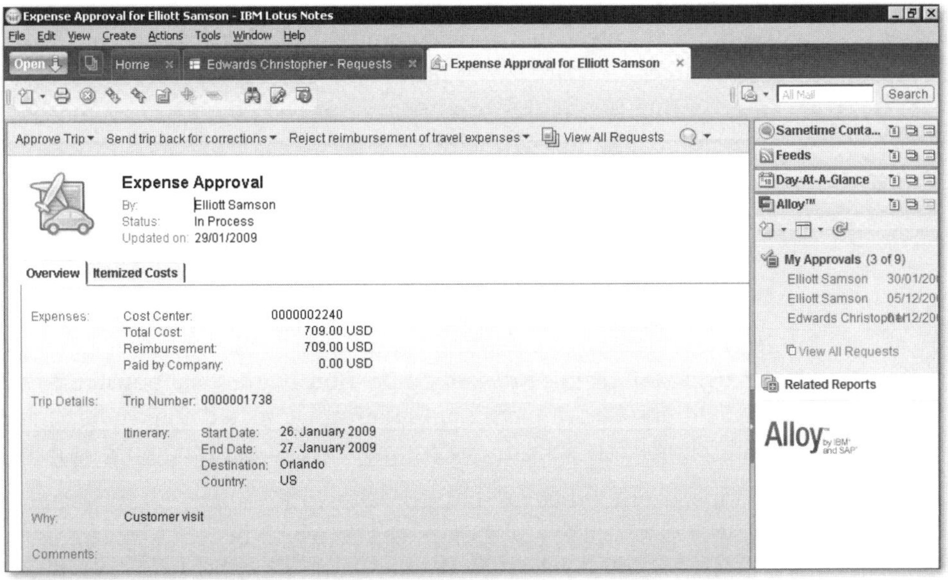

Figure 14.4 Using Lotus Notes to Access SAP Data

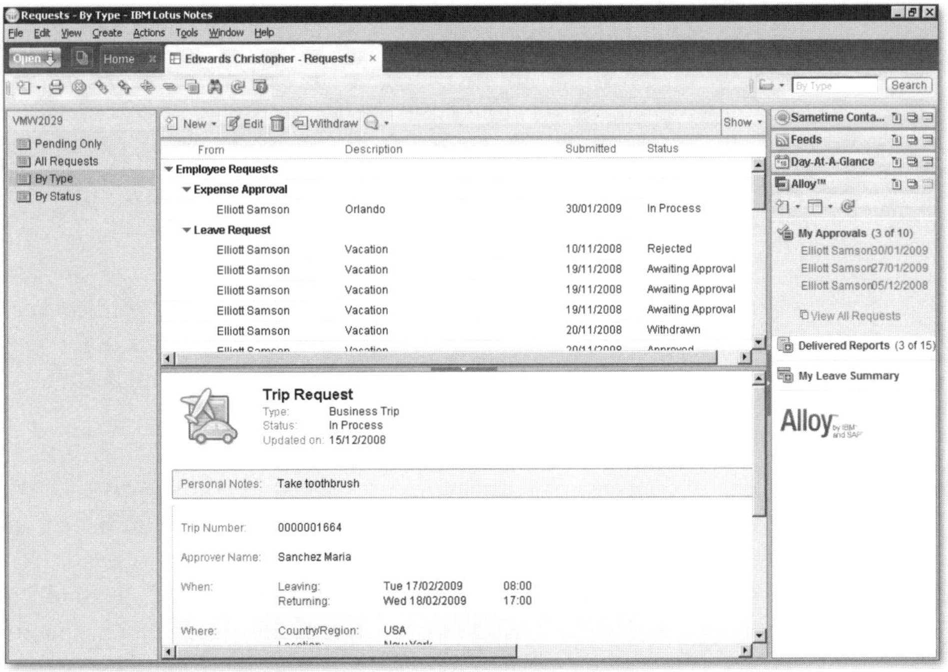

Figure 14.5 Submit and Approve Leave and Travel Requests

Workers can view appropriate contextual information through the Lotus Notes sidebar so that processing leave and travel requests is done within the framework of the approval guidelines established by your company in SAP ERP.

> Workflow Decision Management helps minimize the risks when you're making decisions by bringing your corporate decision steps from other SAP business processes (such as budgeting, recruitment, and purchasing) into the Lotus Notes client.

With Alloy, after you perform transactions or make decisions in Lotus Notes using the features described previously, the data transferred to the SAP enterprise products is automatically updated. This reduces the likelihood of errors introduced by manually re-entering information.

Alloy components

Take a look at the nuts and bolts of Alloy. In essence, Alloy creates a gateway service used to pass messages between the SAP software (e.g., SAP Business Suite or SAP NetWeaver) and the IBM Lotus Domino® server. These messages are passed through the gateway using web services and XML. To initiate this service, SAP and Lotus Domino need the following:

> Client plug-ins that improve performance and flexibility by handling metadata and handle the central Alloy sidebar.

> An SAP Alloy add-on that is deployed on the SAP NetWeaver server to collect and bundle data received from SAP NetWeaver BW and SAP Business Suite. After this information is collected, it is passed to the Lotus Notes client.

> An IBM Lotus Domino Alloy add-on module that likewise collects and bundles data received from Lotus Notes, passes it back to the SAP server, and then hands it off to the SAP Business Suite applications.

What Are the Advantages of Alloy?

Alloy advantages

Because of the type of architecture that is used by Alloy, workers only use a single sign-on (SSO). So when a worker requests information from SAP via Lotus Notes, the Lotus Domino Alloy add-on validates the worker's signature against his profile stored in SAP. If there's a positive validation, the request is passed to the SAP system. This maintains security for your system and data and makes things easier for your employees.

Alloy also supports SAP workflows, which means relevant information from SAP Business Suite applications displays in the Lotus Notes sidebar to give your employees information to make accurate decisions on the spot.

While Alloy comes with a set of standard workflows and reports, it is easy to customize it to reflect the unique processes of your organization. When a manager needs to approve a travel request, for example, the Lotus Notes sidebar can display the current amount of money remaining in the travel budget so he can make the correct decision about the request.

With Alloy and Lotus Notes, if your employees are traveling and working offline, they can view existing SAP reports and make changes. The next time an employee connects to the network, those modifications will automatically be uploaded against the report stored in SAP so that everything stays in sync.

An Everyday Example of Alloy

Let's say late Friday afternoon, one of your employees submits a request to take a trip via the SAP Leave Management application. The next step in the business process requires a manager to evaluate the request and determine whether or not it can be approved.

A typical use of Alloy

It's now Sunday evening, and you decide to get a jump on the work week. When you open your Lotus Notes e-mail, you see the message from your employee requesting vacation time. Because of the Alloy add-ons in SAP and Lotus Domino, the request that was submitted in SAP now appears as a form in your email (see Figure 14.6).

Before you approve this request, you review the relevant information provided in the Lotus Notes sidebar, which includes the department calendar showing the other employees who have requested time off for this same period. In addition, you also see the deadlines for your projects that are coming due during this time. As a final check, you review the summary display of the leave time this employee has already taken and see how much time he has remaining.

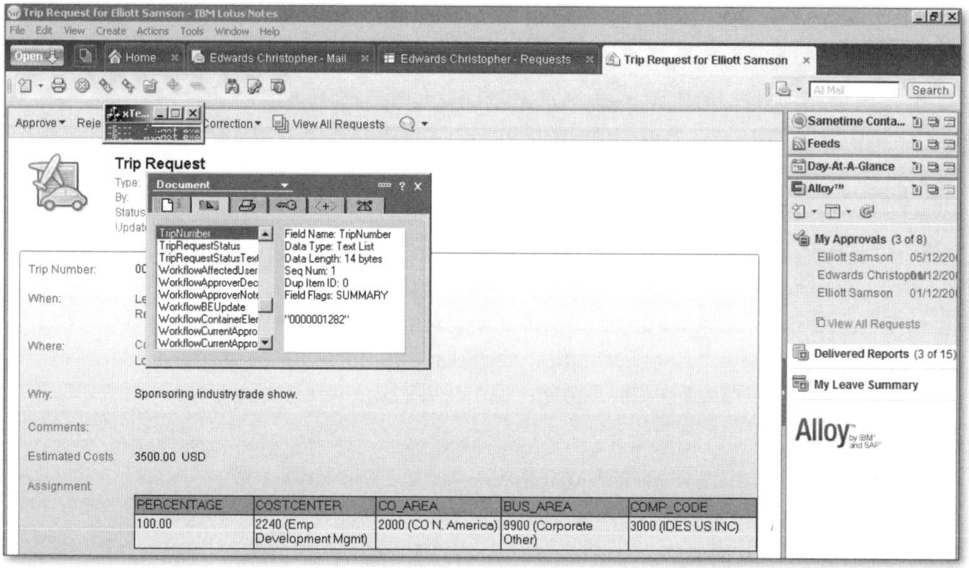

Figure 14.6 Email Notification of Vacation Request via Alloy Add-On in SAP and Lotus Domino

Based on the information provided, you approve the leave request. The approval is then routed back through the Lotus Domino Alloy add-on and the SAP Alloy add-on, where the changes are applied to the SAP Business Suite application, and the request is then submitted to HR as the next step of your business process.

Because you are about to enter a critical phase in one of your projects, you decide to generate a report to show how much time off remains for the people in your department as well as the dates of the upcoming project milestones. Your report displays in Lotus Notes and allows you to drill down through SAP to view all relevant data. This is a great application if you're using Lotus Notes with SAP.

Now let's move on to look at how Adobe's form technology provides another great match with SAP systems by allowing users to enter and share data easily.

The Paperless Office: Adobe Forms

SAP Interactive
Forms software
by Adobe

The office of yesterday was jam packed with paper forms. Perhaps your office today is still groaning under the weight of antiquated forms' processing. With SAP Interactive Forms software by Adobe, you're about to get a lot more efficient, form-wise at least.

The Need to Go Paperless

A 2004 study by GISTICS, an analyst firm specializing in digital asset management, estimated that a single paper-based form costs the average enterprise $75,000 a year in labor and materials. Count up the number of forms used in your organization, and the numbers can become staggering.

When a paper form is used for approvals, there is the ever-present danger that the form will go astray or get lost under piles of paperwork. If the approving manager is on the road, everybody waits until he returns to the office to sign off and get things rolling again.

In addition, paper-based forms require data to be re-entered into systems, opening you up to the possibility of introducing errors and creating extra work for all involved. Paper forms require additional work to centralize, track, access, and audit data. It's almost impossible to extend your business processes to outside partners, customers, and suppliers without further manual processing.

If you have remote or mobile workers, they won't be able to retrieve up-to-date forms or make changes to them if necessary.

 Tip

Think HTML forms are the answer? Think again. HTML forms may allow you to capture data from them, but they can't be used offline, and they're difficult to print.

Streamlining Business Processes

When you implement SAP Interactive Forms, you may not go entirely paperless, but you can become much more efficient in your handling of forms. These are interactive digital forms (see Figure 14.7) that you can actually integrate into the business processes that SAP supports.

The SAP Interactive Forms system creates a bridge between the very structured data that is stored within your enterprise database and the document-based processes you use every day. Data entered into a form by a customer, supplier, or employee can be sent directly to the core databases without further data entry.

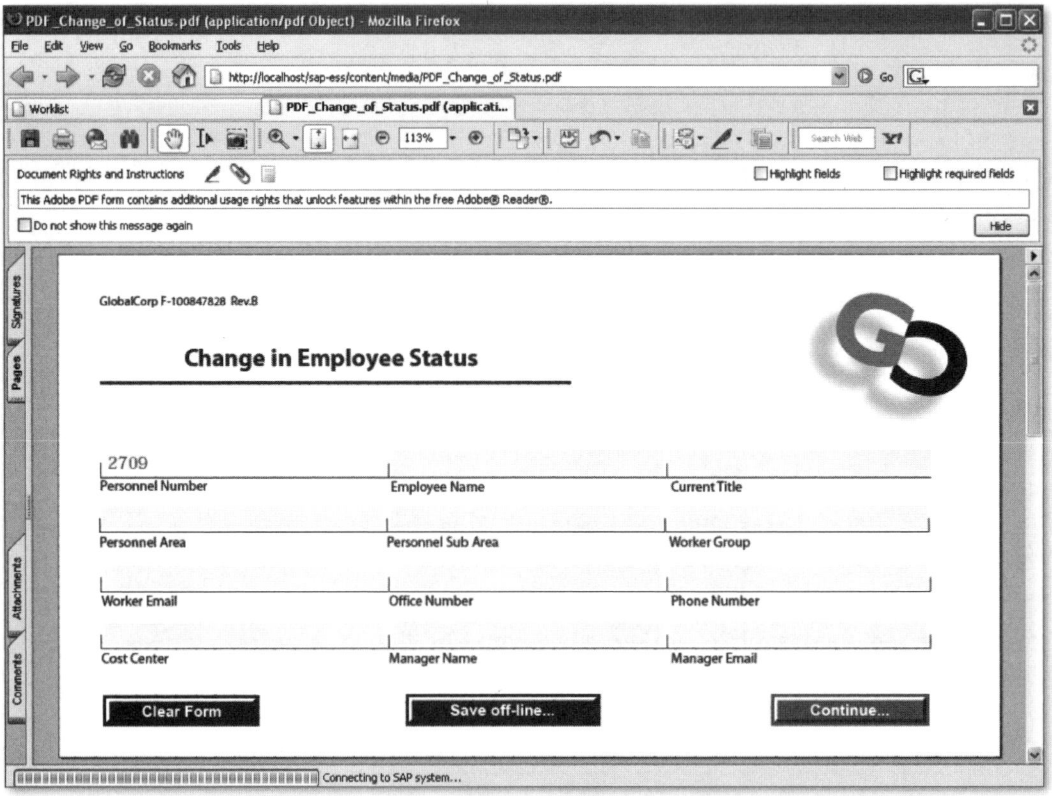

Figure 14.7 An Interactive Form Makes Updating Employee Records Easy

➕ Tip

Forms change on a regular basis, so it's useful that form design and modification is relatively easy. That's because Adobe technology is connected to the SAP NetWeaver development environments for Java and the ABAP programming language.

In the past, if an internal customer placed a larger order, your purchasing clerk may have had to locate a requisition form, complete it, and send it on to another manager for approval. With SAP Interactive Forms, all forms can be requested online, and these forms can already be populated with the requestor's contact and cost center information. SAP's embedded workflow pushes such requests to the approver, ensuring a timely response.

 Tip

> When your workers are on the road, they should have access to forms that connect to your backend system seamlessly. Remote users should be able to upload forms and expect that the home-based systems will update rapidly.
>
> With SAP Interactive Forms, an employee on the road could connect to a system such as SAP CRM, upload forms, and instantly update the backend system. A salesperson could even use a downloaded form on a sales call, complete the form, email it to the home office, and print out a copy for the client to retain as a receipt. If the generation of that form should trigger a next activity in the organization, such as pulling ordered items for shipment, the submission of the form can be set up to act as such a trigger.

Interactive Forms in the Workplace

What will SAP Interactive Forms look like in your workplace? Here are just some of the form processes that can be streamlined:

> Purchase requisitions

> Personnel changes

> Cost center change requests

> Expense reports

> Internal requisitions for products or services

> Job applications

Interactive forms can be prepopulated with common information, including the company contact information or client address and client number, saving time in generating such forms. By linking fields in the forms to SAP applications, you can automatically capture and distribute data, ensuring that your entire system is up to date and accurate.

Forms can be securely sent via email, which is a much more effective way to communicate data than with fax or paper copy distribution. If you have business partners that supply you with data, you can capture

Working with SAP Interactive Forms

that data via forms and even add customer and partner forms into your own business processes. Forms can also be signed with electronic signatures (see Figure 14.8).

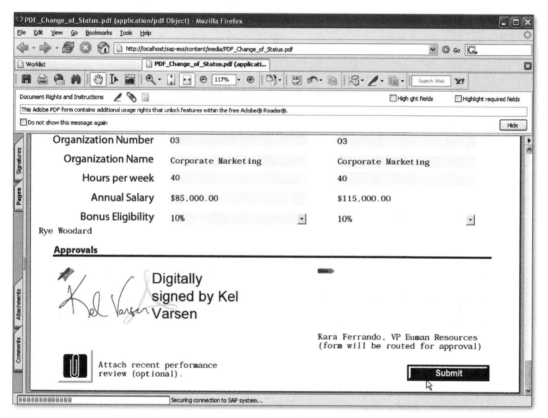

Figure 14.8 Digital Signatures and Attachments to Forms Are an Efficient Way to Communicate

➕ Tip

SAP Interactive Forms supports multiple languages, so if you have an international presence or supplier base, you will find it easy to use these forms for international transactions.

Interactive Forms Extend Outside Your Organization

The concept of using interactive forms does not have to stop at your front door. Imagine if you could use these forms for business processes outside of your organization. Implementing such external business processes reduces costs by eliminating the necessity for rekeying data. Examples include the following:

> A large insurance company can send out an interactive form to a customer to fill out an insurance claim. The form is already prepopulated with customer information, and all the claimant has to do is to fill out the information and send the form back. All information is then electronically stored and forms the basis of the claim.

> Universities are using interactive forms to plan courses. Students can simply mark checkboxes for their chosen subjects. The form can already have some intelligence to ensure that the correct number of study hours is entered. The student then submits the form, and class sizes are updated and appropriate rooms are allocated for the courses.

Interacting outside of your business

These are just two examples of how information can be integrated into business cycles using interactive forms technology.

Conclusion

In this chapter, we explored two joint technologies that SAP has incorporated to make end users' lives simpler:

> Duet represents a joint venture of Microsoft and SAP that seamlessly adds the familiar interfaces of Microsoft Office products into SAP business processes.

> Alloy, like Duet, allows your employees to continue using the tools they are already familiar with — in this case, Lotus Notes — while providing access to data within the SAP Business Suite.

> SAP Interactive Forms software by Adobe produces well designed forms that can be built into your everyday processes to make data entry much more efficient.

Next, in Chapter 15, we'll look at the SAP approach to sustainability.

15 Sustainability

To understand SAP's passion and dedication to sustainability, you need to first understand what sustainability means. One of the most popular definitions comes from the 1987 United Nations Brundtland Commission, which says that sustainability is "meeting the needs of the present without compromising the ability of future generations to meet their own needs." For SAP, this means taking a holistic approach to managing social, economic, and environmental opportunities and risks to achieve profitability, while remaining in compliance and enhancing your reputation. To do this, SAP tries to lead by example by making sustainability an integral part of its own business efforts, while at the same time providing technology solutions through its products that other businesses can use to develop and model their own sustainability programs (see Figure 15.1). In the next section, we'll look at SAP's internal sustainability program and the progress it has made toward achieving its own goals in this area.

Definition of sustainability

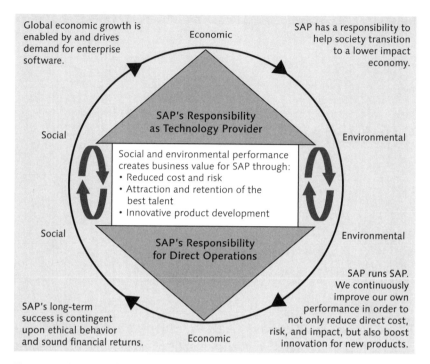

Global economic growth is enabled by and drives demand for enterprise software.

Economic

SAP has a responsibility to help society transition to a lower impact economy.

SAP's Responsibility as Technology Provider

Social

Environmental

Social and environmental performance creates business value for SAP through:
- Reduced cost and risk
- Attraction and retention of the best talent
- Innovative product development

Social

Environmental

SAP's Responsibility for Direct Operations

SAP's long-term success is contingent upon ethical behavior and sound financial returns.

Economic

SAP runs SAP. We continuously improve our own performance in order to not only reduce direct cost, risk, and impact, but also boost innovation for new products.

Figure 15.1 SAP's Dual Responsibility

SAP's Dedication to Sustainability

SAP's commitment and focus on sustainability

To prove its commitment to sustainability, SAP has created an in-house cross-functional organization dedicated to all activities surrounding sustainability. This group is responsible for coordinating both SAP's own sustainability program and helping customers develop their own.

SAP has set goals for itself in three areas: carbon reduction targets, focused social engagements, and corporate governance initiatives.

> **Carbon reduction targets**
  After conducting a self-analysis of its own carbon emissions, SAP is lowering its carbon footprint by reducing company car fuel consumption, hosting more virtual events to reduce business travel, and working toward more energy-efficient designs in its buildings.

> **Focused social engagements**
> SAP works with its partners to help some of the world's poorest people become self-sufficient. By collaborating, local farmers and tradesmen can be included in small supply chain networks and thereby help raise their standard of living.

> **Corporate governance initiatives**
> Being responsible and promoting integrity are ways to keep SAP a sustainable organization. Efforts in this area include being proactive in risk and compliance programs, having employees follow a strict code of ethics when conducting business transactions, and participating in organizations to help promote global sustainability.

To demonstrate its progress toward achieving these goals, SAP released its 2008 Sustainability Report, which we'll examine in the next section.

2008 Sustainability Report

Because of SAP's commitment to sustainability, it has examined numerous social, economic, and environmental trends to determine how it can best meet its dual responsibilities for improving its own environment and that of its customers.

2008 Sustainability Report

One of the first things SAP researched was climate change. Reduction of greenhouse gas emissions is a top priority because of increasing regulation. Several countries already require certain industries to disclose their greenhouse emissions levels. By containing emissions levels and managing energy costs, SAP can realize true cost savings.

Producing green, low-carbon products is seen as a competitive business differentiator for SAP. Increased awareness of hazards to the environment has consumers putting more pressure on companies to find ways of lessening their impact on the environment and creating more environmentally friendly solutions in their products and services. SAP realizes its reputation is at stake and is embracing the challenge by ensuring its customer products require lower energy to run, thereby helping to reduce the technology carbon footprint.

Examining climate change

SAP's internal goals in this area include reducing its own greenhouse gas emissions to its 2000 level by 2020. This will come as a result of reducing business flights, using more energy-efficient buildings, reducing electrical consumption, reducing company car fuel consumption, and reducing paper usage through double-sided printing, reduced packaging, and other initiatives.

Social sustainability The next area of focus for SAP is determining how to incorporate areas of society that are currently excluded into the market system. Because many of the world's poorest areas lack infrastructure, money, educated people, and stable governments, they cannot take part in today's global economy and advances in technology. These factors also restrict those businesses looking to expand their markets in these areas. This leads to less social sustainability and stability.

SAP's goals in promoting social sustainability include getting private industry to focus on poor areas and working to develop small business networks. To achieve this, SAP will help educate the people and provide access to technology and finances to help fledgling businesses. In addition, as these businesses continue to grow, regulatory and environmental considerations must be integrated and imposed. When business growth begins in these areas, additional investment by others, including foreign investment, will follow.

The third priority for SAP is its people. SAP's efforts to promote sustainability can only work if it hires, trains, and develops the people within its organization and ecosystem of partners. Innovation comes from people, so having the right mixture and diversity of people on the SAP team provides the creativity and resourcefulness needed to sustain growth and productivity even in turbulent economic times.

The last focus area for SAP is accountability. SAP remains committed to providing a sustainable organization for its shareholders, employees, and outside groups who have a vested interest in SAP. Through governance and reporting, SAP continues to share its progress in reaching its sustainability goals with all parties. Although bribery and corruption in business are normal in some parts of the world, SAP continues to operate ethically and prohibits the use of unethical practices by its people.

Participation in organizations focused on sustainability These represent SAP's key focal points for its sustainability drive. SAP will continue to issue updates on its internal progress in these areas by following the Sustainability Reporting Guidelines (G3) of the Global Reporting Initiative, and continue its participation in the following organizations to help understand and improve its sustainability program:

> 3C-Combat Climate Change
> AccountAbility
> Business for Social Responsibility
> CSR Europe
> econsense (lab on demographic change)
> International Business Leaders Forum
> International Chamber of Commerce
> Global Reporting Initiative (organizational stakeholder)
> Transparency International (member of the Transparency International Business Principles Steering Group)
> UN Global Compact (10th Principle Advisory Committee, Caring for Climate)

Now we'll look at how SAP stays on track for its sustainability goals.

SAP Sustainability Map

SAP has created a sustainability roadmap for not only itself and its partners to follow but also for its customers (see Figure 15.2).

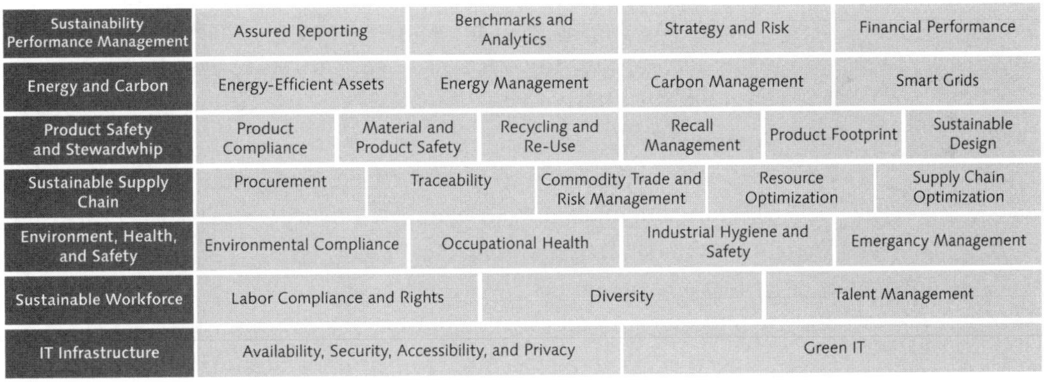

Sustainability Performance Management	Assured Reporting	Benchmarks and Analytics		Strategy and Risk	Financial Performance
Energy and Carbon	Energy-Efficient Assets	Energy Management		Carbon Management	Smart Grids
Product Safety and Stewardwhip	Product Compliance	Material and Product Safety	Recycling and Re-Use	Recall Management	Product Footprint	Sustainable Design
Sustainable Supply Chain	Procurement	Traceability	Commodity Trade and Risk Management	Resource Optimization	Supply Chain Optimization
Environment, Health, and Safety	Environmental Compliance	Occupational Health		Industrial Hygiene and Safety	Emergancy Management
Sustainable Workforce	Labor Compliance and Rights	Diversity		Talent Management	
IT Infrastructure	Availability, Security, Accessibility, and Privacy			Green IT	

Figure 15.2 SAP Sustainability Map

> **Sustainability Performance Management**
> These tools provide a model for taking action on sustainability and reducing the associated risks, as well as providing tools for benchmarking and reporting your results while reducing the time and costs associated with these efforts.

287

> **Energy and Carbon**
>
> With these tools, your company gains insight into its energy usage and carbon footprint. You then learn the best mix of energy sources for your organization, ways to effectively reduce energy costs during the production process, and how to accurately budget for your energy costs.

> **Product Safety and Stewardship**
>
> These functions help protect your company with an integrated set of product material, safety, and compliance reporting tools. Product Safety and Stewardship features help protect product loyalty while minimizing the risks of adverse events affecting product safety.

> **Sustainable Supply Chain**
>
> This is the key to making your organization sustainable. These tools help you examine every facet of your supply chain so that you can find suppliers that adhere to energy conservation and social sustainability practices. Optimize the design of your supply chain and transportation processes to accurately track your supplies and materials and monitor your energy consumption.

> **Environment, Health, & Safety**
>
> Tools to ensure your compliance with industrial hygiene, environmental, safety, and health standards and practices. In addition to compliance tools, this area also has features for regulatory reporting requirements.

> **Sustainable Workforce**
>
> To succeed, you need to have the best workforce. These tools help you hire and manage your people to ensure you have the best group to meet your long-term business goals.

> **IT Infrastructure**
>
> In addition to your people, another one of your organization's best assets is its IT infrastructure. To maintain sustainability, your organization must be able to provide the data your people need, at the time they need it, and in the manner they need it. IT tools that protect your data are agile, energy-efficient, and a necessity in today's business environment. SAP's IT infrastructure tools guide you in meeting these needs.

How Sustainability Improves Profitability

Companies today do not exist in a vacuum but instead are intertwined with other companies, industries, societies, and the environment. For example, what happens in the oil industry can have an impact on the transportation aspect of your supply chain, as well as consumers' abilities to purchase your products. Couple that with stark reports about environmental trends such as global warming and economic volatility, and you find you need help just to keep track of everything. Corporate goals now must focus on being responsible through ethical conduct, reducing their impact and footprint on the environment, and adhering to compliance and regulatory reporting.

To do this, organizations need to make sustainability an integral part of their corporate culture. This begins by a review of your end-to-end processes and by setting targets for sustainability, such as reducing fuel consumption and carbon emissions. The targets you select are the ones that, over time, have the most financial impact on your company. Next, you need to develop policies and procedures on sustainability. Employees, suppliers, and other third-party vendors with whom you deal must understand their role in supporting and adhering to these measures.

Tracking and reporting on your progress are key elements to ensuring that sustainability is working in your company. Because SAP's products can pull data from all sources, both within SAP applications and other non-SAP applications, you can merge financial data from these sources to get a complete picture of how sustainability projects are working in your organization. SAP's Xcelsius software (see Chapter 12, SAP BusinessObjects Solutions, for more details) provides dashboards for visual representation of key metrics and allows you to perform what-if scenarios as conditions change, so you can understand and measure your sustainability ROI. These and other tools within SAP help you form your strategy for managing your sustainability objectives throughout your organization.

Through careful monitoring and tracking of your sustainability progress, you'll find your organization becoming more profitable through cost and energy savings. Your consumers will also help protect your brand loyalty and reputation as your sustainability efforts help differentiate you from your competition, thus making your company more profitable.

Taking Advantage of Industry-Specific Solutions

As we've mentioned, there is increasing pressure for companies to report on their sustainability projects. Consumers and governments worldwide want to see results and proof to ensure you are in compliance. The following items help you manage risks and search out new opportunities to keep you profitable while meeting the demands of global regulation and compliance.

> **SAP Environment, Health, and Safety Management**
> These functions help you reduce the cost of compliance, loss of loyalty, and loss of company reputation. With these tools, you can track new regulations and compliance reporting needs as well as employee and product safety within your organization.

> **Ensure transparency**
> The way to achieve your sustainability goals is by having *transparency*, which means having insight and visibility into your entire organization's operations. With transparency, you have the information you need to make better decisions; eliminate waste, inefficiencies, and unnecessary costs; and remain accountable to your stakeholders.

> **Improving compliance**
> By following SAP's sustainability roadmap and having a transparent organization, you are better able to recognize and react to risks before they turn into problems, which reduces the cost of compliance. This also means including compliance controls and reporting throughout your production and quality processes and throughout your supply chain.

> **Energy and natural resource efficiency**
> As energy and natural resources become more scarce and expensive, it is important for you to take control of how they are being used throughout your organization. In collaboration with its partners, SAP is working on solutions that let companies select more energy-efficient hardware setups and efficient software applications that use virtualization to reduce the amount of computing resources.

Next we'll see how one organization used sustainability practices to increase profitability.

Sustainability Case Study

Table 15.1 introduces you to a case study for a large global provider of technologies for the specialty materials industry. The company needed to report and comply with REACH (Registration, Evaluation, Authorization, and Restriction of Chemicals) regulations that require registration of safety information about the chemical substances they manufacture or import within the European Union.

Company	Global provider of technologies for the specialty materials industry.
Existing Solutions	SAP ERP combined with manual processes to obtain required data and create required reports
Challenge	To establish a global approach to REACH compliance, to improve visibility into inbound and outbound chemical movements, to eliminate manual compliance processes, to provide data to drive market decisions, and to minimize registration costs
SAP Solutions	SAP Environmental, Health, and Safety Management application offered substance volume tracking and the visibility needed. This application also integrated with existing Materials Management functionality and product component data.
Benefits	Elimination of manual compliance processes while creating a global structure for compliance reporting, improvement of the accuracy and quality of compositional data, and well-informed product decisions that still protect increased European revenue

Table 15.1 Sustainability Case Study

The company was facing the challenges of compliance reporting for a complex set of regulations enacted in Europe. Many of its reporting processes were manual and required obtaining data from multiple sources. Working with SAP because of its strong leadership in the chemical industry, the company integrated the SAP Environmental, Health, and Safety Management application to automate manual processes and pull data into a single source. The effort was pilot tested at a plant in a region with fewer regulations and then fully implemented into the company's other plants. The implementation of the SAP Environmental, Health, and Safety Management application provided the just-in-time tracking and analysis the company needed to improve its product portfolio decision making and to better position itself for long-term compliance with global regulations.

Conclusion

In this chapter, you've seen how SAP has made a long-term commitment to sustainability not only within its own organization but also in the products and services it provides to its customers. SAP's focus on social, economic, and environmental solutions will help your organization consume fewer natural resources, reduce your carbon footprint, and provide a measure of differentiation from your competition while remaining profitable.

In the next chapter, we'll examine SAP's productivity tools to help you and your employees better manage data.

User Productivity Tools for Information Workers

The interface and tools that an SAP solution presents to your employees and managers are very important parts of its usefulness. In this chapter, we'll explore SAP's easy-to-use interface, combined with access to data and analytics offered by portals and roles. In addition, we'll look at another powerful feature, the ability for employees and managers to use self-service workspaces to get work done based on their roles. Because SAP NetWeaver enables these technologies, they are available to many of SAP's applications to help boost your productivity. Lastly, we'll show you how access to data from mobile devices opens up opportunities for employees regardless of where they are.

Portals and Roles

A portal is like a technology dashboard that IT can customize to contain certain pieces and that employees can personalize to access the centrally stored data they need — whether analytics, order status information, or customer records (for example). Depending on the role a person plays in your organization, he will be given access to a certain set of data.

Read Chapter 18 for more about SAP NetWeaver

Understanding Portals

Portals are essentially based on the technology used in web browsers, and they offer an interface you can use to access and view information from different data sources. Instead of logging on to a variety of systems or opening several pieces of software, an employee can use a portal to get to all of the information he needs. Workers can also drill down through deeper and deeper levels of information, depending on the level of detail they need.

Beyond just receiving data When you put a portal together with the functionality of SAP applications such as SAP ERP, you can go beyond having employees simply receive data. They can use features of those applications to publish documents to team sites for collaboration, track project progress, and even perform searches that tap into several systems at one time to get results (see Figure 16.1).

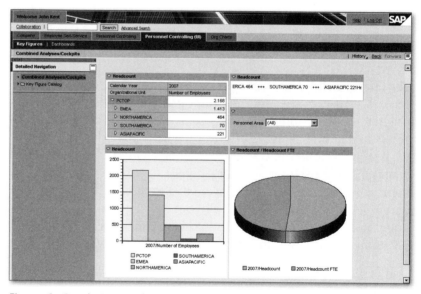

Figure 16.1 Portals Give Workers All of the Tools and Data They Need in One Location

Portals can even connect employees with systems outside of your walls, such as your business partners' or vendors' systems. This allows your partners to have access to up-to-the-minute information they can use to service your company's requirements (e.g., replenishing inventory of a component) and provides you and your partners with an environment for collaboration on various projects or initiatives.

Lastly, portals can provide a window to the functionality of software your employees are already comfortable with, such as Microsoft Outlook for email and scheduling, right from within a single interface.

Portals, which are spaces where data is collected in one place, are one part of the story. The other part is how you can customize and personalize which information goes to whom. For that, you need to understand how roles work and the way that portals are connected to underlying information and functionality in your system.

Understanding iViews

With SAP NetWeaver Portal, your IT employees can build and customize portals using templates, along with HTML code and elements called *iViews*. These iViews are small applications that help connect the portal to the underlying data and applications in your system.

SAP offers thousands of iViews that relate to industry segments such as aerospace or banking. iViews are the pieces that users can move around to personalize their own portals. You can think of these iViews as small boxes of predesigned content, which you can slot into a portal interface. In some cases, one iView will call on another iView to provide related or more detailed content using a process called *eventing*. When you click on content in one iView, you initiate an event that might, for example, call on another iView to provide the backup data for the chart that you were just viewing.

Thousands of iViews

> ➕ **Tip**
>
> Implementing portals doesn't require that you dispose of your legacy programs. Portals can provide a view into a wide variety of systems and applications.

Assigning Roles

Whether you work in a small or large company, each employee probably has a role. One person might work in the human resources department and need access to employee salary and benefits information; and another person who supervises the shop floor has no business accessing employee salary information but absolutely must have information about materials inventory and sales orders at his fingertips.

By assigning a role to an employee, such as HR or production, you can also assign a set of accesses to data that an individual needs to get his job done. An HR professional might have access to personnel records, for example, while a manufacturing person might have access to customer orders or inventory levels. In an SAP system, those roles can be set up and modified to accommodate changes in position or responsibilities.

The ability for IT to customize and for employees to personalize portals helps you make each worker and manager more productive. Role-based capabilities are currently available in SAP ERP Human Capital Management (HCM), SAP ERP Operations, and SAP ERP Financials.

 Tip

> SAP offers portal templates to get you started. These templates are based on typical business processes such as sales. They give you a head start to personalizing templates for the various people in your company.

Tip

> An IT person assigns a role to a worker and provides certain access privileges. Based on that role, an employee can, to a certain extent, personalize his own portals by selecting from a set of options. An assistant in the accounting department can choose the data and tools he needs, as can the CFO, based on his job in the enterprise. Just as you might personalize your ISP's home page by adding the weather report, your horoscope, and sports scores, you can personalize a portal to display different types of information and functionality from a single page.

Customizable portals

For example, an employee in the marketing department might place a marketing project folder, instant messaging, a blog, and an email contact list on his page, along with reports on customer satisfaction and news stories about your product line. The ability of individuals to customize their portals frees up IT people from having to tweak these settings.

Guided procedures

A *guided procedure* is a user-interface component that represents a step-by-step process that a user follows to complete a process. Each step in the guided procedure might impact a different application. IT organizations can use guided procedures that help employees work through the steps of a typical business process, much as a wizard in a typical software program prompts you to move through the steps of setting up a new piece of hardware or changing browser settings.

Now let's see how portals are built and why they're so flexible.

How SAP NetWeaver Supports Portals

SAP NetWeaver is the platform that runs SAP and non-SAP applications, data, and user interfaces, including portals. In the area of portals, it provides several essential elements.

First, SAP NetWeaver contains the repository of enterprise services. As you saw in Chapter 2, The SAP Approach to Enterprise Software, (and will learn more about in Chapter 17, Service-Oriented Architecture), enterprise services allow an SAP application to call on just the functions it needs, rather than an entire application because they break business processes down into bite-sized chunks.

Enterprise services

Next, the the SAP NetWeaver Developer Studio (NWDS) tool and Portal Development Kit (PDK) can be used to design and deploy portal applications. During the design phase, you can use predefined, packaged portal content to expedite your portal implementation. This business content consists of iViews bundled into hundreds of role-specific business packages based on solutions from SAP.

The SAP NetWeaver Portal component provides functionality that allows you to manage the portal infrastructure. The portal also provides collaboration features, such as personal and team workspaces, Wikis, and discussion forums. Finally, the portal supports knowledge management functions, enabling users to find, organize, and access unstructured content stored in SAP and non-SAP data stores.

Wiki: A Web application that allows multiple authors to add, delete, and edit online content

The SAP NetWeaver Portal component is tightly integrated with other functionality in SAP NetWeaver, including SAP NetWeaver Business Warehouse (SAP NetWeaver BW) and SAP NetWeaver Master Data Management (SAP NetWeaver MDM). These components consolidate and harmonize data to deliver information and analytics through portals that users can work with in their daily tasks.

SAP NetWeaver Portal

> **Tip**
>
> The SAP NetWeaver Process Integration component (SAP NetWeaver PI) is the tool that helps you exchange data between SAP and non-SAP applications. With SAP NetWeaver PI, you can take XML data and convert it into an iView.

Within portals, you can build self-service functionality that enables employees to handle common business processes themselves to save time. The next section looks at collaborative tools and self-service.

Collaborative Tools

To help you improve productivity in your enterprise, SAP makes several useful collaboration tools available. Let's review these in the upcoming subsections.

Workspaces

Workspaces (previously called *collaboration rooms*) are essentially portals where people working on the same project inside and outside of your company can share data and communicate. Workspaces come in two types: personal and team. Each type can include calendars and schedules, lists of tasks, areas for discussions and chats, and even the sharing of applications.

SAP E-Recruiting

Additional collaborative features — either built into SAP NetWeaver or available through SAP applications — include the ability to check others' calendars and schedule them for meetings, instant messaging features, shared folders, and broadcasting report views to others via SAP NetWeaver BW. One great example of collaborative features is SAP E-Recruiting, where a hiring manager and an HR professional can collaborate on the hiring process for a position or positions.

Discussion Forums and Wikis

SAP NetWeaver Portal also enables organizations to set up discussion forums and Wikis. These collaborative tools help users publish information and collaborate quickly in decision and documentation processes. Discussion forums allow people to share ideas about various topics and participate in group decision making. Wiki pages allow many users to reach consensus on definitions on projects, plans, and other key information. Simple, web-based user interfaces reduce learning time and make it easy to work with people securely both inside and outside of your organization.

Collaborative features such as workspaces and Wikis are wonderful, but what about the employees who practically live on the road? For them, mobile productivity helps them get work done and stay in touch.

Self-Service

There was a time in the business world when managers would dictate information to secretaries who would then type that information into a document. It took two people and sometimes a few drafts to get a simple memo written, approved, signed, and sent out. Not that long ago, this model changed and managers began to type their own memos and letters into computers, cutting out the middle-person and saving money and time.

Self-service workspaces

A self-service workspace is a similar concept; it provides users with role-based access to applications and information required to perform certain tasks. Why should you have to play phone tag or email tag with somebody in a travel department to book your trip when you could just fill out an online form, pick your flights and hotel, and be done with it? SAP provides self-service capabilities that enable both employees and managers to streamline several areas of functionality.

➕ **Tip**

There are two types of self-service applications: employee self-service (ESS) and manager self-service (MSS).

Employee Self-Service Workspaces

Via portals, employees can take advantage of several self-service activities (see Figure 16.2). Doing so saves duplication of effort and the errors that sometimes result from duplication of data entry. Once entered, those who deal with the data (e.g., travel expense analysts or company travel agents) can access the data in centralized databases.

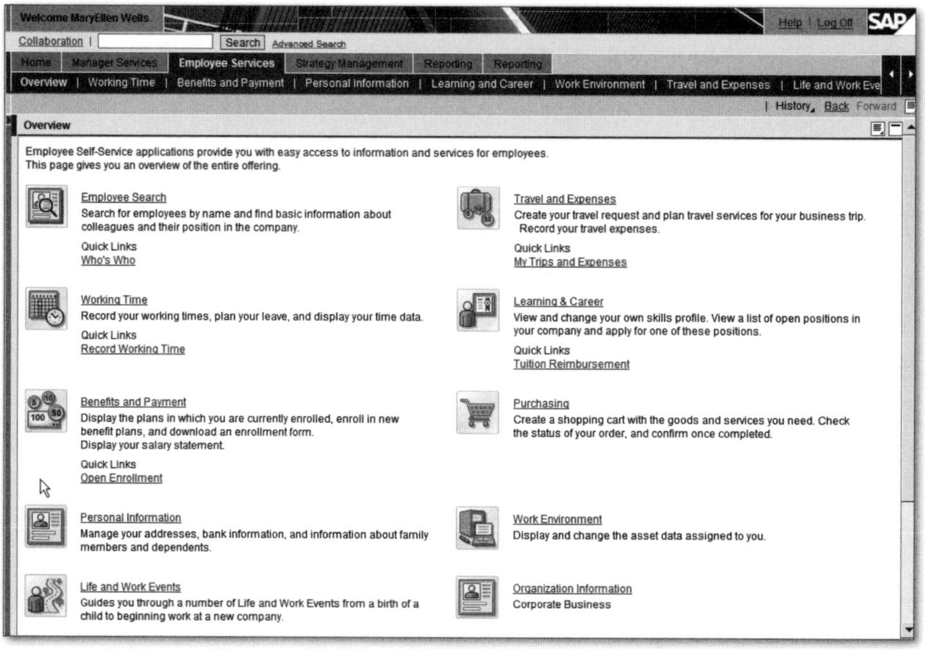

Figure 16.2 Various Activities in an Employee Self-Service Workspace

Areas of ESS include the following:

> **Personal Information Management**
> Employees can access their personal information in HR databases and make changes to data such as home address or emergency contact.

> **Business Travel and Expense Management**
> Employees can set up business travel and record travel expenses.

> **Time Management**
> Employees working on projects or on an hourly basis can report the hours they've worked, request leave, and review their working schedules.

> **Corporate Learning**
> Employees can access training schedules, get manager approval, and sign up for classes.

> **Corporate Information Management**
> Employees have access to general corporate information such as security policies and the employee handbook.

> **Benefits Management**
> Employees can enroll in benefits programs and view current benefits participation.

> **Life and Work Event Management**
> Employees can update data on life event changes, such as marital status or the birth of a child, and view their employment history.

> **Payment Administration**
> Employees can deal with various salary and compensation issues.

> **Internal Opportunities**
> Employees can review job openings, submit applications, and check on the hiring status.

Who can use ESS and MSS?

> **Procurement**
> Employees can buy products or services, or request maintenance or repair for equipment using self-service.

ESS can be used by just about everybody in your company. MSS, on the other hand, is uniquely suited to those who wear the manager hat.

 Tip

A specialized self-service workspace is called a *work center*. Work centers allow employees to create portals that are focused on certain types of work, for example, by business unit or a group such as Manufacturing or HR. Rather than adding this work-specific content to the employee's main portal interface (which typically includes the employees' schedule, commonly used applications, and analytics related to the overall job), you can create work centers.

SAP Work centers

For example, a manufacturing manager might include his schedule, contacts, and analytics about manufacturing productivity on the portal he opens every morning, but he might call up a management work center where he accesses all job performance information, staffing projections, employee vacation schedules, salary information, and so on when working on employee-related issues.

Manager Self-Service Workspaces

Managers will be on the receiving end of some ESS requests, specifically those that require approvals such as leave requests, training approvals, or purchasing requests. In addition, there are some manager-specific self-services that help to streamline any manager's job, including the following:

Access analytics

> **Budget**
Budget planning and monitoring features help managers get their numbers in line. Managers can access analytics that help them keep track of variances and make corrections to posted budget numbers.

Tools for compensation planning

> **Staffing**
Recruitment and staff review procedures are two HR-related self-service features. Managers can use tools for compensation planning, viewing attendance records, and handling future staffing planning (see Figure 16.3).

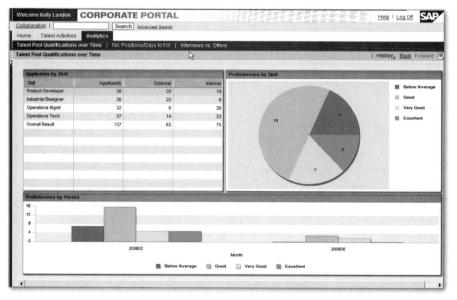

Figure 16.3 Tools for Planning Future Headcount Help Managers with Staffing

➕ Tip

With SAP ERP, you can create a personnel record for each employee with all of the relevant details such as compensation, attendance history, vacation time available, and so on. You can make one set of data available to managers, and another set available to the employee, depending on their need to know.

In addition to self-service workspaces, SAP provides tools that enable collaboration to make people more productive, which we'll examine in the next section.

Mobile Productivity

Mobile computing is essential in a business world, where we rush from appointment to appointment, from one office to another — often in different countries. Staying in touch and being able to tap into your corporate home base has become imperative.

The SAP NetWeaver Mobile component provides an infrastructure that allows people on the move to use links from their mobile devices to SAP core systems. You install SAP NetWeaver Mobile on each mobile device, and then, when used with SAP mobile applications, you can access many of SAP Business Suite's features from mobile devices. IT can work with users to customize a mobile setup that works for their needs.

Mobile devices can use local business logic to process actions, such as entering an order, without having to access the home system. In locations where wireless or dial-up access isn't available, this means that workers can still do their jobs on the road.

Then, back at the office, mobile users can synchronize their devices with the core system to ensure that data is kept current, orders are processed, and other transactions such as generating invoices or customer confirmations are initiated.

Mobile devices

Finally, by using the voice-recognition capabilities built into SAP NetWeaver, workers can use cell phones to submit or request data, or initiate transactions they used to have to handle back at their desks.

Voice recognition

 Tip

Synchronization of SAP NetWeaver Mobile provides a secure encrypted transmission by using the HTTPS protocol that ensures wireless connections are safe for your sensitive data. In addition, role-based authentication, authentication using passwords, and integrity protection keep your office systems safe from outside attacks via mobile devices.

You can use a standard browser for mobile access, or you can customize a user interface via which your mobile workers can access your systems.

 Tip

> If your company has to maintain and repair mobile assets, such as a vehicle fleet or utility stations, you may want to look into SAP Service and Asset Management. Workers in the field can use its features, along with SAP NetWeaver Mobile and SAP Mobile Asset Management (SAP MAM), to deal with asset installation, maintenance, or repair out on the road, and track their activities back to your main system. You can even track maintenance activities based on counter readings (such as an electric meter reading at various locations) and schedule future maintenance.

Conclusion

In this chapter, we've provided you with an overview of some very useful tools to make your workers more productive:

> Portals with role-based access for delivering information to and sharing information with users

> Collaborative tools such as forums and Wikis

> Self-service workspaces that allow people to access many common business processes such as scheduling training for themselves

> Tools for mobile productivity to keep workers in touch with information while on the road.

Now that you understand the useful tools that an SAP system can offer your workers, we're going to delve a bit deeper into the architecture and technology behind the tools.

In Part IV, Technology Overview, beginning with Chapter 17, we'll look at the details of service-oriented architecture (SOA), and then in Chapter 18, we'll discuss SAP NetWeaver, the technology platform on which most of SAP's offerings rest.

PART IV
Technology Overview

17

Service-Oriented Architecture

Not so many years ago, we used computer functionality from software that was installed on computers. *Web services*, also referred to as simply *services*, have introduced a very different way of interacting with technology. Rather than buying one program with a set of predefined functions, services offer flexibility that allows you to pick and choose functionality, and tailor it according to the way your enterprise does business. Services have become the way that enterprises can meet information requirements and other challenges by making it easier to respond to change and modifying and building new solutions quickly and easily.

Enterprise Computing Challenges

Today the kind of quick-change act that services support is simply not possible. Many companies have accumulated a variety of applications and support systems across their enterprise. IT people have had to integrate these systems by jury-rigging connections between these applications and systems using code generated with various programming languages. Trying to make changes quickly often proves difficult, if not impossible. When changes need to be made to an application, it can be costly because of the time that programmers have to invest to write code and the downtime for the application while it's being updated.

Moving from an application-oriented environment

In this application-oriented environment, employees often have to open several different applications to complete a typical business process. If, for example, you want to place an order for a product, you have to send a confirmation to the customer, place the order in your production system, and adjust the current inventory in yet another system. These processes may span several applications and systems in your organization and multiple layers of data entry. What's needed is a way to bridge the various systems and applications in your organization to build complete, enterprise-wide business processes.

Understanding Web Services

Build and customize business functions

For a long time, enterprise technology was based on enterprise applications (software) and the ability to customize these applications to your business by writing proprietary custom code or changing proprietary configuration tables. Over time, as enterprise applications sought to bridge functions in various departments in enterprises, and even reach out to third-party vendors or customers, that custom approach became rather convoluted. Web services can make building and customizing business functions considerably much easier.

What Is a Web Service?

The idea of services grew out of the Internet. If you think about it, the Internet doesn't use discrete kinds of software such as word processors and spreadsheet programs to open documents. Instead, it uses a browser to help a user navigate and pick and choose among all of the information and websites out there, and then delivers what you need in a single interface. Because people have developed standards for the Web, such as the standard way in which HTML is used to create web documents and HTTP is used to access those documents, you can access data from a variety of sources.

Web services can be used to enable different applications to communicate across the Web. These services use HTTP, a standardized platform, but typically they aren't dependent on any one computer operating system, so they aren't controlled by one vendor or one type of software. This concept of "service" translates quite logically to your enterprise. Rather than having to build bridges between applications in your business, you can use a service-oriented approach to access and integrate all of that functionality.

Service-Oriented Architecture

Service-oriented architecture is an architecture that uses services to support business processes. Think about a typical business process that might be made up of several services. If you want to change that process, you simply insert a different service or add a new one. So, if your order process used to involve a credit check, but you decide to stop including a credit check for every order, you simply remove the credit check service, and you have modified your business process. This architecture makes building and modifying business processes much easier and less expensive than writing and modifying custom code.

Service-oriented architecture

So what is the SAP approach to SOA? We'll discuss this next.

Service-Oriented Architecture in SAP

SAP took SOA to the next logical step. If you can combine services to create processes, you should be able to address enterprise-wide functions. To do that, you need to provide aspects of enterprise software, such as data dictionaries that define data types to make services more robust and useful in the business world. The resulting concept crosses all boundaries in your organization to integrate functionality in a standards-based environment. According to SAP, its approach to SOA is "a blueprint for adaptable, flexible, and open IT architecture for developing service-based, enterprise-scale business solutions."

SAP's approach to SOA

How SAP Has Enhanced SOA

Web services are often too granular to be efficient in everyday business operations. For example, you might have to pull services from several different applications and systems to make one business process work. Enterprise services address this issue (see Figure 17.1); they are built on web services, but they include a naming system for services as well as selection definitions.

Enterprise service

These selection definitions help to set parameters for services that correspond to business process parameters. Basically, an enterprise service consists of several web services with a built-in logic related to a typical business process. Enterprise services provide stability to services and the ability to reuse global data types again and again.

Uncertainty & Cost Cutting	Growth Back on the Agenda	IT for Competitive Advantage	IT as a Strategic Lever	IT "Embedded" in Business
Let's be Bold Again	Growth through Innovation	Taking IT to Maturity	Making IT Strategic to the Business	Business at the Speed of Change
Enterprise SOA Launch	mySAP ERP SAP NetWeaver	Suite on SAP NetWeaver BPP Pre-Release	SAP Business ByDesign BPP	Enterprise Services Architecture Delivered
2003	2004	2005	2006	2007

Figure 17.1 SOA is Here to Stay

These services can be used repeatedly in different business processes, making them very flexible and cost-effective. For example, you can use the service of calculating tax in a process for estimating supply costs for your manufacturing plant, or in the tasks involved in calculating a total for a customer order.

Open standards Because enterprise services are based on open standards (standards that aren't vendor-specific), they are more flexible than code that programmers write using specific programming languages such as Java. These web standards are described in a services repository, which, in the case of SAP, is contained within SAP NetWeaver. But how exactly do you connect all of these technical standards with the way you do business every day? That's the real key to the power of SOA.

The Importance of Business Processes

Along with the advent of web services, there was a shift in thinking at SAP that led to formulating its approach to SOA. Although in its earlier days, the folks at SAP created applications just like every other ERP company, over time they realized that business people don't think in terms of software but in terms of the processes they work with on a daily basis, including ordering supplies or hiring a new employee. SAP continued to study business processes and best practices, and with the advent of SOA, they began the move from providing applications to providing business processes via services.

Enterprise services represent the individual steps of a business process. When you need to modify a process using an enterprise services approach, your IT people can work with combinations of these *business objects*. Changing a process is easier because you can model, compose, and generate an enterprise service without having to do much, if any, coding.

Business objects

One other benefit of using services to build and modify applications instead of a static, off-the-shelf software application is that services make it easier to extend your processes across departments, divisions, and even to external partners and resources because you are no longer tied to a particular software or a proprietary customized code. In addition to being flexible, modifying services is far more cost-effective than modifying a hard-coded piece of custom software.

Now, let's take a look at how services are integrated into the everyday world of a business.

How SOA Fits into a Business Setting

Services address common business processes such as processing an order or performing an accounting function; in the real world, though, those processes exist within a wide variety of industries. Each industry has its own procedures and its own terminology. SAP has created *industry scenarios* to organize enterprise services under the umbrella of different industry environments. There are more than 25 industry scenarios made up of enterprise services, including wholesale distribution, retail, professional services, and manufacturing.

Industry scenarios

Business content   Still, each business is unique to itself, so when you buy an enterprise application from SAP, there is a certain amount of configuration you'll need to do. SAP builds in choices to the configuration settings, and by making the choices specific to your industry and company, you can set up the application to meet your needs. These settings, referred to as *business content*, constitute a huge collection of business best practices.

Of course, there is still a provision for those instances where your situation is truly unique. In that case, you may use a combination of business content and individual services to customize the right solution for your specific process.

Enterprise Services Bundles

SAP is committed to developing increasingly more services and business processes in the coming years, to make use of this business content out of the box a reality. SAP is working on developing these business bundles, which will help you realize SOA benefits in your business processes.

Enterprise services bundles   *Enterprise services bundles* are enhancement packages (see Figure 17.2) that provide groups of enterprise services. You can use these bundles to place the functionality of SAP ERP at the disposal of the entire SAP Business Suite. These enterprise services will be provided in enhancement packages for SAP ERP.

The first package, made available in late 2006, focused on HCM, sales, service, production, and credit management. The second package, released in 2007, contains enhancements in wholesale and retail, public services, automobile, and order-to-cash processes. The third package provided improved performance for SAP ERP, and the fourth, released in late 2008, addressed finance, human resources, plant and operations, sales and support, procurement, product development, and enhancements for specific industries.

Each bundle provides a set of services and documentation that explains how the services can be used to build on and reconfigure the processes that are included in any business scenario. Bundles come with explanations of how you can use them with a business scenario, the relevant roles, and descriptions of business objects that make the services work.

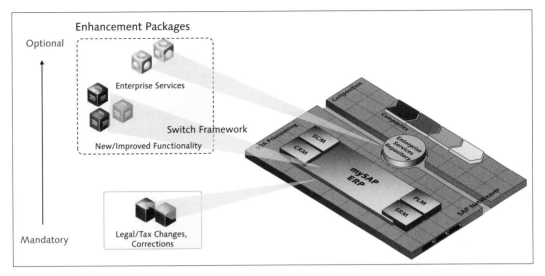

Figure 17.2 Enhancement Packages Add to Your SAP Functionality

You can use SAP NetWeaver's development and modeling tools along with the services in enterprise services bundles to build your own composite applications. This is an easy way to build on the core functions of the SAP Business Suite to meet new requirements that your company may have.

SAP NetWeaver development and modeling tools

SAP is in the process of providing SOA to support all of its products, and enterprise services bundles are integral to SAP's program of enabling services.

 Tip

You can get information about currently available ES bundles in the Enterprise Services Wiki, a section of the SDN/BPX Wiki. The ES Wiki exists to encourage the sharing of information. Anybody who has an ES bundle-related idea can add it to the Wiki. You can find the ES Wiki at *https://wiki.sdn.sap.com/wiki/x/LQ0*.

The technology underlying SOA is SAP NetWeaver, so let's explore how this platform supports the goals of SOA.

SOA and SAP NetWeaver

See Chapter 18 for more about SAP NetWeaver

To make an enterprise services environment work, you must have a central set of tools that stores the services, and call those services when required by a business process. SAP NetWeaver is the platform for running SAP applications and invoking and customizing services for your business. You can also use SAP NetWeaver to compose new enterprise services, using what is referred to as a *model-based approach*, rather than a code-based approach.

Hiding complexity

Though SAP NetWeaver brings a lot of technological muscle to the table, the whole approach of using web services keeps the technical complexity of enterprise applications hidden. How services work is less important than what they do. This hiding of complexity is referred to as *abstraction*. One of the major benefits of SOA is that, instead of opening and working with multiple application interfaces to get work done, users can work with a consistent interface to access all types of functionality and data, and never have to see the underlying complexity because of the way SAP NetWeaver integrates all of the pieces.

But do you have to discard everything you have in place and start from scratch to make the move to SOA? Not at all.

Implementing SOA

Adoption program

You don't have to make the leap from your current computing environment to an enterprise services environment immediately; instead, you can use an incremental approach when you begin implementing enterprise services in your organization. The SOA adoption program from SAP allows you to adopt business processes based on services as you need them, thereby slowly building an enterprise services landscape for your business in a cost-effective way. You can customize your adoption path to enterprise services.

Conclusion

Go to Part V for more on implementing SOA in your company

We have explored several benefits of SOA in this chapter, but it's worth summarizing those benefits here.

A service-oriented approach to your enterprise will provide the following:

> The ability for your employees to access the functionality they need through a single interface, rather than by opening multiple applications, thereby saving them time. This also cuts down on the time spent training them to use different software applications.

> A way for your IT department to build and modify business processes more easily, without disrupting your business operations.

> The ability to reuse services in existing business processes so you can build new processes quickly, without having to rewrite underlying code.

> An environment in which your company can respond to change quickly, allowing you to innovate and switch your business strategy without being dependent on complex IT procedures before you can make changes.

> An approach that lets you leverage existing IT investments, and incrementally implement an enterprise services structure.

The bridge that SOA provides between business strategies and technical functionality can be an important one to help your business become more efficient in the future.

In the next and final section of this book, we'll look at what's involved in implementing SAP NetWeaver and various SAP applications in your enterprise. Let's begin this by proceeding to Chapter 18, which covers SAP NetWeaver.

18

SAP NetWeaver as a Technology Platform

SAP NetWeaver is the technology platform for all SAP applications. In the same way that Microsoft Windows is the operating system for the Microsoft applications you use on a daily basis (for example, Microsoft Office), SAP NetWeaver provides services that allow you to run both SAP and third-party products. The services it provides include a runtime environment for enterprise applications, data integration capabilities, and tools for enhancing and creating applications.

At the end of 2008, SAP NetWeaver functions and tools were in use in some 46,000 customer systems. With the acquisition of BusinessObjects in early 2008, NetWeaver began a move from a focus on composite application tools such as SAP NetWeaver Portal and Visual Composer to SAP BusinessObjects alternatives, especially regarding a phase out over time of SAP BEx Report Designer. However other aspects of NetWeaver will stay unchanged.

This chapter describes how enterprises can use SAP NetWeaver, explains its various components, and provides an outlook for the future development of this technology.

The Role of SAP NetWeaver in Your Enterprise

SAP NetWeaver provides enterprises with a range of functions and tools for integrating and running SAP and third-party products. The platform also provides a technology basis for building and operating a service-oriented architecture. It comprises functions for creating new applications and services and for enhancing existing ones, which allow you to design your IT infrastructure in keeping suit with your business strategies. So how exactly does this work?

SAP NetWeaver and SOA

This section provides an overview of the functions and application options provided by SAP NetWeaver. We will discuss the specific components of SAP NetWeaver, on which these functions are based, later in this chapter.

An Integration Platform

SAP NetWeaver integrates users, information, and processes on a single platform. It facilitates communication between users, the administration of and access to data in diverse IT systems, and the execution of business processes across these systems.

Using the existing IT infrastructure represents one way of using SAP NetWeaver's integration functions. It is irrelevant whether this IT infrastructure consists of third-party products, of SAP applications, or a combination of both. If the processes in your enterprise are executed in different types of systems and data is saved in various applications, SAP NetWeaver helps users to locate and consolidate the relevant data in these systems. SAP NetWeaver also takes account of the technical properties and requirements of the various systems and allows these to be managed centrally.

SAP NetWeaver integration

In this way, SAP NetWeaver supports access to all of the data in these systems and reduces technical complexity for users and system administrators. In addition, SAP NetWeaver enables the exchange of data between applications and allows the functions of all SAP applications and tools to be integrated. The section entitled *SAP NetWeaver Components*, which appears later in this chapter, explains how this is achieved.

A Composition Platform

Another way to use SAP NetWeaver is to enhance the existing IT infrastructure and make it more flexible. SAP NetWeaver provides the tools that allow you to create new business applications based on existing applications using web services, the ABAP and Java programming languages, or other industry standards. SAP calls this process "composition."

Sequencing of useful business applications

You can, for example, develop new custom applications to meet specific requirements in your enterprise, create portals to enable central access to the functions and data that end users require to do their work, or use subfunctions from SAP applications to build composite applications (see Chapter 13) that combine existing services in completely new business processes.

 Business Content

In addition to tools for developing new applications, SAP NetWeaver includes business content, which is comprised of integrated templates and industry-specific applications that can be used "out of the box."

Enterprise Services Repository

SAP NetWeaver includes a repository of enterprise services, from which you can compile business processes of your own. An enterprise service is the smallest unit of an application that performs a business function; for example, the creation of an order or a check to determine the creditworthiness of a customer. Enterprise services have standardized interfaces and their functions and components are described in a standardized form. This means that you can re-use the same enterprise service in various applications without needing to re-program its function for each application.

Descriptions of Interfaces and Functions

In terms of technology, enterprise services use recognized web service standards like XML (Extensible Markup Language), WSDL (Web Service Description Language), and UDDI (Universal Description, Discovery and Integration) to describe interfaces and functions.

You can use modeling tools to create custom enterprise services without programming, which means that you need not concern yourself with the technical details of enterprise service implementation. When you use SAP NetWeaver, the underlying complexity is not visible to you because you do not need to use programming languages or web standards. Instead, you can model the individual functions in the language of the relevant business departments.

The latest version of the Enterprise Services Repository already contains more than 2,000 enterprise services. In addition to service management, it also includes business process models and business object models, which provide templates to facilitate the creation of your own business processes.

Figure 18.1 depicts the role of SAP NetWeaver as a process and composition environment for SAP landscapes. Here, SAP NetWeaver is shown as a comprehensive environment for the integration of Business Suite applications and external applications. The data that is to be accessed is "abstracted" so that it is no longer relevant which technology is used to access it. The composition platform and its tools enable the creation of individual, flexible, service-oriented applications, which — like the Business Suite applications — access the services in the Enterprise Services Repository.

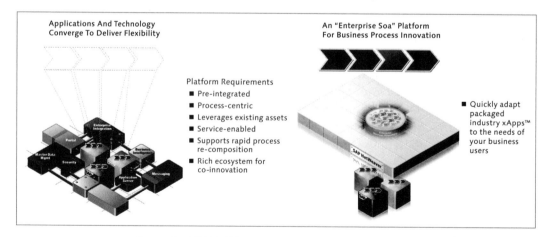

Figure 18.1 SAP NetWeaver — An Integrated IT Landscape

Management of Information and Reports

The third major field of application for SAP NetWeaver comprises the management of information and the creation of reports. The data warehousing and knowledge management functions of SAP NetWeaver help you to more efficiently structure the information that is distributed across all the various systems in your enterprise and improve access to that information. These functions can be used to search for data so that all employees in the enterprise can access consistent information.

In addition, SAP NetWeaver offers tools for analytical applications, which help managers make better business decisions based on up-to-date and meaningful reports.

Making better business decisions

Collaboration between employees is also enhanced through the shared use of data with SAP NetWeaver. Other functions enable, for example, mobile access to important data, which means that employees on business trips can still access the systems they need.

Now that you have been introduced to the functions of SAP NetWeaver, we will turn our attention, in the section below, to the SAP NetWeaver solution map and explain the IT practices that are supported.

The SAP NetWeaver Solution Map

Figure 18.2 shows the SAP NetWeaver solution map. As you can see, SAP NetWeaver supports seven IT practices, which you can use directly or indirectly to tackle business-related challenges. Each of these seven IT practices in turn comprises several scenarios, which allow you to implement the practice step by step. If you take a look at the dynamic solution map on the SAP website (*www.sap.com*), you will notice that each scenario further contains more detailed areas and components, which are required for the implementation of the individual IT practices.

IT practices and scenarios

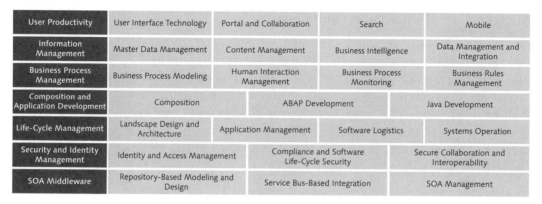

User Productivity	User Interface Technology	Portal and Collaboration		Search	Mobile
Information Management	Master Data Management	Content Management		Business Intelligence	Data Management and Integration
Business Process Management	Business Process Modeling	Human Interaction Management		Business Process Monitoring	Business Rules Management
Composition and Application Development	Composition		ABAP Development		Java Development
Life-Cycle Management	Landscape Design and Architecture	Application Management		Software Logistics	Systems Operation
Security and Identity Management	Identity and Access Management		Compliance and Software Life-Cycle Security		Secure Collaboration and Interoperability
SOA Middleware	Repository-Based Modeling and Design		Service Bus-Based Integration		SOA Management

Figure 18.2 The Solution Map for SAP NetWeaver Technology

Fields of application for SAP NetWeaver in an enterprise

The IT practices consist of the following functions:

> **User Productivity**
User productivity enablement covers issues relating to the software user interface. It provides users with access to software applications and information via an interface that is tailored to meet their requirements. User productivity enablement also includes functions for cross-enterprise collaboration and knowledge management — which means that you can even collaborate with external partners on a project, share documents, and have centralized access to unstructured data.

> **Information Management**
This functional area provides central master data management and a single repository for supplier, customer, and production data, including user-defined and third-party vendor data. Another tool in this area is the SAP Enterprise Search. Because knowledge drives today's business, users need a fast and secure means to access information and data regardless of the source or system on which it resides. The SAP Enterprise Search tool has a web-based interface that delivers results to your people when and where they need them.

> **Business Process Management**
These functions help you monitor your business processes so that you avoid duplication and reduce errors in complicated tasks. By embedding SAP Business Rules Management in your business processes, you ensure that your organization is able to align your processes with your overall business strategies. Business rules can be

developed and then tested and modified by those departments impacted, so that they can be refined to meet their needs. In addition, a repository controls the versioning and access to your business rules so that the business rules within your business processes are the most current.

> **Composition and Application Development**
> The composition tools allow you to create, deploy, and maintain applications that support your business processes. SAP NetWeaver supports application development with the Eclipse-based NetWeaver Developer Studio, Adobe's Interactive Forms, ABAP, and J2E.

> **Life-Cycle Management**
> In this area of SAP NetWeaver, your organization can develop a more robust IT landscape through the elimination or consolidation of redundant IT systems and the archiving of old data. While you streamline your IT systems, these SAP NetWeaver tools also ensure that records retention and data reporting are maintained for compliance purposes.

> **Security and Identity Management**
> While the amount of information and the demand for that information continue to increase, SAP's Security and Identity Management tools help your IT department secure the identities of those who access this information (internally and externally), as well as protect your data and intellectual property from virus threats and hacking.

> **SOA Middleware**
> These tools provide the smooth communication link between all of your organization's systems and data regardless of the platform or source.

The following sections discuss in detail the various components and tools in SAP NetWeaver that you need to implement and execute the various IT practices.

SAP NetWeaver Components

SAP NetWeaver consists of seven technical components, which can be used individually or in tandem to meet various business requirements and implement various IT practices. These components, which cover everything from effective data management to enhanced integration, constitute the essential core of SAP NetWeaver.

SAP NetWeaver Application Server

SAP NetWeaver Application Server (SAP NetWeaver AS) provides the runtime environment for all SAP applications. It therefore serves as a cornerstone for any SAP landscape, without which no SAP system can be operated. SAP NetWeaver AS consists of two tightly integrated parts, one serving as a programming and runtime environment for ABAP, and the other for Java.

SAP NetWeaver AS provides similar services in both; for example, transaction administration, user administration, tools for creating custom applications, and an infrastructure that enables a distributed development of new applications by multiple developers at the same time.

Infrastructure for using web service technology

The infrastructure of SAP NetWeaver Application Server also serves as a basis for using web service technology, as well as tools for developing standards-based services and extremely flexible web applications. In this way, it supports the entire process of creating new applications, including completion of installation and setup. The key components of this infrastructure are briefly introduced below.

ABAP applications

> **ABAP Workbench**
  The ABAP Workbench is a highly integrated collection of tools for developing applications in the ABAP programming language. This language was developed by SAP over 25 years ago, and has been in a state of continuous evolution ever since. ABAP is optimized to ensure efficient and secure processing of structured datasets, and fulfills the requirements of modern software design, thanks to the object-oriented programming capabilities of its ABAP Objects component. The ABAP Workbench provides all tools required to develop ABAP applications, including an editor, a debugger, a dictionary of data types, and a framework for interface design with Web Dynpro technology (for more details, refer to the section entitled "SAP Tools for Developers" below).

Java applications

> **SAP NetWeaver Developer Studio**
  The SAP NetWeaver Developer Studio (NWDS) is a development environment based on the Eclipse open-source framework. The

tools in the Developer Studio allow you to develop Java/J2EE business applications and web service applications. The Web Dynpro Java component of the SAP NWDS provides you with the option of creating user interfaces for your business applications. For more information about the SAP NWDS, refer to the section entitled "SAP Tools for Developers" below.

> **Other Tools**
The SAP NetWeaver toolbox also includes a repository for version management and a data storage medium, which uses the local file system to save relational databases on a central server. Meanwhile, you can manage changes that occur due to business or organizational restructuring with the Change Management function and with transport services, which distribute new functions to the relevant systems.

> **SAP NetWeaver Application Server Security Standards**
The security standards implemented in SAP NetWeaver Application Server include HTTPS, SSL (*secure sockets layer*), and LDAP (*lightweight directory access protocol*). Functions for secure communication between client and server, authentication and SSO (*single sign-on*), modern user administration in the form of CUA (*centralized user administration*), digital certificates, digital signatures, and audits (a method for system monitoring and reporting of all changes) are also provided.

⚙ Open Standards

Thanks to the use of open standards (vendor-independent standards), you can install SAP NetWeaver Application Server on any open technology platform.

SAP NetWeaver Business Warehouse

It is of crucial importance to today's enterprises to have immediate, real-time access to the data required for management decisions. Unfortunately, the information stored by an enterprise is often distributed among various systems and data stores and, in some cases, is available in two or three different versions.

Making information available when needed

325

Data warehousing concepts

SAP NetWeaver Business Warehouse (BW) provides an infrastructure for all business intelligence and data warehousing functions. A data warehouse serves as a central store for historical enterprise data from various sources. Data from all business areas can be integrated in SAP NetWeaver BW, and can then be made available as needed in the form required for strategic decision-making.

Refer to Chapter 12 for more detail about Business Objects and its impact on NetWeaver's contents

Because of SAP's acquisition of BusinessObjects in 2008, there have been some changes to NetWeaver BW. At one point, for example, the name of BW was changed to NetWeaver Business Intelligence (BI). But with the acquisition of BusinessObjects which brings its own BI solution to the table, the name was once again changed to NetWeaver BW, and in the future this feature is likely to be phased out in favor of BusinessObjects premium offerings.

> **Data Warehousing**

The data warehousing function of SAP NetWeaver BI enables the retrieval of key data, business modeling of that data, the creation of data warehouses, modification of the data architecture to suit business structures, and the management of data from various sources.

Searching large volumes of data

> **Analysis and Data Mining**

The functions provided in the Business Intelligence area include *online analytical processing* (OLAP), *data mining* (a function that allows you to search for patterns in large volumes of data), and *alerts*. These functions allow you to access and represent data, identify patterns, and detect exceptions to standard procedures.

Microsoft Excel and web based planning and budgeting

> **Framework for Business Planning**

A framework for business planning allows you to establish a reliable planning workflow based on your business processes. You can execute planning from different perspectives (bottom-up or top-down) based on consolidated business data. Business-planning functions also support the use of Microsoft Excel as well as web-based planning and budgeting.

> **Business Insights**

Business insight functions allow you to create queries, reports, and analyses. With the functions provided for designing web applications, you can create analysis reports and publish business intelligence applications on the Internet or on your enterprise's intranet.

> **Measurement and Management**
> The SAP NetWeaver BW functions for measurement and management allow you to manage business content, metadata, and collaboration business intelligence. You can also create report templates to ensure data consistency.

Consistent data

> **Open Hub Services**
> *Open hub services* enable the distribution of high-quality, audited enterprise information to applications using web services. These services also include the exchange of mass data and modeling functions.

> **Information Broadcasting**
> You can use *information broadcasting functions* to distribute information to a large number of users in a personalized and secure form. The information can be distributed according to a schedule or based on key events. This information may take the form of a document or a current report and may be attached to personal e-mails or published on the Internet.

> **SAP NetWeaver BW Accelerator**
> *SAP NetWeaver BW Accelerator* is used to enable fast access to business intelligence. The functions of BW Accelerator make queries more efficient and accelerate background processes using compression, parallel memory processing and search technologies.

SAP NetWeaver Portal

The SAP NetWeaver Portal is a component that allows users to unify all applications they use in their day-to-day work (for example, various SAP systems, third-party components, or Internet pages) in a single, browser-based interface. Users can define how these applications are displayed and organized, so that each employee has his/her own unique, personalized user interface. Since the design of the user interface is usually determined by an employee's role and function within the enterprise, rather than by his personal preferences, we refer to this approach as a role-based approach.

Role-based interface

With the SAP NetWeaver Portal, information and applications are no longer confined to their original user interfaces and can instead be accessed from any screen by any user in the enterprise in a standardized or personalized form. The Portal also supports the exchange of

Integration

data based on very simple drag and drop functions. The benefits of this are obvious. Users can retrieve all of the information they need directly from their work stations, and only need to log on to a single system (the Portal) to access a range of other systems.

The term integration is used to describe the way in which a single interface is used to unite various systems. Open standards and web services are used to integrate the various applications in the Portal. Pre-defined business content enables a fast and cost-effective implementation of the portal and integration of existing systems.

Collaboration functions

The user interface of the SAP NetWeaver Portal also allows users to collaborate on joint projects with colleagues, both within and outside of the enterprise and, for example, to work on certain files at the same time. These collaboration functions allow users to exchange information in real time in virtual workspaces called *collaboration rooms*.

Finally, the Knowledge Management functions of the SAP NetWeaver Portal help users to search, organize, and access content saved in the enterprise. Classification tools (for example, an index server and search engine) can be used to structure data, publish information in web-based applications, and manage business content more efficiently.

SAP NetWeaver Process Integration

SAP NetWeaver PI (SAP NetWeaver Process Integration) provides additional integration technologies. However, rather than integrating applications in a user interface, these enable process-oriented collaboration between applications; in other words, an automated exchange of data without user intervention.

SAP NetWeaver PI supports collaboration between SAP and non-SAP applications within and across enterprises. Process integration is based on standards-based XML messaging, and all process-dependent data is modeled using web-service standards.

Maintaining, storing and changing integrated information

SAP NetWeaver PI is also delivered with pre-defined business content. This incorporates information about interfaces and assignments between applications, business scenarios, and business processes (referred to as *mapping*) in the central Integration Repository and Integration Directory. You can maintain, store, and change this integrated information using the modeling and development tools that are also provided.

You can use the adapters provided in SAP NetWeaver PI to set up a connection to systems from other providers; for example, with IDoc or BAPI interfaces, or with file, messaging, database, or web service interfaces. Finally, functions are also provided for B2B integration (B2B = *business-to-business*). These support communication with business partners, even if they cannot access SAP NetWeaver.

> ### ⚙ SAP NetWeaver Process Integration
>
> SAP NetWeaver Process Integration (SAP NetWeaver PI) bundles the SAP NetWeaver PI component with a range of Java-based tools in a complete package, which is optimized for the running of service-oriented applications "between" individual systems.

SAP NetWeaver Master Data Management

Master data is data relating to products, customers, or employees, which never or only rarely changes as part of day-to-day business (unlike transaction data). This data includes names, addresses, material numbers, and so on. *SAP NetWeaver Master Data Management* (SAP NetWeaver MDM) helps you manage this data and therefore provides a foundation for service and business process management.

Master data

SAP NetWeaver MDM allows you to consolidate and cleanse master data records relating to the same object from various systems (referred to as duplicates) and to then save these in a central repository. In this way, SAP NetWeaver MDM enables consistency of data across systems.

In addition, SAP NetWeaver MDM allows you to maintain master data and to distribute it to the various systems connected, while also guaranteeing the quality of this data. Global attributes ensure the availability of identical master data in all systems. You can track and verify the active status during distribution, which gives you more control over the process.

Maintaining and distributing master data

You can use the SAP NetWeaver MDM user interface to perform administrative tasks, such as handling data exceptions and assigning access rights to business processes and role-based information. In terms of data administration, you can also use the interface to configure the merging of data sources, define business rules, and set distribution parameters.

Catalog management

You can choose among several tools for working with internal content. These allow you to manage images, texts, and PDF documents, browse and publish web catalogs, modify and send print catalogs, and create reports based on synchronized data.

SAP NetWeaver Mobile

Mobile applications

SAP NetWeaver Mobile provides the technology basis for developing and operating mobile applications based on NetWeaver. This component also enables the use of composite applications for mobile business.

Remote employees

Users can use the functions on mobile devices, even if they are not connected to the system. Data can also be saved on mobile devices without a connection, and then synchronized with back-end systems later. A special development environment in SAP NetWeaver Mobile helps developers create and modify mobile solutions. In addition, an administration console enables centralized administration of mobile solutions and access to these.

The following three client technologies, which have been optimized for specific user roles and various mobile end devices, are provided in SAP NetWeaver Mobile:

> **Mobile Java Client**
  This software is used by PDAs (personal digital assistants) or handheld devices that access online applications like Mobile Asset Management.

> **Mobile .NET Client**
  This technology was designed for devices with Microsoft Windows systems that are used to run CRM applications for field-service employees, for example.

> **Mobile Browser Client**
  Mobile devices that are permanently connected to a web server use this technology in conjunction with WAP, WLAN, Bluetooth and GPRS.

SAP Auto-ID Infrastructure

This component provides RFID capabilities. RFID technology (*Radio Frequency Identification*) is used to create, store, and transmit electronic data via radio waves. This electronically communicated data can be read by IT systems. RFID is used for non-contact identification of objects by means of a reader that can read an RFID chip or transponder (for example, on a cardboard box).

The SAP Auto-ID Infrastructure creates a gateway that allows IT systems to access RFID data. Using this SAP NetWeaver component, you can integrate all automated communication and sensing devices, including RFID readers and printers, Bluetooth devices, and bar code scanners. The technology receives and controls automated signals to make this possible.

Integration of all device types

If you set up a connection between the SAP Auto-ID Infrastructure and the business processes in the back-end system, you can access data in real time, which significantly accelerates processing. The Integrator, an application in the SAP Auto-ID Infrastructure, incorporates RFID technology into logistics processes.

⚙ Areas of Application for RFID

The Auto-ID Infrastructure meets the requirements of large retailing chains, which re-tag goods with RFID chips. RFID can also be used to track drugs electronically in the pharmaceutical industry.

SAP Tools for Developers

In addition to the main components of SAP NetWeaver described above, the SAP technology platform also provides tools for implementing, developing, and managing your IT systems. These tools are introduced in this section.

The developers in your enterprise can use various SAP NetWeaver tools to modify or enhance the SAP solution. These include the large development environments for ABAP and Java, as well as specialized tools for modeling composite applications and user-friendly interfaces, and for creating Portal content and analyses.

ABAP

ABAP is a programming language developed over 25 years ago by SAP for the development of business applications. In the last ten years, ABAP has also provided developers with the ability to develop applications in accordance with the object-oriented programming paradigm. ABAP's distinguishing features include transaction security, stability, a sophisticated data type concept, and, of course, its extensive range of development tools.

ABAP is the programming language in which the core applications of SAP ERP and most back-end areas of the other Business Suite applications were written.

ABAP Workbench

The ABAP Workbench provides a central point of access to all ABAP development tools. Unlike other programming languages (e.g., Java) the ABAP Workbench is the only development platform for ABAP, and it is only available as part of an SAP NetWeaver Application Server.

Tools   The ABAP Workbench contains all of the tools you need to plan, develop, test, and compile ABAP programs.

These include:

> The ABAP Editor for writing code
> The ABAP Debugger for testing programs and detecting errors
> The Class Builder for creating and managing classes for object-oriented programming
> The Web Service Framework for creating and managing ABAP web services
> A range of other tools to help you test and improve all aspects of your programs

Development infrastructure   The sophisticated development infrastructure of the ABAP Workbench means that different developers can work on the same project simultaneously without any conflicts. The Workbench is also connected to the "transport system," which enables fast and reliable distribution of newly developed programs to the relevant target systems.

Web Dynpro ABAP

Web Dynpro ABAP is a new, important tool in the Workbench. It provides a development environment for modern user interfaces. You can use this tool to create ergonomic interfaces that are based on the latest programming principles (for example, a clear division between business and presentation logic, the need for modeling, and so on) and can be used on a wide range of end devices. Web browsers, PDAs, and mobile cellular phones are supported.

Java

The Java programming platform was developed by Sun Microsystems and released in 1995. Java is freely available and free of charge. Java enables exclusively object-oriented programming. The language is particularly suitable for the development of multi-functional, web-based user interfaces, as well as for applications that connect various systems or users in various applications (*composite applications* and *collaboration* functions).

SAP uses Java, for example, as a language for the SAP NetWeaver Portal, for analytical applications, and for the development of *composite applications*.

SAP NetWeaver Developer Studio

The SAP NetWeaver Developer Studio (NWDS) is the SAP development environment for J2EE-based, multilayer applications. This component is based on the Eclipse open source framework, for which SAP offers a comprehensive collection of modeling, development, and maintenance tools. A few examples of the many tools available are provided below:

Eclipse

> Tools for developing J2EE applications

> Tools for developing Java web services

> Tools for developing Web Dynpro applications

> Debugging tools

> Tools for managing distributed development projects (Java Development Infrastructure)

Web Dynpro Java

Web Dynpro interface technology is provided for Java, just as it is for ABAP (see the above section entitled "ABAP"). The underlying functions of Web Dynpro Java are the same as in Web Dynpro ABAP. You can simply choose between the two variants depending on the developer's preferred development language or the language of the back-end application.

SAP Composite Application Framework

SAP CAF
Composite applications (which were previously known as xApps) are applications that consist of services from diverse applications. You can use the *SAP Composite Application Framework* (CAF) to create and use SOA-compliant composite applications. The CAF includes, for example, development tools, an abstraction layer for objects, a user interface, and libraries of sample processes, which you can employ to create and use composite applications.

With SAP CAF, you can combine business processes from existing objects from various systems, rather than having to program code for objects and processes when you require a new application. The object access layer of SAP CAF allows you to run composite applications in any system landscape, regardless of the system in which they originated. The object access layer is a central interface, which controls system communication using web services and SAP NetWeaver PI. For more information about SAP CAF, see Chapter 13.

Several other CAF tools are also provided; for example, tools that allow you to develop user interfaces and *guided procedures* (functions, similar to wizards, which guide users through business processes), as well as pre-defined collaboration functions, which help you to quickly implement mechanisms for virtual collaboration between team members.

SAP NetWeaver Visual Composer

Portal iViews
The *SAP NetWeaver Visual Composer* (VC) tool allows you to create model-based business applications. With this tool, you build user interfaces either based on templates or by using simple drag and drop functions and then defining the data flow between the individual components. In this way, you can create an application without writing a single line of code. When you create a model, the relevant code is generated automatically.

The Visual Composer is integrated into the SAP NetWeaver Portal and SAP NetWeaver BW. .

⚙ SAP NetWeaver Composition Environment

The SAP NetWeaver Composition Environment (SAP NetWeaver CE) bundles SAP's tools for developing Java-based composite applications in a single product, which is relatively lightweight when compared to the SAP NetWeaver platform as a whole. The SAP NetWeaver CE can run independently of other NetWeaver tools in a separate development system, and enables a particularly tight integration of all tools mentioned in this section.

It also includes two completely new NetWeaver components, which are available for the first time with version 7.1.1 of the Composition Environment: SAP NetWeaver Business Process Management and SAP NetWeaver Business Rules Management. These tools are used for low-level modeling of complete business processes across physical system boundaries. This allows application development to move a significant step closer to the business departments.

SAP Solution Manager

While SAP Solution Manager is discussed in detail in Chapter 21, we will provide a short introduction at this point. SAP Solution Manager is a tool for implementing, operating, and upgrading IT solutions based on SAP NetWeaver.

⚙ SAP Solution Manager Availability

SAP Solution Manager is included in your annual maintenance fee for the SAP solutions installed in your enterprise.

SAP Solution Manager comprises a core palette of tools, which offer technical support for the operation of system landscapes.

The functions in SAP Solution Manager are primarily intended to enable the implementation, operation, and optimization of SAP solutions. However, Solution Manager can be used for non-SAP software also. An essential part of the design of its functions is the connection between business processes and the underlying IT infrastructure. In other words, SAP Solution Manager is not intended to be used solely for the monitoring of technical systems by administrations. It also always takes into account the functional interaction between various applications in a business process.

Its functions, which are described in more detail in Chapter 21, include the following:

> Roadmaps for implementing Business Suite solutions within an enterprise as a whole and in a coordinated manner across various areas of the enterprise

> Documentation functions for all processes of your SAP solutions and all changes made to your systems

> Functions to accelerate the preparation and execution of software tests

> A Service Desk to help your IT support personnel record and process problems with applications

> Functions for central monitoring and analysis of systems, business processes, and interfaces

> An online connection to SAP support organizations, which allows you to request regular maintenance services and help from SAP in the event of serious problems

SAP NetWeaver Case Study 1

Table 18.1 provides an overview of the case study discussed in this section.

Enterprise	A large Asian university
Existing solutions	Various software applications from third-party providers and SAP ERP software based on SAP R/3
The challenge	To consolidate data and cleanse inconsistent data in the individual systems and applications
SAP solutions	SAP NetWeaver Portal and SAP NetWeaver BW
Benefits	Consolidated and consistent data, self-service functions, a single point of access for applications and data

Table 18.1 SAP NetWeaver Case Study 1

This large Asian university has more than 6,000 employees and 30,000 students enrolled in a wide range of courses spanning various disciplines. The university needed a solution that would enable enhanced collaboration between the various departments and administrative uses, as well as shared use of data.

The Challenge

Various IT solutions were implemented in the university over the years. The ERP software for finance, HR, and logistics that was implemented in 1994 was still based on an old release (SAP R/3). The university management recognized the need to consolidate the large volume of administrative master data and to eliminate inconsistencies. For this reason, it decided to implement SAP NetWeaver to integrate various data sources used by several isolated systems and applications.

The SAP Solution

It emerged that two SAP NetWeaver components were particularly well suited to meeting the university's requirements. Both SAP NetWeaver BW and SAP NetWeaver Portal offer a single point of access *Single Point of Access* (SpoA) to data. They also allow users to use self-services functions in the Portal to access data and create reports.

SAP NetWeaver BW and SAP NetWeaver Portal

Since SAP NetWeaver BW accesses data structures in SAP R/3, retrieving data from the system did not present a problem. It was also a relatively simple matter to program reporting based on the underlying data for SAP NetWeaver BW. The first phase was completed in less than six months. This phase was shorter than originally planned, thanks to the use of existing business content, pre-defined reports, and analysis tools integrated into SAP NetWeaver. In addition, SAP NetWeaver tools accelerated the mapping of queries and reports in web applications.

Efficient reports

At the end of this phase, the university was able to access data relating to Asset Accounting, Project System, settlement, room reservations, enrollment, course fees, and employee and student numbers. As a result, it was possible to create reports on HR and financial data. It was also possible to incorporate the staff/student ratio into the analyses.

With the SAP NetWeaver Portal, users no longer needed to log on to several systems. Instead, they could use *single sign-on* (SSO) to log on

Single sign-on

to the Portal once only. They then had easy and secure access to all of the information and applications they required. In addition, a portal-based interface allowed users to familiarize themselves with the system within a short space of time without any training.

Finally, the university museum used the search engine (*Search and Classification*) of the SAP NetWeaver Portal to create catalogs for new exhibits in XML format. All employees with Portal access can use the integrated SAP search engine to search for the data they require.

Outlook

Following the implementation of SAP NetWeaver BW and the SAP NetWeaver Portal, the university management now plans to extend their use of BI functions. It is planned that training and performance management information will be added to the data warehouse, where it will be accessible to the HR department. Furthermore, additional areas are to be optimized using planning functions. These include the administration of assets, budgets, and spending. The Registrar's Office also hopes to use the functions of SAP NetWeaver BW to create reports and analyses based on student data.

The collaboration functions of the SAP NetWeaver Portal would allow messages and information to be published on a website for students. The university is also considering using the SAP NetWeaver search engine to access information from file servers and other sources.

SAP NetWeaver Case Study 2

In this section, we examine the use of SAP NetWeaver in a second enterprise. Table 18.2 provides a brief overview of this case study.

Enterprise	A software development and consulting enterprise
Existing solutions	Databases developed by the customer and an accounting system with background processing, IBM xSeries hardware with Microsoft Windows 2000 Server
The challenge	To eliminate unnecessary entries and incorrect data, to enhance employee services, to establish an option for external access to the system and faster invoice processing

Table 18.2 SAP NetWeaver Case Study 2

SAP solutions	SAP NetWeaver Portal, SAP NetWeaver BW and SAP NetWeaver Application Server, SAP ERP, SAP CRM, SAP SEM, SAP Self-Services
Benefits	Internet-based collaboration between internal and external systems, data entry in real time

Table 18.2 SAP NetWeaver Case Study 2 (Cont.)

This IT enterprise specializes in the development of software and system components. Its workforce of over 700 employees provides support for customers with plug-in software applications for financial institutions, the public sector, and distributors.

The Challenge

Management at the company desired an IT environment that would support strategic objectives and meet employee requirements. They also wanted the solution to enable the sharing of information and to improve data accuracy. Since many of the employees work in the field service rather than in the office, it was essential that the solution would also permit interaction between internal and external systems. A further challenge was presented by the accounting system, which was unable to process invoices as quickly as required. Employees of the enterprise had developed their own integrated databases for the accounting system, for which background processing was also used. This resulted in a number of inconsistencies. The enterprise therefore required a single, integrated database for the accounting and information systems.

The SAP Solution

Management at the enterprise decided to implement a brand new system, comprising SAP ERP and SAP NetWeaver with specific SAP solutions such as SAP CRM and SAP SEM

The SAP ERP software provided functions for accounting, sales and distribution, and HR. Three SAP NetWeaver components — SAP NetWeaver Application Server, SAP NetWeaver Portal, and SAP NetWeaver BW — provided support for data integration and the creation of user-friendly interfaces for remote access by employees. Users

SAP NetWeaver and specific solutions

can now use the SAP NetWeaver Portal to access the particular systems they need. A browser environment with SSO access allows them to access several systems, such as groupware and SAP systems, as well as web systems provided by SAP NetWeaver Application Server. SAP NetWeaver BW integrates information by bundling all data from the SAP applications.

Thanks to the use of SAP NetWeaver, data accuracy and integration were successfully optimized. As a result, the enterprise is able to make faster and better strategic decisions. In addition, field-service employees can now access key systems, which means that they can enter data on various devices faster than before, even while on the move. The enterprise's IT team replaced the existing system with a completely new SAP solution. This established a basis for maintaining and enhancing the solution in the future, in order to keep pace with changing business requirements.

Conclusion

This chapter provided an introduction to SAP NetWeaver technology, which is a prerequisite for service-oriented architectures and supports other SAP applications. You are now familiar with the following aspects of SAP NetWeaver:

> Integration options
> Modeling tools
> Data administration and analysis tools
> Components such as SAP NetWeaver BW, SAP NetWeaver Portal, and SAP NetWeaver Application Server
> Tools for developers, including ABAP Workbench und SAP NetWeaver Developer Studio
> Outlook for future developments

This technology platform, with its far-reaching functional scope, provides the basis for any SAP application you may implement.

The next and final part of this book is devoted to the implementation and operation of SAP software. It also provides detailed information about the functions and features of SAP Solution Manager.

PART V
The Solution in Place

Preparing for an SAP Implementation

Whatever piece of the SAP solution landscape you're contemplating putting in place, doing so can take time, money, and effort. Before you jump in, you might want to get an idea of what's involved and also what resources exist to help you out. You'll be glad to hear that there are a lot of support tools, methodologies, and programs in place to take you step-by-step through an SAP implementation. This chapter covers some of the most useful support tools, methodologies, and programs.

> ▶ **Note**
>
> For a more in-depth exploration, read *Managing Organizational Change during SAP Implementations* (SAP PRESS, 2007).

Important Considerations

Before we explore the support and help available to you, take a moment to try to understand what a typical SAP implementation will involve. You need to understand four key elements before you proceed:

> The state of your own business

> How your business fits with industry best practices

> The potential costs involved

> How to anticipate and deal with change

Let's examine these elements one by one, starting with assessing your business.

Assessing Your Own Business

Understand your unique characteristics

Every business is unique in that it has its own structure, processes, industry-related procedures, customer base, geographic locations, and so forth. To put an enterprise solution in place, you need to understand your unique characteristics to find the right fit. Assessing your business and its needs is a very important part of taking the plunge with SAP. In fact, if you don't understand the goals of your company and where you want to go, you can't implement any enterprise solution effectively. For example, you must identify your most pressing problem to decide which solutions to implement first. You have to understand and document your current processes to automate them, and so on.

You should bring together all of the relevant people in your organization, so that IT people understand the business strategies, goals, and priorities for solving business challenges, and business people understand the existing IT landscape. Because SAP products can be incrementally integrated with your current systems, determining what changes will bring about the greatest benefit will help you to implement them strategically and cost-effectively.

Understanding How Your Business Fits in Your Industry

Analyze industry needs

Even though every business is unique, each business also has some things in common with other businesses in their industry. Using SAP Best Practices, built into SAP Business Suite products, helps provide out-of-the-box solutions that have worked for many companies in your industry.

SAP Best Practices provide a prototype you can use to accelerate your move to SAP. You get a methodology for using the prototype, documented scenarios that reflect both a business and technical point of view, and preconfigured SAP solutions. There are SAP Best Practices for the following industries, among others:

> Apparel and footwear
> Automotive
> Chemicals
> Consumer products
> Deal business management
> Engineering, construction, and operations
> High tech
> Industrial machinery and components
> Life sciences
> Professional services
> Public sector
> Retail
> Utilities

Cross-industry best practices are those that are useful for most businesses, regardless of their industry. These include the following:

> SAP Best Practices for Business Intelligence (SAP Best Practices for BI)

Cross-industry best practices

> SAP Best Practices for Business Planning and Consolidation
> SAP Best Practices for Business Warehousing (SAP Best Practices for BW)
> SAP Best Practices for Data Migration
> SAP Best Practices for Governance, Risk, and Compliance (SAP Best Practices for GRC)
> SAP Best Practices for Human Capital Management (SAP Best Practices for HCM)
> SAP Best Practices for Supply Chain Management (SAP Best Practices for SCM)
> SAP Best Practices for Customer Relationship Management (SAP Best Practices for CRM)
> SAP Best Practices for Strategy Management

SAP Best Practices prototypes are reusable and help you get an SAP ERP Business Suite solution in place faster and more cost-effectively.

Understanding Implementation Costs

Estimating the cost of your SAP implementation

It's not easy to help you estimate the costs of an SAP implementation. That would be like trying to guess what your vacation is going to cost without knowing your destination, how long you'll be gone, how far you have to travel, how many family members will be joining you, or what activities you will participate in when you get there. However, for small and mid-sized companies, you can increasingly find a *fixed price offer* depending on the scope of the implementation. But what we can do is give you some factors to consider that contribute toward the final cost of your SAP implementation.

There are several pieces of an SAP implementation that you have to consider:

> Are you implementing a small business solution such as SAP Business One, or are you customizing a combination of SAP Business Suite functionalities with SAP NetWeaver, a couple of pieces of SAP ERP, and one other package such as SAP CRM?

> Are you gradually implementing pieces of SAP functionality, or do you want to implement a total solution as soon as possible?

> Do you have legacy systems that could integrate with SAP NetWeaver to save you money?

> Will you need a great deal of consultation to help you design and implement your solution or to customize processes, or do you have internal resources who can help with some of this work?

> Will your employees have to be trained in the new system?

> How many user licenses will you need, and what costs will you encounter in migrating data to the new system?

> How extensively will you want to customize the user interface?

> In which countries or regions will you be implementing the solution? Will localization be required?

An SAP account executive can work through all of these questions with you to help you estimate your total cost of ownership (TCO).

Dealing with Change

Don't forget to put a change management plan in place. Change management involves preparing your organization for change by strategically introducing new technologies or procedures in a way that engages them and provides them with the tools they need (such as training) to be successful. When an SAP implementation encounters problems, it is often because the organization and its employees weren't ready for the change and not because of the technology. There are two important things to remember about dealing with change:

> Change management plan

> > A new system for managing your business processes is likely to highlight areas of your current processes that are weak or even non-existent. People can be offended by the suggestion that they are not handling things in the most efficient way possible. Remind them that to solve problems, you have to identify them first. Identifying problems is not a process of assigning blame but of focusing on a better way to get work done. Involve your people in the process, and they will feel like a part of your future success.

> Change is a people issue

> > Change is difficult, even for the most flexible among us. Keep that in mind as you find employees suddenly married to an old system that they used to gripe about. Provide clear justification for the change and information about the anticipated rewards. Document and celebrate milestones as you implement the new system.

Though you may have many partners involved in your implementation, your employees are the people who will work with the new system day in and day out, so don't forget them as you work through the process. Next, we'll introduce you to a variety of resources that can help you begin planning for an SAP implementation.

Planning for Success

Adopting any SAP solution means that you're entering the world of service-oriented architecture (SOA), an approach to enterprise computing that brings a lot of benefits. You'll be glad to hear that you're definitely not alone when you begin to implement an SAP solution. SAP has created an entire program to help you adopt the SOA model for your business, called the *SOA adoption program*. In addition, there are people and organizations that can help you determine how to leverage SOA and begin to map out your SAP solution.

The SOA Adoption Program

SOA is designed to deliver benefits by using existing systems and reducing the costs of changing or developing new processes. However, an SAP approach to SOA is also designed to provide support for business processes through an entire organization, which is no small task. An organization doesn't put an SOA into effect overnight. You need more than a technology implementation; you need education, direction, and time to get all of the pieces in place.

 Tip

SAP has introduced a program called *Standardized E2E* (End-to-End) *Operations* to help with the operations portion of SOA adoption. This is the phase in which you refine what you put in place. The first piece of this program is an organizational model that assigns roles to all involved stakeholders, including tools for collaboration and SLA-based support processes. Standardized procedures are also established. Tools are implemented for executing the described procedures.

SAP Solution Manager, which you'll learn more about in Chapter 20, supports the various SAP standards for solution operations, and individual work centers provide access to all functions that different stakeholders need to get their role-based jobs done. Finally, the stakeholders have to be educated to use the E2E Solution Operations procedures. SAP's role-based education and certification program for E2E Solution Operations meets this need.

The SOA adoption program was designed to help you envision an SOA environment for your business and find the best path to it. There are four phases to this program: *discovery*, where you find out what SOA can do for you; *evaluation*, when you build a roadmap for making the move to SOA and SAP NetWeaver; *implementation*, the phase in which you plan, build, and run the services you will use as the foundation of your business processes; and *operations*, when you go live and refine what you've put in place.

The SOA adoption program includes the following:

> Roadmaps that are like blueprints for your SOA adoption. These roadmaps show you how you can merge SAP's enterprise applications with SAP NetWeaver functionality to achieve a services-based environment.

The roadmap for SOA

> Discovery Server is a preconfigured system that allows you to try out SOA and SAP NetWeaver in your own business.

> Enterprise Services Workplace (ES Workplace) allows you to browse through packaged enterprise services and test them to see how they might work in your enterprise.

> Industry Value Networks help you collaborate with others to develop business solutions.

> The Business Process Expert (BPX) community has the goal of bridging the gap between IT and business strategies by helping these two camps find a common language. The role of the business process expert (also called business analyst, business consultant, or process consultant) in an organization is largely a result of introducing a service-oriented approach to business solutions.

> SOA Innovation is another community that offers information in the form of brochures, demos, and webcasts from experts to help you find your way to an SOA environment in your company.

An SAO adoption program can help, but what about those times when you need a one-on-one helping hand? There are several options from which you can choose.

SAP and the SAP Community

In addition to the various planning and adoption tools outlined so far in this chapter, there's a virtual army of resources out there that can help you get started.

SAP account representatives are not just salespeople. They're your team leaders for designing a solution, assembling a team of advisors, and working with you to develop an analysis of your needs. An account representative will also stick with you throughout your implementation to ensure that you're getting what you need from SAP.

SAP account representatives — more than just sales people

Tip

To find an account representative, go to *www.sap.com/contactsap/directory* for a list of SAP offices around the world. Contact your closest office to begin working with an account representative right away.

SAP consultants — consultant certification

SAP consultants have been certified by SAP to help companies with their SAP implementations. There are more than 140,000 certified specialists, including application, technology, and development consultants, as well as solution architects. Currently, there are three levels of consultant certification: *associate* (fundamental knowledge), *professional* (proven project experience), and *master* (expert grasp and broad project experience within complex projects).

SAP third-party certification

SAP supports third-party vendors who want to integrate their software with SAP software. SAP Integration and Certification Centers (SAP ICC) can offer help in connecting you with third-party solutions and advising you on integration issues. Visit *www.sdn.sap.com* to find information on these ICC programs.

In addition to these people and groups, SAP provides help in the form of SAP Services, a broad program designed to provide you with what you need to have a successful implementation.

Making the Best of Enhancement Packages

Enhancement packages

Full system upgrades and installations can be extremely costly in terms of time, money, and resources, not to mention the disruption to your day-to-day business activities. If your company already has SAP ERP installed and running but wants to improve general business functionality or specific industry functionality to remain competitive, consider an SAP enhancement package.

Enhancement packages bring you the flexibility to install only those portions of software that directly impact the process or function you want to improve. After these specific components are in place, you can then re-activate the impacted processes, and your system will react only to those changes.

Who Can Help You Implement?

SAP Services is an extensive network of people and programs that offers tools, consulting, and service plans to help your company get up and running with an SAP solution throughout the entire planning, building, and running process.

SAP Services

In this section, we look at SAP Services through the planning, building, and running phases of an implementation, and then take a closer look at what SAP Consulting has to offer.

SAP Service Portfolio

SAP describes its service offerings in a model that breaks them down into three key phases of an implementation: planning, building, and running. Each of these phases is further broken down into categories of services: complete execution, expert guidance, quality management, and enablement (see Figure 19.1).

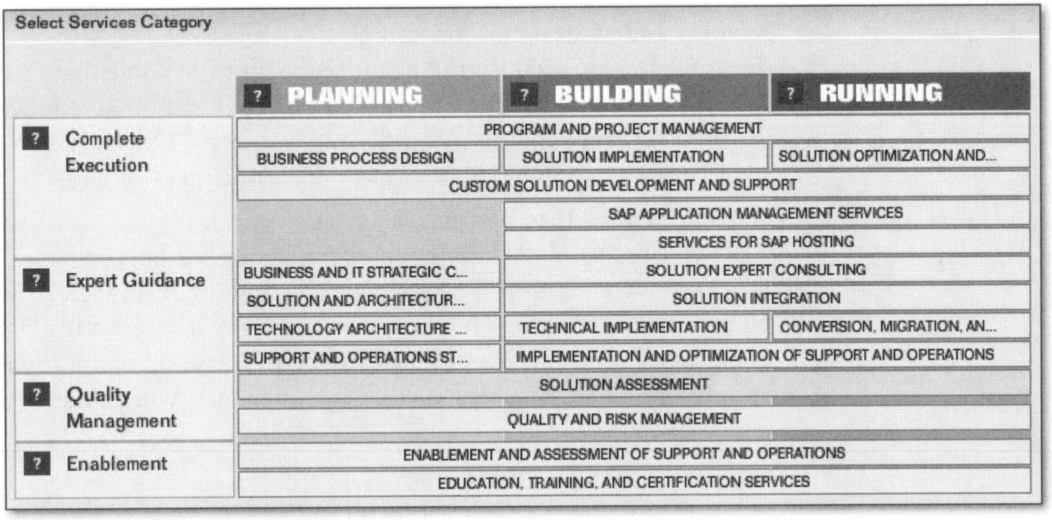

SAP services portfolio

Figure 19.1 SAP's Services Portfolio Breakdown

In the next three sections, we explore the details of each of these phases.

SAP Services Portfolio: Planning Phase

The planning phase helps your business define what your processes are and where they need improvement. In this phase, you determine the direction for your IT strategy through a variety of services:

> **Program and Project Management**
> These services include program management, project management, and change management services. You work through initial planning, organizing, and staffing, as well as controlling the project.

> **Business Process Design**
> These services include process analysis, redesign, innovation, improvement, determining best practices, and quality assurance.

> **Custom Solution Development and Maintenance**
> These services include the development of applications and interfaces. The features include planning your help-desk support, solution testing as part of installing support packages and upgrades, and software maintenance.

> **Business and IT Strategic Consulting**
> This is where you identify and quantify the business value that you can expect from improving the efficiency of your enterprise. In this category, you get solution planning, analysis of your business process and business requirements, and value assessment services.

> **Solution Architecture Design**
> These services involve helping to integrate your business solutions into your overall enterprise architecture. Activities in this category include developing an implementation approach; establishing scope, costs, and timelines; designing the process and application landscape; and setting benchmarks against which you can assess your operations.

> **Technology Architecture Design**
> This is where you break down high-level system architecture into the technical requirements of your implementation project. Activities include system landscape strategy, internal release rollout, determination of distributed and centralized systems, and software change management.

> **Support and Operations Strategy**
> This is the part of the planning phase where you set up support

structures, establish the appropriate level of support, calculate your TCO, and pinpoint the strategy for your system operation.

> **Solution Assessment**
These services help you identify and minimize technical risk in your implementation, target integration issues, and check the technical feasibility of an implementation project. They also help you identify weak points in your existing solution.

> **Quality and Risk Management**
These services help you identify and manage implementation risks, provide a review of the project's progress, and analyze the technical design.

> **Enablement and Assessment of Support and Operations**
These services help you to assess and set up support structures and processes. Training workshops help your support organization understand how to analyze and solve system problems.

> **Education Training, and Certification Services**
These services help educate users, consultants, and project teams. Consulting, customized training, documentation, and computer-based tools are provided to users, including a range of courses and certifications on SAP solutions and infrastructure.

When you move beyond the planning phase, you're ready to begin building your solution, which is where the building phase categories of services come into play.

SAP Services Portfolio: Building Phase

When planning is done, you're ready to begin to roll out new applications, customize interfaces, and integrate all of the pieces. The building phase includes several services, such as those that involve custom solutions, solution implementation, technical implementation, and solution assessment. Some of these categories overlap with those in the planning phase but with a focus on implementing the solution.

> **Program and Project Management**
These services include program management, project management, and change management services.

> **Solution Implementation**
These services support implementation and rollout of new appli-

cations. Activities include blueprinting business process requirements, tailoring applications to business requirements, resolving conceptual and technical issues, cycle testing, and load and stress testing.

> **Custom Solution Development and Maintenance**
> These services involve customized development of applications and interfaces. In addition, you get enhancements to packaged applications and templates. Other services cover outsourcing of the maintenance for your development projects, helpdesk support, solution testing while installing support packages and upgrades, and software maintenance.

> **SAP Application Management services**
> These services include helpdesk and second-level support, process support and infrastructure design, and system management and monitoring. This category of services can also involve remote application administration for solutions that are run onsite or offsite.

> **Services for SAP Hosting**
> These services include selecting hosting and application management services that cover everything from evaluation to implementation to application hosting. Out-of-the-box solutions can be scaled to meet your specific needs.

> **Solution Expert Consulting**
> These services involve dedicated SAP solution experts with direct access to SAP development. These resources are available onsite or operating remotely to address solution, process, and technical issues, and work with your project team to instruct them in software features and functions. The ongoing evaluation of tools and processes helps you avoid problems as you begin building your solution.

> **Solution Integration**
> These services deliver detailed design, implementation, and management services that link applications and integrate them with your IT infrastructure. SAP integration experts help to match up SAP and non-SAP solutions. These services help you optimize the architecture and interfaces of your solution, and adopt strategies for converting your data.

> **Technical Implementation**
> These services support the technical implementation and rollout of new applications by providing tools, methodologies, and best practices. Consultants help you translate high-level system architecture into implementation project technical requirements. Activities include configuration of your IT environment, definition of an IT security policy, and movement of data, operating systems, and databases from legacy systems to the SAP solution.

> **Implementation and Optimization of Support and Operations**
> These services deal with system administration, which includes reviewing the main aspects of your operations such as interface settings, database administration, backup, recovery, and security settings. In addition, data volume management services help to reduce the size and growth of your database and offer a customized archiving strategy.

> **Solution Assessment**
> These services help you identify integration issues and risks during the building phase, and check the technical details of your implementation infrastructure, sizing, and volume.

> **Quality and Risk Management**
> These services manage implementation risks, examine your project's progress, and ensure your solution design aligns with your overall business needs.

> **Enablement and Assessment of Support and Operations**
> These services help you build a solution support organization. You set up support structures and processes and train your support organization.

> **Education, Training, and Certification Services**
> These services bring consulting, customized training, documentation, and the latest computer-based tools to your users.

SAP Consulting

One of the major support efforts of SAP Services is SAP Consulting. SAP Consulting offers two programs to help you: Technical Implementation and Solution Implementation. Here, briefly, is what each program delivers to your enterprise.

SAP Consulting provides services

SAP Technical Implementation

To get the technical aspects of your implementation up and running, SAP Consulting provides the following services:

> **SAP Technical Analysis and Design**
> This helps to relate your high-level system architecture to project-specific technical requirements. SAP Consulting looks at your system landscape strategy, software change management approach, and how you'll deal with business continuity throughout the implementation.

> **SAP Technical Installation**
> This provides technology tools for your installation, makes sure your hardware is configured optimally, and checks your system settings and speeds.

> **SAP Globalization and Language Consulting**
> This helps international companies with global implementation, setting up the right system architecture, and dealing with localization issues. Multiple language and time-zone support are included.

> **SAP Security Concepts and Implementation**
> This consulting service helps you get your information security policy defined and in place. Your security policy will be analyzed, and suggestions will be made. In addition, detailed documentation helps you configure and set up your systems for improved security.

> **SAP Technical Migration**
> This helps you determine a strategy for migrating to a new solution or technology. You get guidelines and documentation for every stage, and help with actually migrating your system with tools such as the SAP Legacy System Migration Workbench (SAP LSMW).

> **SAP ABAP and Java Consulting**
> This helps your company develop and integrate your own specific applications to work with SAP solutions.

Now let's move onto the other half of SAP Consulting Solution implementation.

SAP Solution Implementation

Your solution needs more than technology, which is where the solution implementation portion of SAP Consulting comes in. This area of support includes the following:

> **SAP Solution Implementation Consulting**
>
> This helps you map out your implementation by identifying your business and system requirements, performing analysis and design tasks, running requirements workshops to determine your needs, and creating both a business blueprint and process plan to help model your business process goals.

> **SAP Solution Expert Consulting**
>
> This brings best practices and proven methodologies to your solution implementation. In this area of solution implementation, SAP Consulting offers help with understanding all of the features of SAP software, and provides tools for minimizing risk.

> **SAP Configuration**
>
> This gives you guidance and support in customizing SAP solutions to your specific business needs. You get specific requirements for your project and development specifications, a baseline configuration to give you a starting point, and a final configuration strategy for system deployment.

> **SAP Test Management**
>
> This keeps the cost of testing activities low and helps you automate test procedures. SAP Consulting provides a roadmap for your testing activities and uses SAP NetWeaver tools, as well as proven testing methodologies.

SAP Consulting offers a wide range of services, including one for midsize companies called *ASAP Focus methodology*, which you will learn about in the next section.

> ASAP Focus Methodology

ASAP Focus Methodology

For midsize companies, the ASAP Focus methodology from SAP Consulting can make it possible to put an SAP Business Suite solution in place in a little over three months. This program streamlines the processes used by larger companies for IT implementation to meet a midsize business model. The focus in this case is on keeping costs down and keeping the disruption of your business's operations to a minimum. If your organization cannot afford any disruption to its core processes, and you're concerned about controlling costs, this is a good option.

SAP Best Practices Based on SAP Best Practices, such as the SAP Business All-in-One fast-start program and other packaged solutions, this program includes the following:

> A roadmap for putting a predefined solution in place quickly
> Predefined processes that enable you to perform business activities, and data conversion tools to help you work with your existing data within the new system
> Documentation for business processes
> Predefined reports, printed forms, roles for your employees, and test programs

In addition, the ASAP Focus methodology allows your people to put certain pieces of the process in place before you begin working with an SAP team, which can save you money right from the beginning. For midsize businesses, having a way to predict both the timeline and cost of an SAP implementation can be important, and the ASAP Focus methodology is designed to do just that.

In the next section, you'll find some information that can help prepare you for your first contact with SAP, so that you'll be prepared to ask the right questions and make an initial determination about which route might be best for you.

SAP Services Portfolio: Running Phase

The running phase offers several of the same types of services covered in the other phases, such as project management, solution optimization, integration, support organization implementation, and quality and risk management — but with the emphasis on a functioning implementation. At this point, you're monitoring your new solution, ensuring that any new development or outsourcing needs are met, and supporting your implementation with daily helpdesk support. Specific conceptual and technical areas are addressed to ensure that all of your SAP projects are completed successfully.

There is an ongoing evaluation to ensure that your solution is working and incorporating any new technologies or products. Conversion, Migration, and Landscape Optimization services help you make the move to your new system by integrating solution landscapes, which helps to ensure corporate governance. In this phase, there is a review of operations, including interface settings, database administration, backup, and security. There is also ongoing quality and risk management to ensure that your solution reflects the needs of your business.

Now that you understand the scope of services offered throughout the planning, building, and running phases of an SAP implementation, we'll take a moment to review some specific tools and programs that deliver them.

SAP Operations Support Options

After you are up and running in the operations phase of SOA adoption, there are several maintenance options and a support offering from SAP Services, as shown in Figure 19.2. These include SAP Enterprise Support services, the customized SAP MaxAttention program, and a portfolio of support offerings for project-based engagement.

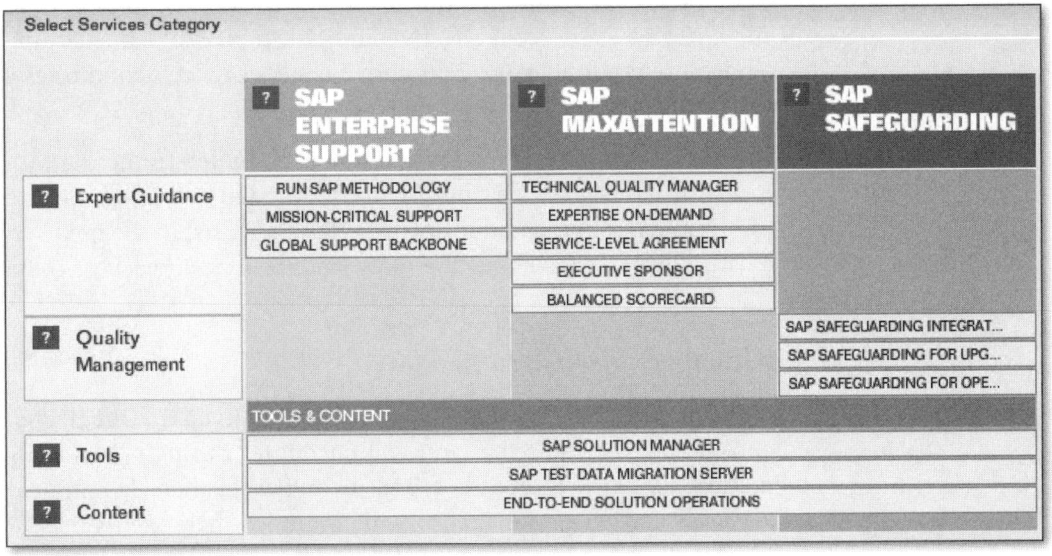

SAP support offerings

Select Services Category	SAP ENTERPRISE SUPPORT	SAP MAXATTENTION	SAP SAFEGUARDING
Expert Guidance	RUN SAP METHODOLOGY	TECHNICAL QUALITY MANAGER	
	MISSION-CRITICAL SUPPORT	EXPERTISE ON-DEMAND	
	GLOBAL SUPPORT BACKBONE	SERVICE-LEVEL AGREEMENT	
		EXECUTIVE SPONSOR	
		BALANCED SCORECARD	
Quality Management			SAP SAFEGUARDING INTEGRAT...
			SAP SAFEGUARDING FOR UPG...
			SAP SAFEGUARDING FOR OPE...
	TOOLS & CONTENT		
Tools	SAP SOLUTION MANAGER		
	SAP TEST DATA MIGRATION SERVER		
Content	END-TO-END SOLUTION OPERATIONS		

Figure 19.2 Pick the Support Option That Matches Your Company's Needs

> **SAP Enterprise Support**
> This provides the holistic management of your SAP solution through 24-hour global support. At this level of support, you get the best business practices and technology required to support your SAP implementation. This support program includes three components: Run SAP Methodology, Mission Critical Support, and Global Support Backbone.

> Enterprise Support also includes the resolution of issues through a service-level agreement (SLA). In addition, you get annual assessments that result in recommendations for actions you can take to lower your risk and improve your processes. A support advisor continuously provides guidance about your implementation and makes suggestions to keep things moving along smoothly.

> **SAP MaxAttention**
> This is for those companies that need more customized support and maintenance options. Onsite specialists work to optimize your SAP software and provide you with ongoing quality management.

> **SAP Safeguarding**
> This is a technical quality management program. It provides a portfolio of assessments, tools, and services that can make your implementation, upgrade, migration, and finally the operation of your IT infrastructure more cost-effective and risk free. SAP Safeguarding services help you manage your core business processes and offer a risk management and service plan.

Find the program best suited for your organization

Your SAP account manager can work with you to determine the program that is best suited for your organization, depending on the size of your implementation and its related risks and costs. In the next section, you'll learn more about the tools that are used in each of these programs.

SAP Services Tools and Programs

Many of the services described previously are delivered through specific tools and programs that you will encounter during your implementation, so we will provide a brief overview of them here. Some of the tools and programs that provide many of the benefits of SAP Services include the following:

> **SAP Active Global Support (SAP AGS)**
> This includes services for planning, implementation, and operations, with an emphasis on helping to continually improve your business processes.

> **SAP Business Process Outsourcing (SAP BPO)**
> This helps you outsource peripheral business processes so you can focus on core business processes. SAP links you up with business process outsourcing (BPO) providers and offers what they call "enabling solutions and services."

> **SAP Custom Development**
> This uses SAP expertise to help you customize solutions. The program includes the services of development architects, project managers, and developers to modify applications, create entirely new applications, or provide advice on application maintenance.

> **SAP Education**
> This helps companies implement solutions faster, reduce the risks of migrating to the new system, lower support costs, and speed up their adoption of new SAP releases. Curricula can be standard or customized, and cutting edge e-learning methods, simulation tools, and support tools help you save money.

> **SAP Ramp-Up**
> This is not for every SAP customer, but only for those who are involved with helping SAP test new products and providing input. This can put your company ahead of the curve technologically.

You may use different pieces of this support toolkit at various stages of your implementation. Again, your SAP account manager can help you orchestrate the best solution for your business.

In the final section of this chapter, we offer some sources for additional information about SAP and implementing an SAP solution.

Getting Information

There are several sources of information about SAP, its products, and services that might help you get the most current information, plan for, and work through an implementation. Some useful resources for information are briefly described here:

www.sap.com

> *www.sap.com* is the SAP website that offers an almost overwhelming wealth of information about SAP's products and their features and benefits, in addition to the articles and white papers, the latest news about SAP, and information about various SAP and SAP community services and support.

SAP Developer Network

> *SAP Developer Network* (SDN) is an online community where those who develop, consult, integrate, or are just curious about learning more about the technical side of SAP can connect.

SAP Service Marketplace

> *SAP Service Marketplace* is an extranet service platform run by SAP and used by SAP, its partners, and customers to collaborate. You have to be granted access to this area, but if you're a partner or customer, you will find this to be a helpful, portal-based environment.

SAP User Groups

> *SAP user groups* are non-profit groups that are independent of SAP. They are made up of SAP partners, customers, and consultants, and they help to provide SAP with information about users' needs as well as providing education to their members.

Books and publications

> *SAP PRESS* offers two books on SAP implementations: *Managing Organizational Change during SAP Implementations* (2007), and *Efficient SAP NetWeaver BI Implementation and Project Management* (2007). Check out these books and other helpful titles at *www.sap-press.com*.

Support in Action: A Case Study

▶ **Note**

See Appendix B, SAP Resources, for a list of resources and the website addresses where you can find them, and (where available) phone numbers to contact them.

To truly understand how an SAP implementation works in the real world, let's look at a case study. Review Table 19.1, and then proceed through the rest of the section.

Company	Large European bank
Existing Solutions	Multiple SAP applications
Challenge	To change its business processes to ensure compliance with Basel II capital accords and gain more flexibility from automated processes and centralized reporting
SAP Solutions	SAP Bank Analyzer applications, SAP NetWeaver BW, SAP Consulting support, SAP Custom Development, SAP Education, SAP Safeguarding, SAP Ramp-Up, SAP Active Global Support
Benefits	Enabled short-term and long-term compliance with Basel II, improved risk management and new functionality for trend analysis, centralized monthly credit data and reporting procedures

Table 19.1 SAP Implementation Case Study

With more than 16,000 employees in 8 countries, this bank needed a way to quickly move into compliance with the complex Basel II accord. Technology was one piece of the puzzle, but the support to quickly implement that technology with a minimum amount of disruption required significant support from SAP and its partners.

It helped that SAP has a long history working with the banking industry. The company had just implemented SAP ERP, which helped to streamline its core business. SAP Consulting took the lead early on, bringing industry knowledge, technical expertise, and a familiarity with the client's data needs to the table. The SAP Solution Manager tool facilitated technical support for various systems, helping to create an audit trail for deployment, operation, and maintenance. SAP Safeguarding services, through the SAP Active Global Support organization, orchestrated performance testing and fine-tuning of the hardware involved in the new system. | **SAP and banking**

The SAP Custom Development organization (part of SAP Services) created a proprietary application to deal with risk-related loan pricing. The new pricing system that SAP experts helped to implement provides improved templates for Basel II compliance. Lastly, a third party that SAP brought in provided a tool for data loading as part of the | **SAP Custom Development**

SAP Bank Analyzer implementation to help with high-volume data processing needs.

Conclusion

In this chapter, we provided you with an overview of the various resources that exist for information and support as you begin to implement an SAP solution. We recommended that you perform an initial self-analysis of your business to understand its goals, industry-related considerations, and how you will deal with the costs and changes that an SAP implementation involves. We also introduced you to the following programs and resources:

> SOA adoption program

> SAP Services portfolio

> ASAP Focus methodology

> SAP Consulting's various programs and support services

Throughout this book, we have tried to give you the latest and most accurate information possible about the specific products, services, and driving concepts behind SAP, so you have a solid grounding in enterprise computing and SAP's offerings. Of course, SAP is known for being responsive to its customers' needs, which means that they constantly update products and services or offer new innovations, so be sure to check some of the resources listed previously and contact an SAP representative to discuss your needs when you're ready to implement an SAP solution.

Now, let's proceed to Chapter 20, where you can learn about SAP Solution Manager and how it can help you support your SAP implementation.

SAP Solution Manager

SAP Solution Manager is the central platform for application management and collaboration, which SAP provides to its customers at no additional cost. You have to use SAP Solution Manager to implement SAP solutions, and with good reason. This very useful platform helps you manage your implementation, but SAP Solution Manager offers much more. It will be with you long after you implement an SAP solution to help you deal with ongoing requirements throughout your solution's lifecycle.

In this chapter, we look at what SAP Solution Manager is, the benefits it offers your business, and the specific functions it delivers. Lastly, we explore a case study where you can see SAP Solution Manager in action.

What Is SAP Solution Manager?

SAP Solution Manager contains tools to support your SAP implementation, monitor your system after it's in place, request support from SAP's support organization, and upgrade your system when you need to grow and change. Quite simply, SAP Solution Manager takes you from the beginning to the end of your SAP experience (see Figure 20.1).

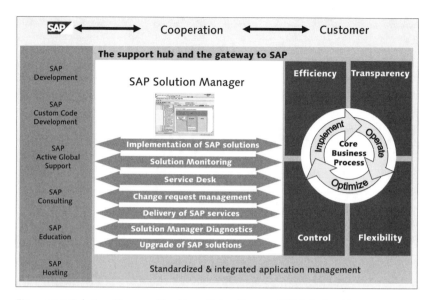

Figure 20.1 Solution Manager Has Many Roles (Source: SAP Solution Manager [2006] Schäfer & Melich. SAP PRESS)

SAP Solution Manager Overview

SAP Solution Manager is included in the cost of your yearly maintenance contract, and you have to use it to implement SAP NetWeaver (and all of the SAP products that rest on SAP NetWeaver) in your organization. SAP Solution Manager provides three categories of offerings, as shown in Table 20.1.

Tool	Application/Technology Management and Maintenance, including:
	> Document
	> Implement
	> Train
	> Test a Deployment
	> Support and Maintain
	> Monitor and Optimize
	> Control Change
	> Manage Incidents

Table 20.1 SAP Solution Manager's Offerings

Content	> Methodologies > Roadmaps > Services > Best Practices
Gateway to SAP	> SAP Active Global Support > SAP Development > Service Delivery Platform

Table 20.1 SAP Solution Manager's Offerings (Cont.)

As you begin to plan your implementation, SAP Solution Manager provides roadmaps that you can follow to work through the various phases of the installation or upgrade process. It also provides frameworks, tools, and services that are useful not only during your implementation but also long after.

Another role of SAP Solution Manager is to document your implementation in detail in a process-oriented documentation repository. The documentation can then be used by support groups or your own IT people to get a view of your IT enterprise computing landscape. If the people involved in your implementation or upgrade leave, you'll have a wealth of historical data for others to draw on as they maintain, upgrade, or troubleshoot your solution.

SAP Solution Manager documentation repository

SAP Solution Manager provides certain functionality that helps to document and expedite your implementation, but those features are based on an underlying approach to how you put pieces of your solution into place, which we'll explore in the next section. Finally, SAP Solution Manager ties you into SAP's support organization, generating information they can use to help you over any bumps that you may encounter on the implementation road.

The SAP Solution Manager Approach

There are six key ideas that provide the foundation for SAP Solution Manager and its various features:

> SAP Solution Manager is designed to help IT employees link technology tools to fit the needs of various business units in a company. It helps IT employees communicate with business users and hide

Business process focus

the technological details from them, focusing instead on their business needs.

Lifecycle support

> When you implement software in your organization, it has a lifecycle that might last years. Applications that spread across your entire enterprise will not only need to be implemented but will also require updating and maintaining. SAP Solution Manager helps you monitor the entire lifecycle of your solution.

Integration

> SAP Solution Manager helps you integrate the various pieces of business processes and account for the various components and interdependencies that are involved. In addition, SAP Solution Manager helps you integrate software from other vendors by providing dedicated integration packages.

Openness, coordination of IT processes, tools, and documents

> SAP supports an open environment spanning any number of systems and platforms. SAP Solution Manager also supports the implementation of SAP products in a way that allows for a variety of products and helps you resolve issues among those products.

Single point of access

> SAP Solution Manager coordinates the IT processes, tools, and documents that you need to implement and operate an SAP solution.

Transparency

> SAP Solution Manager gathers a variety of information about your SAP implementation together and makes it available in one location. This is useful not only for you to locate information about your systems but also to comply with information transparency requirements (see Figure 20.1).

End-to-End (E2E)

SAP Solution Manager is the platform that, based on these six underlying ideas, enables you to implement standards for End-to-End (E2E) solution operations. This means that, after an implementation, you have the experience from thousands of successful projects at your fingertips.

Now that we've given you a rough idea of what SAP Solution Manager is, we'll take the time to look more closely at the features and tools you get with SAP Solution Manager.

SAP Solution Manager Contents

SAP Solution Manager gives you technical support for deploying solutions, operating your systems, and upgrading your solutions long-term. SAP Solution Manager supports both SAP and non-SAP software and will dovetail nicely with upcoming SAP solutions.

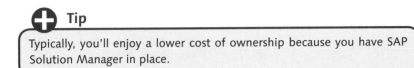

Tip

Typically, you'll enjoy a lower cost of ownership because you have SAP Solution Manager in place.

SAP Solution Manager is strongly focused on your core business; it provides tools and features for your IT people to connect technology to your business processes and strategies (see Figure 20.2). From installing a new piece of enterprise software to managing your existing systems, SAP Solution Manager was designed to make everything work together and help you solve problems rather than creating new ones.

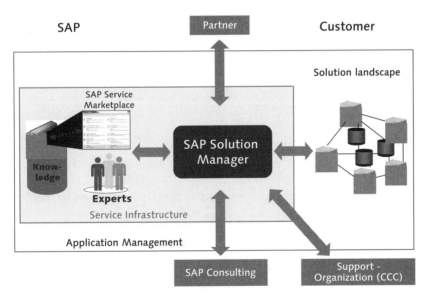

Figure 20.2 How SAP Solution Manager Fits in an Implementation Environment (Source: SAP Solution Manager [2006] Schäfer & Melich. SAP PRESS)

SAP Solution Manager offers a lot of functionality to support your implementation:

Functionality

> Configuration information and a process-centric implementation strategy help you create an implementation blueprint, configure

your system, and deal with the final preparation phases of your implementation. SAP Solution Manager has tools that help you administer your project and deal with cross-component implementations (see Figure 20.3).

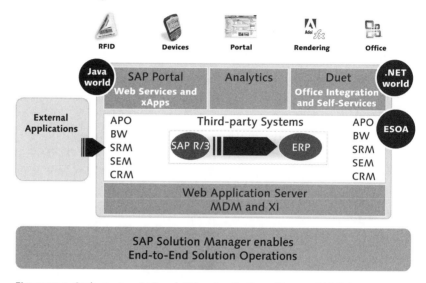

Figure 20.3 Orchestrating SAP and Other Applications (Source: SAP Solution Manager [2006] Schäfer & Melich. SAP PRESS)

> Rollout tools to support standardization of your processes throughout your enterprise with methodologies and predesigned functionality. You can build Business Configuration Sets and put standardized settings in place at your various sites without having to reenter configuration settings locally.

> Support desk functionality that helps you deal with support incidents quickly and saves you money in the area of support costs.

> Monitoring for your systems, business processes, and interfaces, including any dependencies among your various systems.

Monitoring features constantly check for problems and help you avoid disasters. SAP Solution Manager also sends automatic notifications of problems, and helps you know that SAP ERP is functioning as it should.

SAP Safeguarding   SAP Solution Manager provides tools for preparing system tests and making their execution faster. You get one point of access to your entire system and centralized storage of testing material. Service recommendations and connections to SAP support services such as SAP Safeguarding for dealing with technical risk are also included.

How do these features work in practice? Take a look at a case study to see exactly how SAP Solution Manager fits into a typical SAP implementation.

Solution Manager Case Study

Table 20.2 provides you with a snapshot of a case study. Review the table and the remainder of this section to learn more about how Solution Manager worked for one company.

Company	European natural gas supplier
Existing Solutions	Standardized on SAP ERP, SAP NetWeaver BW, SAP Strategic Enterprise Management (SAP SEM), SAP Enterprise Buyer (SAP EB), and industry-specific SAP solutions
Challenge	To implement a CRM solution quickly, while keeping the solution cost-effective
SAP Solutions	SAP Solution Manager and SAP CRM
Benefits	Fast implementation with documentation repository to help support maintenance and future upgrades of system, predefined content provided a foundation for customizing

Table 20.2 Solution Manager Case Study

A Norwegian company that supplies natural gas to European customers is also a major supplier of crude oil. With 24,000 employees and offices around the world, the company was growing and enjoying great success but needed to plan now for future growth. To support its success, the company felt that SAP CRM was a logical fit for its future.

The Challenges

The company needed a CRM solution, including mobile sales features to support about 200 field salespeople in Norway, Denmark, and

Sweden. Extensive downtime was not an option for this $37 billion company, so the company wanted to roll out SAP CRM quickly and efficiently. The company hoped to save money by various methods, including having its own employees assist with the implementation.

The Solution

CRM solution

SAP Consulting worked with the company to structure an SAP CRM solution and suggested using SAP Solution Manager to streamline the implementation. SAP Consulting conducted a two-day workshop with the company's IT employees. Implementation accelerators and an entire set of preconfigured business processes in SAP Solution Manager helped the company get a head start. SAP Solution Manager also gave the IT staff an understanding of both the functionality of Solution Manager and how its tools could support relevant business processes.

The centralized repository for implementation documentation that SAP Solution Manager provided has proven to be a valuable resource for future changes and maintenance. In addition, predefined configuration settings served as a great starting point for customization.

The Benefits

SAP CRM blueprint

The SAP solution set up the blueprint for SAP CRM and configured the entire system. The costs were half of what the company spent on its entire legacy CRM system. SAP Solution Manager enabled an implementation that took less than a year to complete.

In fact, the company's employees could handle more of the process without consultant input because of SAP Solution Manager and the tools it provided. The company's next step is to implement an Internet sales model in partnership with SAP to leverage the features and tools of SAP Solution Manager further.

Conclusion

In this chapter, we've tried to give you an understanding of Solution Manager, which is integral to any SAP implementation, by providing you with the following:

> An overview of the features that SAP Solution Manager offers you to make your implementation more efficient and effective

> The six key ideas underlying SAP's approach to using SAP Solution Manager

> A discussion of the SAP Solution Manager scenarios that deliver key features of SAP Solution Manager

> A case study of SAP Solution Manager in action

As was already mentioned, you're required to use SAP Solution Manager, because it is part of SAP NetWeaver. You will find that it automates your implementation documentation in very helpful ways.

The Next Step

We hope the information in this chapter, as well as the information provided in the preceding chapters, has provided you with a solid foundation for understanding what SAP, the company, is; what products and technologies it offers; and what tools and services it delivers to support you through an SAP implementation.

We hope that this book makes your experience with SAP and its products a smoother and more productive one, letting you make informed choices. Let's move on to the conclusion of this book and recap what you've learned.

21

Conclusion

We have provided the information in this book to give you a solid foundation for understanding what SAP, the company, is; what products and technologies it offers; and what tools and services it delivers to support you through an SAP implementation. Before we leave you, we want to offer some closing advice to help you take the next step.

Helpful Resources

Four appendices that follow offer you several helpful reference tools:

> Appendix A provides a glossary of terms, including SAP product names, enterprise technology terms, and buzzwords in the enterprise computing world to help you find your way in discussions with SAP.

> Appendix B includes lists of additional resources for you to explore, such as SAP Consulting groups, third-party SAP user groups, useful websites for enterprise computing, and regular enterprise computing events.

> Appendix C contains SAP solution maps, including detailed drill-down listings of features in SAP products for your reference.

> Appendix D provides a list of resources used in pulling this book together.

Come back to these resource appendices for help as you proceed with your enterprise computing needs in the future.

Going Forward

Here are a few final thoughts about your next steps with SAP and this book:

> You can use the foundation we have provided to find the right resources, ask the right questions, and understand the terms and product names that your SAP representative or third party consultant might use.

> The introduction we've provided to SOA should get you thinking in interesting directions for your organization's future computing environment.

> The case studies you've read may give you some ideas about the types of benefits your enterprise might discover by going further in your exploration of an SAP solution.

> When you hit a point of confusion in your exploration of SAP, use the glossary at the back of this book to clarify terms, or the explanations in these chapters to help you understand the features of each SAP offering. Don't forget to check SAP's website (*www.sap.com*) for any new information because products may change features from time to time.

We hope that this book has given you knowledge that will make your experience with SAP and its products a smoother and more productive one.

Appendices

A   Glossary

ABAP   (Advanced Business Application Programming) is a programming language for developing applications for the SAP system.

Abstraction   A method of presenting technology so that users see only what they need without exposing the underlying complexity.

Access management   A feature that allows IT people to set up specific accesses for various users on a network.

Adobe Interactive PDF Forms (SAP Interactive Forms software by Adobe)   A digital forms technology used in SAP software for collaborative electronic forms documentation.

Alloy   is an application developed through the joint effort of SAP and IBM to allow Lotus Notes users to access data within the SAP Business Suite.

Analytics   Data analyses typically generated in the form of reports, charts, and so on.

ASUG (Americas' SAP Users' Group)   A nonprofit organization of SAP customer companies dedicated to providing educational and networking opportunities in support of SAP applications and implementation. ASUG also works with SAP in its Partners in Education Program offered at the annual SAP Tech Ed conference.

Authentication   The process of verifying the identity of a computer user to provide access to a system or data.

Best practice   A management concept that involves devising a method or process that most effectively produces a desired outcome. SAP applications use business best practices to automate common business processes. (See also SAP Best Practices.)

Business Application Programming Interface (BAPI)   An application programming interface (source code that systems use to request services from computer applications) with certain business rules attached.

Business content   Predefined sets of business data provided based on a user's role in the company.

Business object   Items in an object-oriented computer application that match an abstract business concept such as an order, invoice, or product. Business objects are used as part of a domain model to encapsulate their associated behavior in programming.

BusinessObjects   A business intelligence company purchased by SAP in 2008 (see Chapter 12 for details).

Business process   A set of related steps performed to create a defined result in a business setting. SAP applications support typical business processes such as invoicing.

Business process outsourcing   Contracting with an external vendor to manage a discrete business process, such as payroll processing.

Business-to-business   Services or products delivered not to end users but to another business, such as transportation services.

Change management   A structured approach to the process of strategizing and managing change for individuals, teams, and departments in an organization.

Collaboration room   Online portals where members of a team can collaborate by sharing documents, applications, schedules, and tasks, along with communicating via chats or discussions.

Compliance   The process businesses use to comply with regulations such as Sarbanes-Oxley or health and safety regulations.

Composite application   An application that rests on other applications or components to use their service-enabled functions and data to build business scenarios.

Composition platform   SAP NetWeaver is a composition platform that you can use to build model-based business processes using services.

Corporate Services   One of the four main applications areas of SAP ERP that offers tools such as real estate management, enterprise asset management, and travel management.

Dashboard   A user interface, typically provided through a portal, that offers tools and data in a centralized location.

Data warehouse   A centralized repository for an enterprise's data.

Database   An electronic collection of information organized for easy access by computer programs.

Duet   A joint venture of Microsoft and SAP that allows the use of SAP functionality and business intelligence

through the Microsoft Office environment.

Electronic form   See Adobe Interactive PDF Forms.

Embedded analytics   Incorporating business intelligence within operational applications and business processes.

Employee self-service (ESS)   One of two self-service features provided by SAP NetWeaver that enables employees to access data and complete processes related to their roles in a company, such as submitting vacation leave requests or signing up for employee training. (See also Manager self-service [MSS].)

Encryption   The process used to obscure information so that it cannot be read without special tools or knowledge to unscramble it.

Enterprise   Any business or organization.

Enterprise computing   Computer systems and processes used within an enterprise.

Enterprise Resource Planning (ERP)   A type of application that is used to integrate all of the data and processes of a business or organization with the goal of maximizing the efficiency of operations. (See also SAP ERP.)

Enterprise service   A web service used to execute one step of a business process. Enterprise services can be used and combined to build business processes. (See also Web service.)

Enterprise Services Repository (ES Repository)   The centralized storage place in SAP NetWeaver for services, business objects, and business processes, along with metadata (data that provides information about the characteristics of other data).

Governance   Strategic directives for an enterprise to follow; corporate policies and procedures.

Granularity   An approach to defining services that breaks them down in relation to the steps of a business process. See also Business process.

Guided procedure   A wizard-like workflow tool in SAP NetWeaver that guides users through collaborative business processes using templates.

HTML (Hypertext Markup Language) A markup language used to create web pages, which describes the characteristics of text in a document involving a request from a client to a server and a response.

HTTP   (Hypertext Transfer Protocol)   A method of accessing information stored on the web.

HTTPS   A secure form of HTTP using encryption. (See also HTTP, Encryption.)

Independent Software Vendors (ISV)   Software vendors who have had an SAP-related software solution certified, thereby earning the right to participate in SAP's Industry Value Network process in support of larger SAP customers.

Industry solution map   Industry-specific maps from SAP that guide users and help them focus on core processes and functions relevant to their types of business.

Industry Value Network   Any of eight industry-focused organizations that involve customers, partners, and

SAP employees who work together to innovate solutions within particular industries.

Integration   The ability for data generated by one software application or device to be used by another device or software application.

Interactive forms   See Adobe Interactive PDF Forms.

Invoice Monitoring System (IMS) A feature of SAP ERP that preprocesses invoices to deal with a variety of invoice exceptions.

iView   Small applications that typically run in a portal and connect to the underlying data and applications in your system.

Key performance indicator (KPI) Both financial and non-financial measurements that help to quantify and analyze strategic performance objectives of an organization.

Knowledge management   Various efforts by an enterprise to create, classify, and represent information and distribute it throughout the organization.

Lifecycle Data Management   Part of SAP Product Lifecycle Management related to using SOA to manage product-related data.

Lifecycle Process Support   Part of SAP Product Lifecycle Management for integrating SAP PLM with other SAP Business Suite applications.

Manager self-service (MSS)   One of two self-service features provided by SAP NetWeaver that enables managers to access data and complete processes related to their management roles in a company such as hiring or creating budgets. (See also Employee self-service [ESS].)

Master Data Management   See SAP Master Data Management.

Mobile Infrastructure   See SAP Mobile Infrastructure.

Model-driven development   See Modeling.

Modeling   A system of programming that describes what a software application's function is by defining relationships between components.

NetWeaver   See SAP NetWeaver.

Outsourcing   See Business process outsourcing.

Portal   Typically a main site on the web or on an intranet that provides capabilities users can personalize for their needs.

Procurement   Acquiring goods or services at the optimum price and quality.

Protocol   In object-oriented software applications, protocols are used to help objects communicate with each other.

RFID   (Radio Frequency Identification) Tags that enable a device to remotely read data; used for activities such as inventorying stock in stores or warehouses.

Risk management   Identifying and planning for potential risk in business, including performing risk analysis, monitoring, and developing responses for possible risk scenarios. SAP GRC Risk Management is a portion of an SAP solution for Governance, Risk, and Compliance.

Role-based   The concept of providing information and services to end users based on their role in an enterprise.

SAP R/3   The SAP client/server architecture-based software introduced in 1992, which was a predecessor of SAP ERP.

SAP Best Practices   A set of preconfigured business templates based on industry best practices to accelerate implementations and upgrades. Used substantially in SAP Business All-in-One fast-start program.

SAP Business All-in-One fast-start program   An integrated software system built on business SAP Best Practices for the small to midsize company.

SAP Business ByDesign   Formerly known as A1S, this is the new SAP hosted offering for mid-market customers. A complete integrated solution with easy configuration, targeted specifically for the mid-market.

SAP Business One   SAP's offering for the smaller end of the mid-market.

SAP Business Suite   A comprehensive business solution from SAP that includes SAP ERP, SAP CRM, SAP PLM, SAP SCM, and SAP SRM.

SAP Composite Application Framework (SAP CAF)   A part of SAP NetWeaver; development environment for services used to create composite applications.

SAP Customer Resource Management (SAP CRM)   Part of the SAP Business Suite that deals with managing the business interactions and relationships with customers.

SAP Developer Network (SDN)   A centralized resource for those developing applications on the SAP NetWeaver platform. SDN involves software developers, systems integrators, and consultants and can be viewed at *http://sdn.sap.com*.

SAP ERP   A suite of software applications from SAP that focuses on the core business requirements of midsize to large companies, including areas of Human Capital Management, Financials, Operations, and Corporate Services.

SAP ERP Corporate Services   The area of SAP ERP that provides centralized management of cost-intensive corporate processes, including real estate; enterprise assets; project portfolios; corporate travel; environment, health, and safety compliance; quality; and global trade services.

SAP ERP Financials   The area of SAP ERP that helps you predict performance, manage compliance, and automate financial accounting and supply chain management.

SAP ERP Human Capital Management (SAP ERP HCM)   The area of SAP ERP that helps you manage human resources processes, including talent management, workforce deployment, and core HR processes such as hiring and training.

SAP ERP Operations   The area of SAP ERP that involves managing procurement and the flow of materials, the manufacturing lifecycle, and sales and service.

SAP Manufacturing   An SAP software package that enables you to integrate manufacturing with other areas of your business operations and detect exceptions in your operation.

SAP Master Data Management (SAP MDM)   A system for managing data that receives and sends out data to the various databases in your enterprise. With SAP MDM, you can create a universal database and even store information about relationships between databases.

SAP Mobile Business   SAP software that enables you to access SAP Business Suite solutions via mobile devices. (See also SAP Mobile Infrastructure.)

SAP NetWeaver   SAP's technology platform for most of its solutions. It allows for the integration of various application components and for composing services using a model-based approach. SAP NetWeaver is also the location of a centralized services repository whereby technologies enable activities such as mobile computing.

SAP NetWeaver Business Warehouse (SAP NetWeaver BW)   A component of the SAP NetWeaver platform that offers data warehousing functionality via repositories of data, and tools for information integration.

SAP NetWeaver Mobile   A part of SAP NetWeaver that provides an open standards platform used to give access to data and processes via a variety of channels. SAP NetWeaver Mobile is the technology that works with SAP Mobile Business to provide access to mobile devices. (See also SAP Mobile Business.)

SAP NetWeaver Process Integration (SAP NetWeaver PI)   A feature in SAP NetWeaver that allows you to integrate processes, thereby allowing applications to communicate with each other.

SAP NetWeaver Visual Composer   A modeling tool included in SAP NetWeaver used to create customized user interfaces.

SAP Product Lifecycle Management (SAP PLM)   An SAP software solution that helps a company manage product development, management of projects, product structures, and quality.

SAP Service and Asset Management An SAP software solution for managing service delivery and management and optimization of assets.

SAP Solution Manager   A solution support set that includes tools, content, and access to SAP to help companies deploy SAP products.

SAP Supplier Relationship Management (SAP SRM)   An application that is part of the SAP Business Suite, which helps organizations manage the procurement process.

SAP Supply Chain Management (SAP SCM)   An application that is part of the SAP Business Suite used to coordinate supply and demand; monitor the supply chain to manage distribution, transportation, and other logistics; and provide collaborative and analytical tools.

SAP TCO Model   A framework for modeling total cost of ownership for SAP ERP software, which provides an analysis of specific customer data to support SAP implementations.

SAP Tech Ed   An annual SAP conference spotlighting technical knowledge and skills related to SOA and SAP NetWeaver, including hands-on workshops and technical lectures.

SAPPHIRE   SAP-run annual conferences that take place in a variety of cities and countries to expose business decision makers to SAP's latest offerings.

Sarbanes-Oxley Act   (SOX) A US regulation initiated in 2002 to regulate financial reporting and accountability in response to corporate scandals such as Enron and WorldCom.

Scalability   The ability of a system to be grown or built on easily.

Scenario   A set of business processes that can be performed in sequence to reach a desired outcome. An example of a scenario in SAP is Procure2Pay, managing an entire procurement process.

Service   See Web service and Enterprise service.

Service-oriented architecture (SOA) A software architecture that allows for the use of services with an exchange relationship to build business processes. In SAP, SOA refers to SAP's blueprint for implementing a service-oriented architecture to use services as building blocks for business processes, based on open standards. (See also Enterprise service.)

Shared services center   A method of sharing pieces of business process scenarios via a centralized location, often used in outsourcing business processes to third parties.

SOA adoption   A support program offered by SAP to help enterprises move toward a service-oriented architecture environment.

Solution Composer   An SAP tool used to manipulate SAP Solution Maps and Business Solution Maps to visualize, plan, and implement various IT solutions in an enterprise.

Solution Manager   See SAP Solution Manager.

Solution map   A table of SAP software applications organized within a single solution category that define a set or requirements either within or across industries.

Standardization   Setting up a single technical standard that various entities can agree to.

Supply Chain Management (SCM) See SAP Supply Chain Management.

Talent Management   An area of the SAP ERP HCM application that provides features for managing HR-related processes, including recruitment, hiring, training, performance, and compensation management.

Total cost of ownership (TCO) See SAP TCO model.

User interface   The visual definition of a communication between a software program and a user.

Value-based services for SAP solutions   A method of evaluating the potential value of the implementation of SAP products or product enhancements.

Vertical solution   An industry-specific solution. See also Industry solution map.

XML   Extensible Markup Language, used to share data across a variety of information systems.

Web service   Web application programming interfaces (APIs) that can be accessed via a network. Web services encapsulate a function of an application in a way that it can be accessed by another application.

Web Service Description Language (WSDL)   A way of describing web services using XML to hide complexity and focus on functionality.

Work center   A kind of user portal that focuses on a certain set of tools or data that supports one kind of work or functionality.

Work trigger   A role-based initiation of data or other functionality being pushed to a user based on a need to know.

B   SAP Resources

Many resources for helping you with your SAP implementation are discussed in detail in Chapters 19, Preparing for an SAP Implementation, and 20, SAP Solution Manager. Here we present a useful list of resources broken down into categories with associated website addresses.

SAP Communities and Alliances

Several organizations exist both within SAP and independently to provide free information or for-a-fee consulting, including business alliance partners and user groups:

> Americas SAP Users Group (ASUG): *www.asug.com*
> Business Process Expert Community: *www.sap.com/platform/ecosystem/bpecommunity*
> IBM/SAP Alliance: *www-03.ibm.com/solutions/sap/us/index.html*
> Intel/SAP Alliance: *www.intelalliance.com/sap/*
> Microsoft/SAP Alliance: *www.microsoft.com/isv/sap/*
> SAP Australian User Group (SAUG): *www.saug.com.au/*
> SAP Enterprise Services Community: *www.sap.com/platform/ecosystem/escommunity/index.epx*
> SAP Industry Value Network: *www.sap.com/platform/ecosystem/ivn*
> SAP Developer Network: *www.sdn.sap.com*
> SUN/SAP Alliance: *www.sun.com/third-party/global/sap/*
> User Group of England: *www2.warwick.ac.uk/services/finance/sap/usergroups/*

Certification

If you're interested in SAP certification, you can get information from SAP or the company that administers the tests, Pearson. You'll find these websites helpful:

> Pearson Vue: *www.vue.com/sap/*
> SAP Education: *www.sap.com/services/education/certification*

Websites and Blogs

There are many useful websites with information about topics such as enterprise resource planning (ERP), customer resource planning, ERP analytics, and topics specific to SAP products, including the following:

> SAP ITToolbox: *www.sap.ittoolbox.com*

> SAP ITToolbox Blogs: *www.sap.ittoolbox.com/blogs*

> The SAP Fan Club: *www.sapfans.com*

> The ERP Fan Club and User Forum: *www.erpfans.com*

> SAP Online Events: *www.sap.com/community/pub/events.epx*

> CIO Magazine Enterprise Resource Planning page: *www.cio.com/research/erp*

> ERP Guide: *www.managementsupport.com/erp.htm*

> SearchSAP: *www.searchsap.com*

> SearchCRM: *www.searchcrm.com*

> 2020Software: *www.2020software.com*

Publications

Several print and online magazines provide regular articles on topics such as ERP, and SAP PRESS, the publisher of this book, offers a broad range of books on SAP-related topics. Some sources for publications are listed here:

> *Business 2.0*: *www.business2.com*

> SAP Info: send email to *press@sap.com* to ask about subscribing

> *SAP Insider*: *www.sapinsideronline.com*

> *SAP Professional Journal*: *www.sappro.com*

> *SAP NetWeaver Magazine*: *www.sapnetweavermagazine.com*

> SAP PRESS offers a range of books on SAP and its products, solutions, and technologies: *www.sap-press.com*

Conferences

If you're interested in attending an SAP or ERP-focused event, there are several of these events that occur throughout the year, including the following:

- › SAP SAPPHIRE: *www.sapsapphire.com*
- › SAP World Tour: *www.sap.com/company/events/worldtour2007*
- › SAP Technology Tour: *www.sap.com/company/events*
- › AGS Road show: *http://www.sap.com/about/events/agsroadshows/index.epx*
- › SAP conferences and seminars from WIS: *www.wispubs.com/products Events.cfm*

SAP Services

As you read about SAP services in Chapters 17, *Service-Oriented Architecture,* and 18, *SAP NetWeaver as a Technology Platform,* many SAP organizations and programs exist to help you succeed. Here are some that you should check out:

- › SAP Active Global Support: *www.sap.com/services/support*
- › SAP Business Process Outsourcing: *www.sap.com/services/bpo*
- › SAP Consulting: *www.sap.com/services/consulting*
- › SAP Custom Development: *www.sap.com/services/customdev*
- › SAP Education: *www.sap.com/services/education*
- › SAP Financing: *http://www.sap.com/services/bysubject/sapfinancing/index.epx*
- › SAP Ramp-Up: *www.sap.com/services/rampup*
- › SAP Service Marketplace: *www.sap.com/services/servsuptech/smp* (partner or customer ID required)
- › SAP Best Practices: *www.sap.com/services/servsuptech/bestpractices*
- › SAP Solution Manager: *www.sap.com/platform/netweaver/components/solutionmanager/*

SAP Offices

If you're ready to contact SAP and discuss your needs further, use this listing of offices worldwide to find the appropriate resource.

Office Directory: United States

Regional SAP Headquarters

SAP America Inc.
Strategic Planning & Support Office
3999 West Chester Pike
Newtown Square, PA 19073
Phone: +1-610-661-1000

U.S. Products and Services
Phone: +1-800-872-1727

SAP Business One Response Center
Phone: +1-888-227-1727

Branch Offices/Sales Partners

SAP America Inc. — Atlanta
20 Perimeter Summit Boulevard
Suite 2100
Atlanta, GA 30319
Phone: +1-404-943-2900
Fax: +1-404-943-2950
Products and Services: +1-800-872-1727

SAP America, Inc. — Bellevue
601 108th Avenue, N.E. — 19th Floor
Bellevue, WA 98004
Phone: +1-425-943-6920
Fax: +1-425-943-6801
Products and Services: +1-800-872-1727

SAP America, Inc. — Boston
3 Van de Graaff Drive
Burlington, MA 01803
Phone: +1-781-852-8900
Fax: +1-781-852-9000

SAP America Inc. — Chicago
5 Westbrook Corporate Center
Suite 1000
Westchester, IL 60154

Phone: +1-708-947-3400
Fax: +1-708-947-3404
Products and Services: +1-800-872-1727

SAP America Inc. — Cincinnati

312 Walnut Street
Suite 1600
Cincinnati, OH 45202
Phone: +1-513-762-7630
Fax: +1-513-762-7602
Products and Services: +1-800-872-1727

SAP America Inc. — Cleveland

6100 Oak Tree Blvd.
Suite 200
Independence, OH 44131
Phone: +1-216-986-2780
Fax: +1-216-986-2791
Products and Services: +1-800-872-1727

SAP America Inc. — Dallas

5215 N. O'Connor Blvd.
Suite 800
Irving, TX 75039
Phone: +1-972-868-2000
Fax: +1-972-868-2001
Products and Services: +1-800-872-1727

SAP America, Inc. — Denver

6400 S. Fiddler's Green Circle, Suite 1400
Greenwood Village, CO 80111
Phone: +1-303-222-2300
Fax: +1-303-222-2301
Products and Services: +1-800-872-1727

SAP America Inc. — Detroit

One Towne Square
Suite 1550
Southfield, MI 48076
Phone: +1-248-304-1000

Fax: +1-248-304-1001
Products and Services: +1-800-872-1727

SAP America Inc. — Exton
350 Eagleview Blvd.
Suite 110
Exton, PA 19341
Phone: +1-610-903-8000
Fax: +1-610-903-8006
Products and Services: +1-800-872-1727

SAP — Fremont
47257 Fremont Blvd.
Fremont, CA 94538
Phone: +1-510-651-5990
Fax: 510-651-6306
Products and Services: +1-800-872-1727

SAP America Inc. — Houston
10111 Richmond Avenue
Suite 600
Houston, TX 77042
Phone: +1-713-917-5200
Fax: +1-713-917-5201
Products and Services: +1-800-872-1727

SAP America Inc. — Irvine
18101 Von Karman Ave.
Suite 900
Irvine, CA 92612
Phone: +1-949-622-2200
Fax: +1-949-622-2201
Products and Services: +1-800-872-1727

SAP America Inc. — Miami
5301 Blue Lagoon Drive
Suite 790
Miami, FL 33126
Phone: +1-305-476-4400
Fax: +1-305-476-4401
Products and Services: +1-800-872-1727

SAP America Inc. — Minneapolis

7760 France Avenue South
Suite 1100
Bloomington, MN 55435
Phone: +1-952-886-7432
Fax: +1-952-886-7431

SAP America Inc. — Morristown

89 Headquarters Plaza
North Tower, 3rd Floor
Suite 306
Morristown, NJ 07960
Phone: +1-973-631-6199
Fax: +1-973-631-6171
Products and Services: +1-800-872-1727

SAP America Inc. — Palo Alto

3410 Hillview Ave.
Palo Alto, CA 94304
Phone: +1-650-849-4000
Fax: +1-650-849-4200
Products and Services: +1-800-872-1727

SAP America Inc. — St. Louis

Two City Place Drive
Suite 200
St. Louis, MO 63141
Phone: +1-314-812-2500
Fax: +1-314-812-2505
Products and Services: +1-800-872-1727

Worldwide Country Sites

There are two useful sites to start with to locate SAP offices worldwide
or to send them an email and let them put you in touch with the right
person:

> International SAP offices: *www.sap.com/usa/contactsap/countries/
> index.epx*

> Contact SAP via email: *www.sap.com/contactsap/index.epx*

C   SAP Solution Maps

Throughout this book, we have provided information on SAP products and the highest level solution maps for these products. Each of these solution maps has additional information within its major categories that can be a handy reference for you as you consider various SAP solutions.

In this appendix, we provide you with solution maps and detailed listings of product features for SAP ERP, SAP Customer Relationship Management, SAP Supplier Relationship Management, SAP Product Lifecycle Management, SAP Supply Chain Management, and SAP Business One (Figures C.1 through C.6 and Tables C.1 through C.38). We've also noted the relevant chapter where you can go for detailed information about each of these products.

 Important Note

Some of the features mentioned here are available through SAP partners, or are planned but not yet available at the time of this writing. Check with your SAP representative to find out how to obtain all the features you need for your particular enterprise situation.

SAP ERP

See Chapters 4, 5, and 6 for more information about SAP ERP, whose features are detailed in Figure C.1 and Tables C.1 through C.8.

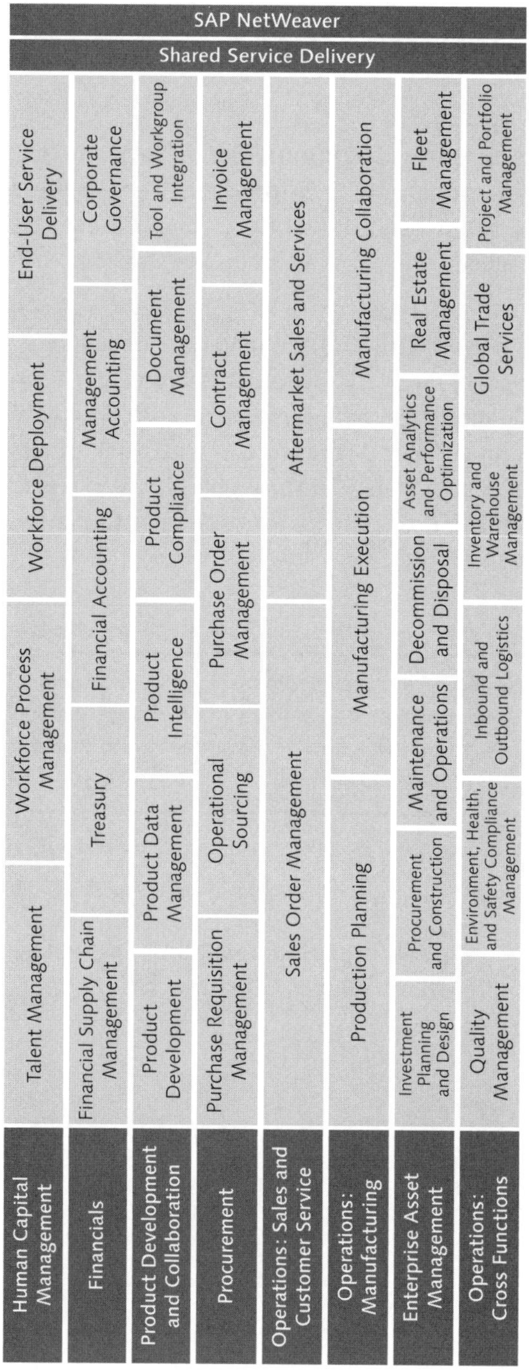

SAP NetWeaver				
Shared Service Delivery				
Human Capital Management	Talent Management	Workforce Process Management	Workforce Deployment	End-User Service Delivery	
Financials	Financial Supply Chain Management	Treasury	Financial Accounting	Management Accounting	Corporate Governance
Product Development and Collaboration	Product Development	Product Data Management	Product Intelligence	Product Compliance	Document Management / Tool and Workgroup Integration
Procurement	Purchase Requisition Management	Operational Sourcing	Purchase Order Management	Contract Management	Invoice Management
Operations: Sales and Customer Service	Sales Order Management		Aftermarket Sales and Services		
Operations: Manufacturing	Production Planning		Manufacturing Execution	Manufacturing Collaboration	
Enterprise Asset Management	Investment Planning and Design	Procurement and Construction	Maintenance and Operations	Decommission and Disposal	Asset Analytics and Performance Optimization / Real Estate Management / Fleet Management
Operations: Cross Functions	Quality Management	Environment, Health, and Safety Compliance Management	Inbound and Outbound Logistics	Inventory and Warehouse Management	Global Trade Services / Project and Portfolio Management

Figure C.1 SAP ERP

Category	Application
Talent Management	Competency Management
	Recruiting
	Employee Performance Management
	Talent Review & Calibration
	Employee Development
	Enterprise Learning
	Succession Management
	Compensation Management
	Talent Management Analytics
Workforce Process Management	Employee Administration
	Organizational Management
	Global Employee Management
	Benefits Management
	Healthcare Cost Management
	Time and Attendance
	Payroll and Legal Reporting
	HCM Processes and Forms
	Employee Self Service/Manager Self Service
	Employee Interaction Center
	Workforce Planning
	Workforce Cost Planning & Simulation
	Workforce Benchmarking
	Workforce Process Analytics & Measurement
	Strategic Alignment
Workforce Deployment Management	Project Resource Planning
	Resource and Program Management
	Retail Scheduling
End User Service Delivery	Manager Self Services
	Employee Self Services
	Employee Interaction Center

Table C.1 SAP ERP Human Capital Management

Financial Supply Chain Management	Treasury	Financial Accounting	Management Accounting	Corporate Governance
› Electronic Bill Presentment and Payment › Collections Management › Credit Management › Dispute Management	› Treasury and Risk Management › Cash and Liquidity Management › In-House Cash › Bank Communication Management	› General Ledger › Accounts Receivable › Accounts Payable › Contract Accounting › Fixed Assets Accounting › Bank Accounting › Cash Journal Accounting › Inventory Accounting › Tax Accounting › Accrual Accounting › Local Close › Financial Statements › Travel Management	› Profit Center Accounting › Cost Center and Internal Order Accounting › Project Accounting › Investment Management › Product Cost Accounting › Profitability Accounting › Transfer Pricing	› Audit Information System › Management of Internal Controls › Risk Management › Whistle Blower Complaints › Segregation of Duties

Table C.2 SAP ERP Financials

Product Deployment	Product Data Management	Product Intelligence	Product Compliance	Document Management	Tool and Workgroup Integration
› Product Development › Development Collaboration	› Product Structure Management › Recipe Management › Specification Management › Change and Configuration Management	› Product-Centric View	› Product Compliance › REACH Compliance	› Document Management	› CAD Integration

Table C.3 SAP ERP Product Development and Collaboration

Purchase Requisition Management	Operational Sourcing	Purchase Order Management	Contract Management	Invoice Management
› Purchase Requisition Processing	› Sourcing › Purchasing Optimization › Compliance Management	› Purchase Order Processing › Delivery Schedule Processing › Commodity Management	› Operational Contract Processing › Scheduling Agreement › Trading Contracts	› Invoice Processing › SAP Invoice Management by Open Text › Flexible Invoice Reconciliation

Table C.4 SAP ERP Procurement

Sales Order Management	Aftermarket Sales and Services
› Account Processing	› Service Sales
› Internet Sales	› Service Contract Management
› Managing Auctions	› Customer Service and Support
› Inquiry Processing	› Installed Base Management
› Quotation Processing	› Warranty and Claims Management
› Trading Contract Management	› Field Service
› Sales Order Processing	› Depot Repair
› Contract Processing	
› Billing	
› Incentive and Commission Management	
› Returnable Packaging Management	
› Consignment	
› Commodity Management	

Table C.5 SAP ERP Operations: Sales and Customer Service

Production Planning	Manufacturing Execution	Manufacturing Collaboration
› Production Planning	› Manufacturing Execution	› External Processing
› Capacity Planning	› Shop Floor Integration	› Quality Collaboration
› Lean Planning	› Supervision and Control	
	› Manufacturing Analytics	

Table C.6 SAP ERP Operations: Manufacturing

Investment Planning and Design	Procurement and Construction	Maintenance and Operations	Decomission and Disposal	Asset Analytics and Performance Optimization	Real Estate Management	Fleet Management
› Business Planning	› Supplier Qualification and Candidate Selection	› Technical Assets Management	› Asset Transfer and Disposal	› Integrated Asset Accounting	› Portfolio Management	› Fleet Administration
› Investment Management	› Bidding and Contract Management	› Workforce Management	› Document Management	› Asset and Maintenance Reporting	› Commercial Real Estate Management	› Fleet Maintenance
› Asset Portfolio Management	› Procurement Process	› Preventive and Predictive Maintenance	› Collaborative Disposal Management	› Asset Performance Management	› Corporate Real Estate Management	› Transportation Logistics
› Collaboration Specification and Design	› Document Management	› Maintenance Planning and Scheduling	› Project Management	› Reliability Centered Maintenance	› Facilities Management	› Capacity Planning
› Maintenance Engineering	› Project Management	› Work Order Management	› Waste Management	› Asset Life-Cycle Costing		› Fleet Analysis
› Interfacing CAD Systems	› Collaborative Construction	› Approval Processing	› Asset Compliance	› Damage Analytics		
› Project Management	› Project and Investment Controlling	› Contractor Management	› Asset Remarketing	› Object Statistics		
	› MRO and Services Procurement	› Refurbishment		› Spend and Supplier Performance Analytics		
		› Mobile Asset Management including RFID Enablement		› Predictive Condition Monitoring		
		› Service Parts and Inventory Management		› Operator Dashboards		
		› Interfacing CAD, GIS, and SCADA Systems		› Budget Tracking		
		› Work Clearance Management		› Maintenance Cost Planning		
		› Shutdown Planning				
		› Asset Tracking with RFID				
		› Takeover/Handover for Technical Objects				

Table C.7 SAP ERP Enterprise Asset Management

Quality Management	Environment, Health, and Safety Compliance Management	Inbound and Outbound Logistics	Inventory and Warehouse Management	Global Trade Services	Project and Portfolio Management
› Quality Engineering › Quality Assurance/ Control › Quality Improvement › Audit Management	› EHS Management › Recycling Administration	› Inbound Processing › Outbound Processing › Transportation Execution › Freight Costing › Product Classification › Duty Calculation › Customs Communication Service › Trade Document Service › Trade Preference Processing	› Cross Docking › Warehousing and Storage › Physical Inventory	› Export Management › Import Management › Trade Preference Management › Restitution Management	› Portfolio Management › Project Management › Resource Management

Table C.8 SAP ERP Operations: Cross Functions

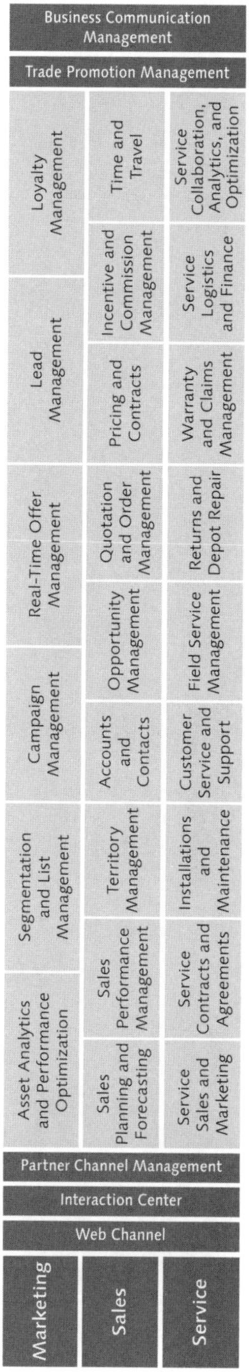

Figure C.2 SAP CRM Solution Map

Marketing Resource Management	Segmentation and List Management	Campaign Management	Real-Time Offer Management	Lead Management	Loyalty Management
> Market Research	> Multiple Data Source Access	> Campaign Planning	> Offer Portfolio Management	> Multiple Interaction Channels	> Loyalty Program Management
> Budget Planning	> High Speed Data Search	> Graphical Campaign Modeling	> Real-Time Event Detection and Recommendation	> Automated Qualification	> Loyalty Campaign Management
> Scenario Planning	> Preview Lists	> Campaign Optimization	> Interaction Assistance	> Rule-Based Distribution	> Reward Rule Management
> Marketing Planning and Budgeting	> Pre-Filtered/Personalized Attribute Lists	> Campaign Simulation	> Self Learning and Optimization Mechanism	> Lead Dispatching	> Membership Management
> Budget Control	> Sampling and Splitting	> Marketing Calendar	> Offer Simulator	> Web-Based Lead Generation	> Membership Management in Web Channel
> Product and Brand Planning	> Embedded Predictive Modeling	> Campaign-Specific Pricing	> Data Mapping Tool	> Lead Partner Management	> Membership Management in Interaction Center
> Cost and Volume Planning	> Personalized Filters	> Multichannel Campaign Execution	> Configuration and Migration Tool	> Mass Generation	> Membership Management in CRM WebClient UI
> Marketing Plan Analysis	> Quick Counts	> Multiwave Campaign Execution	> Offer Performance Analytics	> Response Recording	> Member Activities and Points Management
> Marketing Calendar	> Segment Deduplication	> Event-Triggered Campaign Execution	> Agent Performance Analytics	> Lead Surveys	
> Marketing Organization	> Suppression Filters	> Real-Time Response Tracking	> Channel Performance Analytics	> Automatic Generation of Follow-Up Activities	
> Workflow and Approval	> Target Group Optimization	> Cost/Financial Reporting		> Lead Analysis	
	> Clustering	> Personalized (E)Mails			
	> Data Mining	> Bounce Handling			
	> Decision Trees	> Call Lists Campaign ROI			
	> ABC Analysis	> Interactive Scripting			
	> List Management – List Format Mapping	> Target Group Analysis			
	> Duplicate Checks	> Campaign Analysis			
	> Postal Validation				
	> Data Cleansing				
	> Data Enrichment				
	> List Quality				
	> Lead and Activity Imports				
	> List Analysis				

Table C.9 SAP CRM Marketing

Sales Planning and Forecasting	Sales Performance Management	Territory Management	Accounts & Contacts	Opportunity Management	Quotation & Order Management	Pricing and Contracts	Incentives & Commission Management	Time and Travel
› Strategic Planning › Flexible Modeling › Rolling Forecast › Collaborative Planning › Supply Chain Integration › Planning-Cycle Monitoring › Performance Reviews › Sales Planning and Forecasting Guides › Account Planning › Opportunity Planning	› Pipeline Performance Management	› Market Segmentation › Territory Assignment and Scheduling › Territory/Organizational Mapping › Rule-Based Synchronization for Mobile Devices › Sales Analysis by Territory › Interface to Third-Party Territory Planning Tools	› Visit Planning › Fact Sheet › Interaction History › Activity Management › Email and Fax Integration › Relationship Management › Marketing Attributes › Customer-Specific Pricing › Account Planning › Customer Analysis › Account Classification › Data Quality Management	› Opportunity Planning › Team Selling › Competitive Information › Account-Specific Sales Processes › Automatic Business Partner Assignment › Pricing › Activities › Follow-Up Transactions › Product Configurations › Anticipated Revenue › Buying Center › Sales Project Management › Opportunity Hierarchies › Sales Process and Selling Methodologies › Opportunity Analysis	› Quotations › Package Quotation › Order Capture › Automatic Business Partner Assignment › Order Status Tracking › Pricing › Price Change Approval › Order Validation Check › Credit Management and Credit Check › Payment Card Processing › Automated Follow-Up Processes › Product Authorization and Restriction › Product Configuration › Bill of Material › Availability Check › Rebates › Billing › Fulfillment Synchronization › Quotation and Order Analysis › Cross-/Upselling › Reordering/Listings › Web Catalog	› Value and Quantity Contracts › Sales Agreements › Authorized Customers › Contract Completion Rules › Collaborative Contract Negotiation › Release Order Processing › Cancellation Handling › Fulfillment Synchronization › Automatic Business Partner Assignment › Product Configuration › Contract Status Tracking › Credit Management and Credit Check › Pricing › Customer-Specific Pricing › Promotional Pricing › Contract Analysis	› Direct and Indirect Sales Compensation › Incentive Plan Modeling › Configuration Templates › Roll Up Hierarchies/Indirect Participants › Contracts and Agreements Handling › Individual Plan Exceptions › Target Agreement Adjustments › Posting and Settlement › Commission Simulation › Commission Status Management	› Time Reporting › Expense Reports › Receipt Itemization › Track Receipts, Mileage, Deductions, and Border Crossings › Integration with Activity Management › Cost Assignment

Table C.10 SAP CRM Sales

Service Sales and Marketing	Service Contracts and Agreements	Installations and Maintenance	Customer Service and Support	Field Service Management	Returns and Depot Repair	Warranty and Claims Management	Service Logistics and Finance	Service Collaboration, Analytics, and Optimization
› Service Catalogs › Service Marketing and Campaigns › Service Opportunity Management › Service Solution Selling	› Service Agreement Management › Service Contract Management › Usage Based Contract Management › Service Level Management	› Installed Base and Objects Management › Installation and Configuration › Counter and Readings Management › Service Plan Management	› Service Requests Processing › Knowledge Management › Case Management › Complaints Processing	› Service Order Management › Resource Planning › Service Confirmation Management	› Returns Processing › Loaner Management › In-House Repair Processing › Quality Management Integration	› Warranty Management › Warranty Claims Processing › Recall Management	› Logistics Integration › Service Parts Management › Financial Integration › Billing	› Multichannel Integration › SOA Ready Service Processes › Business Workflow, Alerts, and Rules › Service Forecasting, Planning, and Analysis

Table C.11 SAP CRM Service

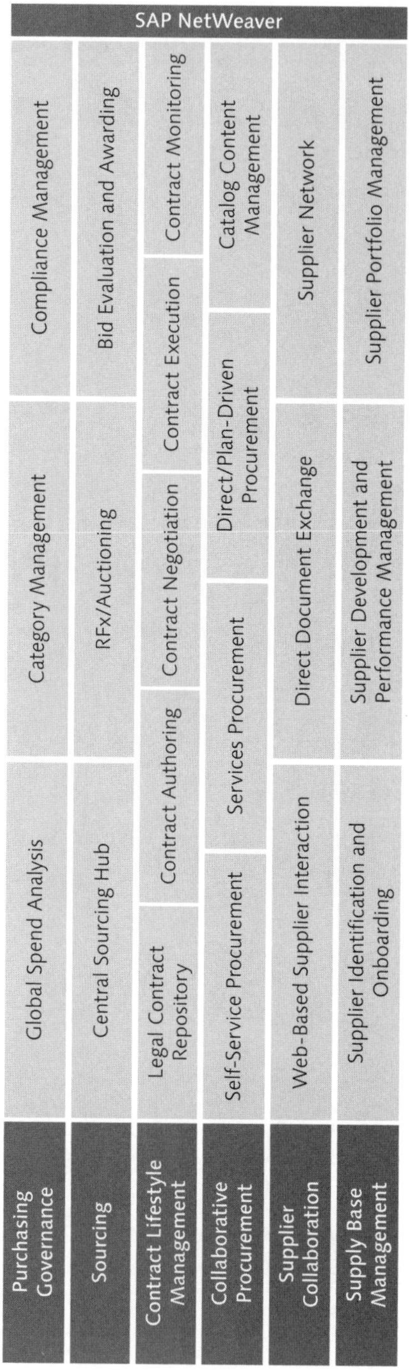
SAP NetWeaver
Purchasing Governance
Global Spend Analysis
Category Management
Compliance Management
Sourcing
Central Sourcing Hub
RFx/Auctioning
Bid Evaluation and Awarding
Contract Lifestyle Management
Legal Contract Repository
Contract Authoring
Contract Negotiation
Contract Execution
Contract Monitoring
Collaborative Procurement
Self-Service Procurement
Services Procurement
Direct/Plan-Driven Procurement
Catalog Content Management
Supplier Collaboration
Web-Based Supplier Interaction
Direct Document Exchange
Supplier Network
Supply Base Management
Supplier Identification and Onboarding
Supplier Development and Performance Management
Supplier Portfolio Management

Figure C.3 SAP SRM Solution Map

Global Spend Analysis	Category Management	Compliance Management
› Consolidated Spend Reporting	› Category Strategy Planning › Category Definition › Methodology Setup › Program Management › Project Management › Buyer Performance Management	› Purchasing Policy and Compliance Analysis › Buyer Compliance Reporting › Business Unit Compliance Reporting › Supplier Compliance Analysis › Embargo Screening › Contract Compliance Management

Table C.12 SAP SRM Purchasing Governance

Central Sourcing Hub	RFx/Auctioning	Bid Evaluation and Awarding
› Automatic Source of Supply Allocation › Procurement Consolidation Workbench › Demand Aggregation	› Project Preparation › RFx Preparation › RFx Processing › RFx Multi-Round Processing › Integrated Design Collaboration and Validation › RFx to Auction Conversion › Reverse Auction	› Analyze Responses › Award of Bid › Event Reporting › Bid Simulation and Optimization

Table C.13 SAP SRM Sourcing

Legal Contract Repository	Contract Authoring	Contract Negotiation	Contract Execution	Contract Monitoring
› Create Master Agreement Template › Create Master Agreement › Upload Contract Document › Search Contract Repository	› Clause and Template Library › Legal Contract Authoring with DUET › Legal Contract Authoring without DUET › Internal Legal Contract Collaboration	› External Collaboration for the Legal Contract › Renegotiation of an Operational Contract	› Integration of Legal and Operational Contract in ERP › Central Operational Contract Repository › Using Contracts for Source of Supply Assignment › Flexible Pricing and Discounts › Integration Between Contract and SRM Catalog › Quota Arrangements › Records Management Integration › Contract Distribution for Global Outline Agreements › Enhanced Control and Risk Mitigation of Currency Fluctuations	› Contract Compliance Management › Monitoring Expiration of Contracts › Maverick Buying Analysis

Table C.14 SAP SRM Contract Management

Self-Service Procurement	Services Procurement	Direct/Plan-Driven Procurement	Catalog Content Management
› Manual Requirements Definition › Approval of Requisition › Goods Receipt › Invoice Processing › Analyzing Self-Service Procurement	› Service Request Management › Integrated Requisition Creation – Materials Management › Service Delivery Entry › Invoice Processing › Analyzing Services Procurement	› Planned Requirements Processing › Goods Receipt › Invoice Processing › Analyzing Plan-Driven Procurement	› Managing Catalog Content › Catalog Data Search › Supplier Managed Content

Table C.15 SAP SRM Collaborative Procurement

Web-Based Supplier Interaction	Direct Document Exchange	Supplier Network
› Order Collaboration › Design Collaboration › Confirmation › Invoice Processing › Financial Settlement › Supplier Managed Content	› Order Communication › ASN/Service Entry › Invoice Communication	› Supplier Onboarding Services › Document Exchange Services

Table C.16 SAP SRM Supplier Collaboration

Supplier Identification and Onboarding	Supplier Development and Performance Management	Supplier Portfolio Management
› Supplier Self-Registration and Profile Data Administration › Integrated Request-for-Information Processing › Integration with External Supplier Repositories	› Supplier KPIs and Measure Definition › Supplier Scorecard Management › Supplier Performance Evaluation and Reporting › Supplier Audits › Action Management	› Analysis (Cost, Contract, Supplier Evaluation, Compliance, and Risk) › Management of Supplier Status › Supplier and Product Segmentation › Portfolio Management Planning and Forecasting (Long Term Planning)

Table C.17 SAP SRM Supply Base Management

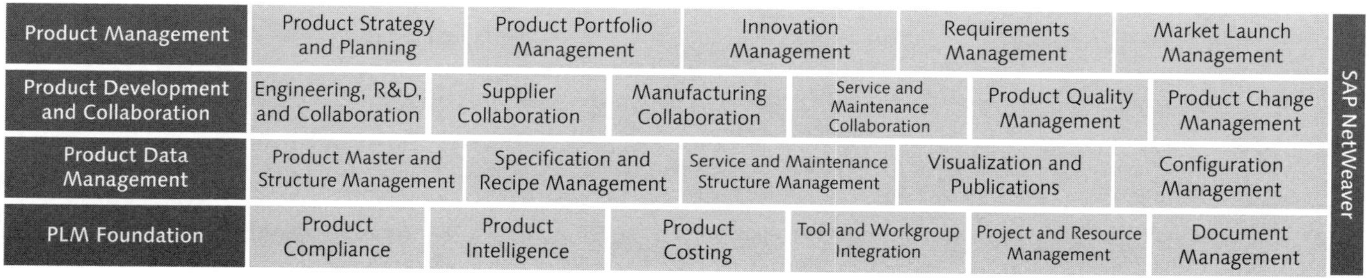

				SAP NetWeaver	
Product Management	Product Strategy and Planning	Product Portfolio Management	Innovation Management	Requirements Management	Market Launch Management
Product Development and Collaboration	Engineering, R&D, and Collaboration	Supplier Collaboration	Manufacturing Collaboration	Service and Maintenance Collaboration	Product Quality Management / Product Change Management
Product Data Management	Product Master and Structure Management	Specification and Recipe Management	Service and Maintenance Structure Management	Visualization and Publications	Configuration Management
PLM Foundation	Product Compliance	Product Intelligence	Product Costing	Tool and Workgroup Integration	Project and Resource Management / Document Management

Figure C.4 SAP Product Lifecycle Management

Product Strategy and Planning	Product Portfolio Management	Innovation Management	Requirements Management	Market Launch Management
› Product Strategy and Planning › Product Roadmap › Product Risk Management › Product IP Management	› Product Portfolio Management	› Idea and Concept Management	› Requirements Management	› New Product Introduction › Post-Launch Review

Table C.18 SAP PLM Product Management

Engineering and R&D Collaboration	Supplier Collaboration	Manufacturing Collaboration	Service and Maintenance Collaboration	Product Quality Management	Product Change Management
› Product Development › Development Collaboration › Engineering Change Collaboration › Engineering (ETO) › Engineering (MTO)	› Sourcing and Supply Planning › Supplier Audits › Supplier KPIs and Measure Definition › Supplier Scorecard Mangement › Supplier Performance Evaluation and Reporting	› Prototyping and Ramp-Up › Integrated Product and Process Engineering (iPPE) › Interfacing CAD, GIS, and SCADA systems	› MRO and Services Management › Warranty and Claims Management › Asset Management	› Quality Engineering › Quality Improvement › Failure Mode and Effects Analysis (FMEA)	› Change and Configuration Management

Table C.19 SAP PLM Product Development and Collaboration

Product Master and Structure Management	Specification and Recipe Management	Service and Maintenance Structure Management	Visualization and Publications	Configuration Management
› Product Structure Management › Integrated Product and Process Engineering (iPPE) › Routing Management and Process Development › Conceptual Product Structure › Variant Configuration › Sales Configuration Management	› Recipe Management › Specification Management	› Phase-In Equipment › Corrective Maintenance › Phase-Out Equipment	› Dynamic Publications	› Catalog Management › Part Management › Classification and Search

Table C.20 SAP PLM Product Data Management

Product Compliance	Product Intelligence	Product Costing	Tool and Workgroup Integration	Project and Resource Management	Document Management
› Product Compliance › Global Label Management › Audit Management › Product Safety › Hazardous Substance Management › Dangerous Goods Management › Waste Management	› Reporting, Query, and Analysis › Enabling Enterprise Search › Providing Business Object Search	› Product and Service Cost Management › Cost and Quotation Management	› MDA Integration › EDA Integration › CASE Integration › Digital Manufacturing › Packaging and Labeling › Media and Artwork	› Project Planning and Scoping › Resource and Time Management › Project Execution › Strategic Portfolio Management › Strategic Resource Management › Phase-Gate Management	› Document Management

Table C.21 SAP PLM Foundation

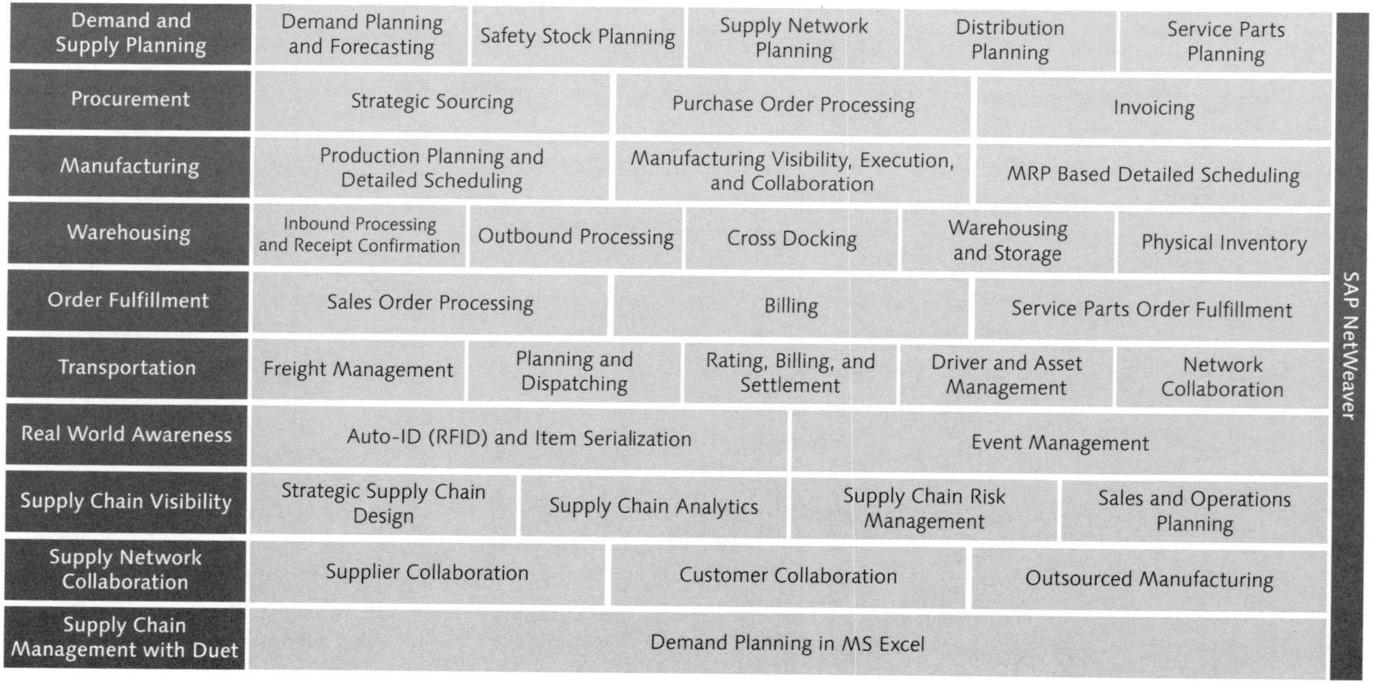

SAP NetWeaver					
Demand and Supply Planning	Demand Planning and Forecasting	Safety Stock Planning	Supply Network Planning	Distribution Planning	Service Parts Planning
Procurement	Strategic Sourcing	Purchase Order Processing		Invoicing	
Manufacturing	Production Planning and Detailed Scheduling	Manufacturing Visibility, Execution, and Collaboration		MRP Based Detailed Scheduling	
Warehousing	Inbound Processing and Receipt Confirmation	Outbound Processing	Cross Docking	Warehousing and Storage	Physical Inventory
Order Fulfillment	Sales Order Processing		Billing		Service Parts Order Fulfillment
Transportation	Freight Management	Planning and Dispatching	Rating, Billing, and Settlement	Driver and Asset Management	Network Collaboration
Real World Awareness	Auto-ID (RFID) and Item Serialization		Event Management		
Supply Chain Visibility	Strategic Supply Chain Design	Supply Chain Analytics	Supply Chain Risk Management		Sales and Operations Planning
Supply Network Collaboration	Supplier Collaboration		Customer Collaboration		Outsourced Manufacturing
Supply Chain Management with Duet	Demand Planning in MS Excel				

Figure C.5 SAP Supply Chain Management

Demand Planning and Forecasting	Safety Stock Planning	Supply Network Planning	Distribution Planning	Service Parts Planning
› Statistical Forecasting	› Basic Safety Stock Planning	› Heuristic	› Distribution Planning	› Strategic Supply Chain Design
› Causal Forecasting	› Advanced Safety Stock Planning	› Capacity Leveling	› Responsive Replenishment	› Parts Demand Planning
› Composite Forecasting		› Optimization	› Vendor Managed Inventory (VMI)	› Parts Inventory Planning
› Life-Cycle Planning		› Multilevel Supply and Demand Matching		› Parts Supply Planning
› Promotion Planning		› Subcontracting		› Parts Distribution Planning
› Data Handling		› Scheduling Agreement		› Parts Monitoring
› Collaborative Demand Planning		› Aggregated Supply Network Planning		
› Macro Calculation				
› Planning with Bills of Materials				
› Characteristics-Based Forecasting				
› Transfer of Consensus Demand Plan				
› Customer Forecast Management				

Table C.22 SAP SCM Demand and Supply Planning

Strategic Sourcing	Purchase Order Processing	Invoicing
› Long-Term Planning › Bid Management › Contract Management › Catalog Management › Source Determination	› Conversion of Demands to Purchase Orders › Confirmation and Monitoring Purchasing Activities › Procurement Visibility	› Receiving an Incoming Invoice › Verifying and Incoming Invoice › Release of Blocked Invoices

Table C.23 SAP SCM Procurement

Production Planning and Detailed Scheduling	Manufacturing Visibility, Execution, and Collaboration	MRP Based Detailed Scheduling
› Production Planning › Detailed Scheduling › Multilevel Supply and Demand Matching › Materials Requirements Planning	› Make-to-Order › Repetitive Manufacturing › Flow Manufacturing › Shop Floor Manufacturing › Lean Manufacturing › Process Manufacturing › Batch Management › Manufacturing Intelligence Dashboard › Manufacturing Visibility	› Production Planning › Detailed Scheduling

Table C.24 SAP SCM Manufacturing

Inbound Processing and Receipt Confirmation	Outbound Processing	Cross Docking	Warehousing and Storage	Physical Inventory
> Determination of External Demands > Acknowledgment of Receipt within Logistics > Advanced Shipping Notification > Value-Added Services > Yard Management > Delivery Monitoring > Goods Receipt > Material Valuation > Kit to Stock > Goods Receipt Optimization > Internal Routing > Deconsolidation	> Delivery Processing and Distribution > Delivery Monitoring > Value-Added Services > Yard Management > Goods Issue > Proof of Delivery > Fulfillment Visibility > Warehouse Order Processing > Kit to Order > Production Supply	> Planned Cross Docking > Opportunistic (Unplanned) Cross Docking > Transportation Cross Docking > Retail Merchandise Cross Docking > Opportunistic Cross Docking > Production Cross Docking and Production Supply Cross Docking	> Strategies > Slotting/Warehouse Optimization > Native Radio Frequency Processing > Task Interleaving and Resource Management > Multiple Handling Units > Inventory Management > Storage and Stock Management > Quality Management Integration > Production Supply > Visibility of Warehouse Activities > Decentralized Warehouse > Labor Management > Warehouse Cockpit > Material Flow System > Graphical Warehouse Layout > Decentralized/Centralized Deployment Options	> Planning Phase of Physical Inventory > Counting Phase of Physical Inventory > Monitoring of the Physical Inventory Activities

Table C.25 SAP SCM Warehousing

Sales Order Processing	Billing	Service Parts Order Fulfillment
› Rules-Based Available-to-Promise (ATP) › Multilevel ATP Check › Capable-to-Promise (CTP) › Product Allocation › Backorder Processing	› Creation and Cancellations of Invoices › Transfer Billing Data to Financial Accounting	› Parts Marketing and Campaign Management › Parts Order Processing › Complaints Processing

Table C.26 SAP SCM Order Fulfillment

Freight Management	Planning and Dispatching	Rating, Billing, and Settlement	Driver and Asset Management	Network Collaboration
› Capture Transportation Requests › Dynamic Route Determination › Credit Limit Check › Send Confirmation › Distance Determination Service › Workflow Management	› Load Consolidation › Mode and Route Optimization › TSP Selection › Transportation Visibility › Shipping	› Supplier Transportation Charges › Customer Transportation Charges › Transportation Charge Rates › Integrate Invoice Request to FI/CO System	› Asset Maintenance › Driver Maintenance	› Collaboration Shipment Tendering › Seamless Integration › Trigger Customs Procedure

Table C.27 SAP SCM Transportation

Auto-ID (RFID) and Item Serialization	Event Management
› Partner Applications and xApps › Pre-Configured Business Processes › Serialization Data Management › Hardware and Device Management	› Procurement Visibility › Fulfillment Visibility › Transportation Visibility › Manufacturing Visibility › Supply Network Visibility › Outbound/Inbound RFID › Railcar Management › Container Track/Trace

Table C.28 SAP SCM Real World Awareness

Strategic Supply Chain Design	Supply Chain Analytics	Supply Chain Risk Management	Sales and Operations Planning
› Supply Chain Definition › Supply Chain Monitoring › Alert Monitoring	› Service Fill Monitor › Service Loss Analysis › Supplier Delivery Performance Rating › Inbound Delivery Monitor › Collaboration Performance Indicator › Key Performance Indicators › Supply Chain Performance Management › Operational Performance Management › Supply Chain Analytical Applications › Supply Chain Analytics	› Identify Risks › Measure Risks › Manage Risks › Monitor Risks	› Demand Analysis and Update › Supply Analysis › Executive S&OP Analysis

Table C.29 SAP SCM Supply Chain Visibility

Supplier Collaboration	Customer Collaboration	Outsourced Manufacturing
› Release Process	› Responsive Demand Planning	› Contract Manufacturing Purchasing
› SMI Process	› Responsive Replenishment Planning	› Supply Network Inventory
› Purchase Order Process	› Min-Max Replenishment	› Work Order Process
› Dynamic Replenishment Process	› Demand Forecast Collaboration	
› Kanban Process		
› Delivery Control Monitor Process		
› Invoice Process		
› Self-Billing Invoice Process		

Table C.30 SAP SCM Supply Network Collaboration

Demand Planning in MS Excel
› Planning Online
› Planning Offline

Table C.31 SAP SCM Supply Chain Management with Duet

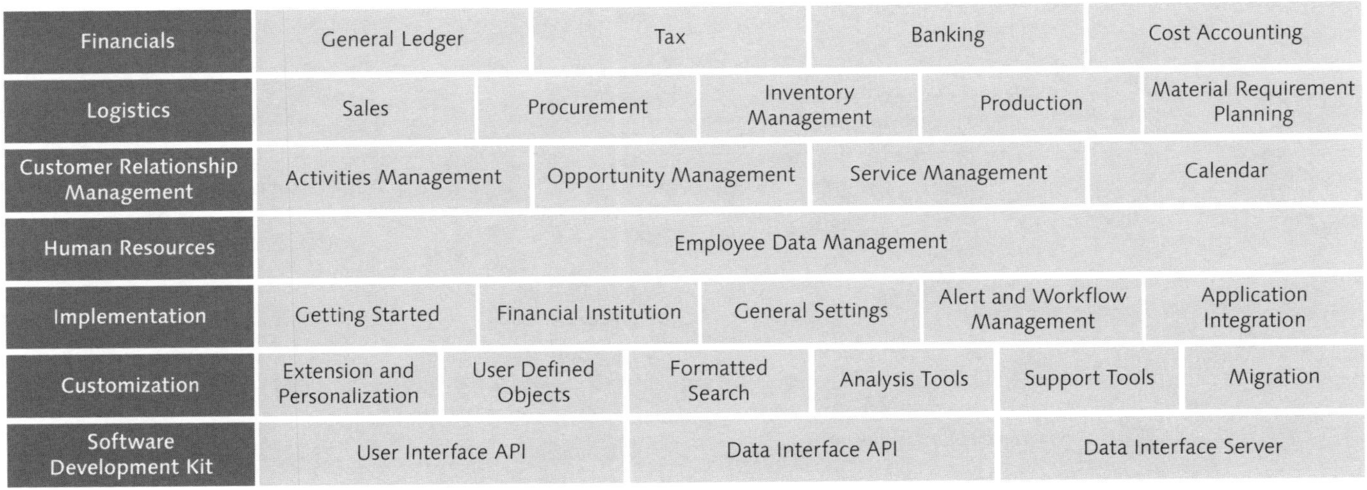

Figure C.6 SAP Business One Solution Map

Financials	General Ledger	Tax	Banking	Cost Accounting	
Logistics	Sales	Procurement	Inventory Management	Production	Material Requirement Planning
Customer Relationship Management	Activities Management	Opportunity Management	Service Management	Calendar	
Human Resources	Employee Data Management				
Implementation	Getting Started	Financial Institution	General Settings	Alert and Workflow Management	Application Integration
Customization	Extension and Personalization	User Defined Objects	Formatted Search	Analysis Tools	Support Tools	Migration
Software Development Kit	User Interface API	Data Interface API	Data Interface Server		

General Ledger	Tax	Banking	Cost Accounting
> Journal Entries	> VAT (Value Added Tax)	> Incoming Payments	> Profit Centers
> Journal Vouchers	> VAT Calculation (Europe)	> Check Register	> Distribution Rules
> Reverse Transactions	> VAT Correction (Portugal and Belgium)	> Credit Card Management	> Profit Center Report
> Recurring Postings	> Withholding Tax	> Deposits	
> Posting Templates	> Deffered Tax (Spain, France, Italy, Mexico, and South Africa)	> Outgoing Payments	
> Posting Periods	> Stamp Tax (Portugal)	> Checks for Payment	
> Exchange Rate Differences	> Equalization Tax (Spain)	> Pre-Numbered Checks	
> Conversion Differences	> Acquisition Tax (Europe)	> Voiding Checks	
> Chart of Accounts	> Tax Declaration Boxes	> Automatic Payment System	
> Account Segmentation	> Tax Exemptions	> Future Payments Monitoring	
> Account Code Generator	> ELSTER Integration (Germany)	> Payment Engine	
> Purchase Accounting	> Tax Only Documents	> Bank Statement Processing	
> Budget Management	> Multiple Excise/Service Tax (India)	> Internal Reconciliation	
> Project Management	> Excise for Inventory Transfer (India)	> Bank Reconciliation Process (USA, Canada, and UK)	
> Fixed Assets		> Bill of Exchange (Belgium, Chile, France, Italy, Portugal, and Spain)	
> Datey FI Interface (Germany)		> Dunning System	
> Folio Numbers (Mexico and Chile)		> Cash Discount	
> Revaluation (Mexico, Chile, Costa Rica, and Guatemala)		> Handling Small Differences in Payments	
> Financial Reports			
> Transaction Journal			
> Document Journal			
> General Ledger			
> G/L Accounts and Business Partners			
> Aging Reports			
> Customer Statement Report			
> Transaction Report by Projects			

Table C.32 SAP Business One Financials

Sales	Procurement	Inventory Management	Production	Material Requirement Planning
› Sales Quotation	› Purchase Order	› Batch Management	› Bill of Material	› Material Requirement Planning Forecasts
› Sales Order	› Split Purchase Order	› Serial Numbers Management	› Production Orders	› Material Requirement Planning Wizard
› Delivery	› Goods Receipt PO	› Stock Transfer		› Order Recommendation Report
› Returns	› Goods Return	› Goods Receipts/Goods Issues		
› A/R Invoice	› A/P Invoice	› Customer/Vendor Catalog Numbers		
› A/R Credit Memos	› A/P Credit Memo	› Perpetual Inventory Management		
› A/R Correction Invoice (Czech Republic, Hungary, Poland, and Slovakia)	› A/P Correction Invoice (Czech Republic, Hungary, Poland, and Slovakia)	› Pick and Pack		
› A/R Reserve Invoice	› A/P Reserve Invoice	› Alternative Items		
› Document Generation Wizard	› Landed Costs	› Inventory Revaluation		
› Creation of Sales Target Documents	› Vendor Invoice for Assets	› Price Lists		
› Backorder Processing	› Warehouse Segregation	› Special Prices		
› Retailer Chain Stores (Israel)	› Multiple Shipping Addresses	› Inventory Reports		
› Gross Profit Calculation	› Customs Bill			
› Structured Marketing Document	› Purchase Accounting			
› Item Availability Check	› Down Payments			
› Intrastat (Europe)	› Freight Charges			
› Down Payments	› Purchase Proposals			
› Drop Shipment	› Open Items List			
› Open Items List	› Purchase Analysis Report			
› Sales Analysis Report	› Creation of Purchasing Target Documents			
› CCD Numbers (Russia)	› Tax Only Documents			
› Tax Only Documents				

Table C.33 SAP Business One Logistics

Activities Management	Opportunity Management	Service Management	Calendar
› Activity › Activities Overview	› Opportunities › Opportunity Analysis Reports › Opportunities Pipeline	› Service Call › Customer Equipment Card › Service Contract › Contract Template Management › Solutions Knowledge Base › Service Reports	› Calendar › Microsoft Outlook Integration

Table C.34 SAP Business One Customer Relationship Management

Payroll	Employee Data Management
› Payroll Accounting	› Employee › Human Resources Reports › HR Connector

Table C.35 SAP Business One Human Resources

Getting Started	Financial Initialization	General Settings	Alert and Workflow Management	Application Integration
> Creation of New Company > Document Numbering > Document Numbering (Belgium) > Determining of Default Values	> Currency Types > Foreign Currency Management > Rounding Methods > Opening Balances > Foreign Currency Exchange Rates and Indexes Table > G/L Account Determination > Financial Report Templates	> Company Details > Accounting Data > Display Settings > Block Documents with Earlier Date > Future Posting Date in Documents > User Shortcuts > User and Authorization Management > Data Ownership	> Approval Procedures > Alert Management	> SAP Business One Integration for SAP NetWeaver > Email > SAP Business One Integration Partner Enablement Package (PEP)

Table C.36 SAP Business One Implementation

Extension and Personalization	User Defined Object	Formatted Search	Analysis Tools	Support Tools	Migration
› User-Defined Fields › User-Defined Menus › User Tables › User Trigger › Layout Designer › Advanced Layout Designer › Multi-Language Support › Export to File › Launch Application › Screen Painter	› User-Defined Object	› Formatted Search	› Query Wizard › Query Generator › Drag and Relate	› SAP Business One EarlyWatch Alert › Support Desk for SAP Business One › User Documentation › Context Sensitive Help › Field Level Help	› Data Transfer Workbench › Data Migration Wizard › Copy Express

Table C.37 SAP Business One Customization

User Interface API	Data Interface API	Data Interface Server
› User Interface API › FormData Event	› Data Interface API	› Data Interface Server

Table C.38 SAP Business One Software Development Kit

D   Bibliography

Books

Melich, M.; Schafer, M.: *SAP Solution Manager*. SAP PRESS, Feb. 2007.

Web Resources

SAP: *www.sap.com*; various product descriptions, white papers, and customer success stories.

Wikipedia: *www.wikipedia.org*; technology definitions.

SAP Presentations and White Papers

Heckner, M.: *Governance, Risk, and Compliance Management*, 2005.

Regutzki, J.: *Enterprise SOA In Practice*, March, 20007.

Swaminath, R.: *Enabling Growth and Innovation: An Introduction to Enterprise Services Architecture*, February 28, 2006.

Kagermann, H.: *Business at the Speed of Change*, April, 2007.

SAP AG: SAP NetWeaver Solution Overview, June, 2006.

SAP AG: Driving Innovative Business Practices with SAP, 2004.

SAP AG: mySAP ERP Solution Overview, June, 2005.

SAP AG: mySAP Financials Solution Overview, August, 2005.

SAP AG: mySAP Human Capital Management Solution Overview, August, 2005.

SAP AG: mySAP ERP Operations Solution Overview, June, 2005.

SAP AG: mySAP ERP Statement of Direction, 2005 to 2007 Outlook, October 2005.

SAP AG: mySAP ERP The Superior ERP Solution, Overview for New Customers, 2004.

SAP AG: Duet: Seamless Access to SAP via Microsoft Office, 2006.

SAP AG: Duet Solution Overview, 2006.

SAP AG: mySAP Product LifeCycle Management, November 2005.

Relevant Business Legislation

Sarbanes-Oxley, *www.sarbanes-oxley.com*

GAAP, *www.fasab.gov/accepted.html*

International Accounting Standards Board, IFRS, *www.IASB.org*

Basel II, Committee on Banking Supervision: Bank for International Settlements, Updated 2005.

Index

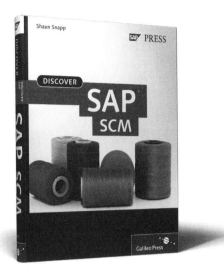

Discover what SAP SCM is by exploring its features, functionality, and more.

Shaun Snapp

Discover SAP SCM

This text offers general overview of the SAP SCM application, which provides broad functionality for enabling responsive supply networks and integrates seamlessly with both SAP and non-SAP software. This text provides detailed coverage of all the functional areas within SAP SCM.

approx. 376 pp., 39,95 Euro / US$ 39.95
ISBN 978-1-59229-305-6, Dec 2009

>> www.sap-press.com

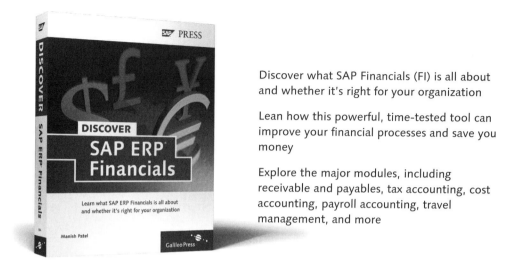

Discover what SAP Financials (FI) is all about and whether it's right for your organization

Lean how this powerful, time-tested tool can improve your financial processes and save you money

Explore the major modules, including receivable and payables, tax accounting, cost accounting, payroll accounting, travel management, and more

Manish Patel

Discover SAP ERP Financials

Business financials are an essential part of every business, large or small. Whether you just need basic accounting or you perform complex financial audits and reporting, your business needs a software tool that meets your needs. Discover SAP Financials explains how SAP can provide this solution. Using an easy-to-follow style filled with real-world examples, case studies, and practical tips and pointers, the book teaches the fundamental capabilities and uses of the core modules of SAP Financials. As part of the Discover SAP series, the book is written to help new users, decision makers considering SAP, and power users moving to the latest version learn everything they need to determine if SAP Financials is the right solution for your organization.

544 pp., 2008, 39,95 Euro / US$ 39.95
ISBN 978-1-59229-184-7

>> www.sap-press.com

Teaches readers what SAP ERP HCM is and how it can benefit their company

Provides a detailed overview of all core functionality

Includes practical insights and real-world case studies to show HCM at work

Greg Newman

Discover SAP ERP HCM

This book is an insightful, detailed guide to what SAP ERP HCM is all about and how it can make companies more effective in managing their own HR processes. The book details all of the major components of SAP HCM, explaining the purpose of the components, how they work, their features and benefits and their integration with other components. It uses real-world examples throughout to demonstrate the uses, benefits, and issues encountered by existing SAP HCM users to ground the book in reality rather than just marketing hype. After reading this book, readers will have a broad understanding of SAP's HCM offering and insight into existing customer experiences with the product.

438 pp., 2009, 39,95 Euro / US$ 39.95
ISBN 978-1-59229-222-6

>> www.sap-press.com

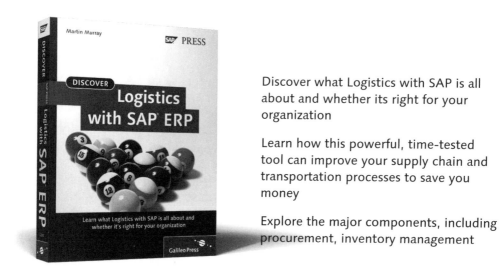

Discover what Logistics with SAP is all about and whether its right for your organization

Learn how this powerful, time-tested tool can improve your supply chain and transportation processes to save you money

Explore the major components, including procurement, inventory management

Martin Murray

Discover Logistics with SAP ERP

With this reader-friendly book, anyone new to SAP or considering implementing it will discover the fundamental capabilities and uses of the Logistics components. You'll learn what's available, and how it works to help you determine if Logistics with SAP is the right tool for your organization. This book is written in a clear, practical style, and uses real-world examples, case studies, and insightful tips to give you a complete overview of the SAP logistics offerings.

385 pp., 2009, 39,95 Euro / US$ 39.95
ISBN 978-1-59229-230-1

>> www.sap-press.com

The new support offering, including concepts, services, and tools

Details SAP standards for solution operations, Run SAP, and Customer COE

Explains extended maintenance, business process optimization, and SAP enhancement packages

Gerhard Oswald, Uwe Hommel

SAP Enterprise Support

ASAP to Run SAP

This book provides IT managers and decision makers with a detailed guide to SAP Enterprise Support. Using a top-down approach, the book begins by explaining why Enterprise Support was introduced, and then details the concrete benefits and concepts of Enterprise Support. It teaches you how and why to use Enterprise Support and covers the new services that have been incorporated. This is the one book you need to really understand how SAP Enterprise Support can work for your organization.

339 pp., 2009, 59,95 Euro / US$ 59.95
ISBN 978-1-59229-302-5

>> www.sap-press.com